The Politics of Humanitarian Intervention

The Politics of Humanitarian Intervention

Edited by
John Harriss

Save the Children

PINTER
London and New York
in association with the
Save the Children Fund and the Centre for Global Governance

First published in 1995 by
Pinter Publishers, *A Cassell Imprint*
Wellington House, 125 Strand, London, WC2R 0BB, United Kingdom
215 Park Avenue South, New York, NY10003, USA

British Library Cataloguing in Publication Data

A CIP catalogue record for this book is available from the British Library

ISBN 1 85567 335 5 (hbk)
ISBN 1 85567 334 7 (pbk)

Library of Congress Cataloging-in-Publication Data

The politics of human intervention / edited by John Harriss.
    p.   cm.
    Includes bibliographical references (p.   ) and index.
    ISBN 1-85567-335-5 (hbk.). ISBN 1-85567-334-7 (pbk.)
    1. Intervention (International law) I. Harriss, John.
JX4481.P56 1995
341.5'84--dc20   95-14316
                                              CIP

Typeset by Patrick Armstrong Book Production Services

Printed by Biddles Ltd., Guildford and King's Lynn

Contents

List of contributors

John Harriss, London School of Economics and Save the Children Fund (SCF), South Asia

John Seaman, Head of Policy Development Unit, SCF

Hugo Slim, Director, Complex Emergencies Programme, Oxford Brookes University

Emma Visman, SCF, Angola

David Keen, SCF Consultant

Martin Griffiths, UN Department of Humanitarian Affairs (Geneva) and formerly Chief Executive Action Aid

Iain Levine, Operation Lifeline Sudan

Mark Weller, University of Cambridge

Paul Taylor, London School of Economics

Abbreviations

ACABQ	Advisory Committee on Administrative and Budgetary Questions
ACC	Administrative Committee for Coordination
AETF	African Emergency Task Force
AICF	Action International Against Hunger
CARE	Co-operative for American Relief to Everywhere
CERF	Central Emergency Revolving Fund
CRS	Catholic Relief Services
CSCE	Conference on Security and Cooperation in Europe
DART	Disaster Assessment Relief Team
DHA	Department of Humanitarian Affairs
DIEC	Director-General for Development and International Economic Cooperation
ECHO	European Community Humanitarian Office
ECOMOG	Economic Community of West African States/Military Monitoring Group
ECOSOC	Economic and Social Council
ECOWAS	Economic Community of West African States
FAO	Food and Agriculture Organisation
IAGE	Inter-Agency Group for Emergencies
IASC	Inter-Agency Standing Committee
IASU	Inter-Agency Support Unit
ICRC	International Committee of the Red Cross
IFRC	International Federation of Red Cross and Red Crescent Societies
IGO	Intergovernmental Organisation
INGO	International Non-Governmental Organisation
IMF	International Monetary Fund
ISCA	International Save the Children Alliance
MSF	Médecins sans Frontières
NGO	Non-Governmental Organisation
NPFL	National Patriotic Front for Liberia
OAS	Organisation of American States
OAU	Organisation of African Unity
OEOA	Office for Emergency Operations in Africa
ODA	Overseas Development Administration
OFDA	Office of Foreign Disaster Assistance (US)
OLS	Operation Lifeline Sudan
Oxfam	Oxford Committee for Famine Relief
SCF	Save the Children Fund
SEPHA	Special Emergency Programme for the Horn of Africa
SPLA	Sudan People's Liberation Army
SPM	Somali Patriotic Movement
UN	United Nations (Organisation)
UNCTAD	United Nations Conference on Trade and Development
UNDP	United Nations Development Programme
UNDRO	United Nations Disaster Relief Organisation
UNFPA	United Nations Fund for Population Activity

UNHCR	United Nations High Commission for Refugees
UNICEF	United Nations International Children's Emergency Fund
UNIDO	United Nations Industrial Development Organisation
UNITA	National Union for the Total Independence of Angola
UNITAF	United Nations Task Force
UNOSOM	United Nations Operation in Somalia
UNPROFOR	United Nations Protection Force (in Bosnia)
USAID	US Agency for International Development
USC	United Somali Congress
WFP	World Food Programme
WHO	World Health Organisation

Preface

John Harriss

The project which has given rise to this book was conceived in September 1992 by Michael Edwards, Head of Information and Research in the Overseas Department of the Save the Children Fund (SCF), and me. Our idea was to try to bring together the Fund's practical field experience of international humanitarian assistance, with the expertise of academics who have studied international organisation and international law. We believed that there was great potential benefit in subjecting the lessons of practice to scholarly critique, and similarly, in testing scholarship against experience. The London School of Economics, with the support of private foundations, had established a Centre for the Study of Global Governance in late 1992, which promised to provide a forum for just this kind of exchange and was directed at the development of ideas for the negotiation and management of global issues. Both the Centre and the Save the Children Fund were persuaded by our arguments and supplied resources that made possible the work contained in this book.

At the time when our project was started, the optimism released by the events of 1989–90, and the idea of a 'New World Order' of greater global cooperation, in place of the divisions of the Cold War, still seemed credible. A new international Commission for Global Governance had been set up, following on from the earlier Brandt and Brundtland Commissions which had also sought to provide new thinking on major international problems. This, and the LSE's serendipitously established Centre, showed that the idea of the exercise of international power in the management of global, social, and economic resources for development (paraphrasing the concept of 'governance' advanced by the World Bank) held promise.

But already, by the autumn of 1992, the failures of the United Nations Organisation in Somalia (documented in the chapter here by Hugo Slim and Emma Visman), and the obvious inconsistencies in the actions of the 'international community', as reflected through the UN, towards the increasing number of 'complex emergencies' that were occurring in the world, gave cause for doubt. The Save the Children Fund had been deeply committed to work in Somalia, even in the absence from that country of the UN and of its Specialised Agencies throughout 1991. As a result of this experience in particular, of those from Iraqi Kurdistan (described here by David Keen) and from many other emergencies in different parts of the world over a good many years, SCF had become known as a forceful critic of the UN. From SCF's point of view, part of the purpose of engaging with academic specialists in international affairs was in order to explore the implications and ramifications of the ideas which had emerged from practice, and to find out how justified they are.

Sadly, the doubters have been offered much further evidence in the past eighteen months with which to support their views. In 1994–95 the civil war in Rwanda, which led the Secretary-General of the UN to make a public statement of failure, and the continuing tragedy of Bosnia — to name only those events which were most in the eye of the television cameras — seemed to pronounce the total failure of the international system. Events have moved on so rapidly, and in such negative ways, that some of the ideas and analysis in this book may now seem terribly idealistic. There is indeed a tension between the pessimistic tone (or is it the 'realism'?) of John Seaman's chapter, which anticipates the increasing marginalisation of the UN, and the concerns of the chapter by Martin Griffiths, Iain Levine and Mark Weller, and of that by Paul Taylor, which propose ideas, principles and procedures for improving the capacity of the UN and of the wider, polycentric, international system in tackling complex emergencies. Rather in sympathy with Seaman's views, the Director-General of SCF (UK), Nicholas Hinton, made a speech at the Royal Society of Arts in February 1994, in which he challenged the continued existence of the UN in its present form. Yet SCF continues to believe that 'the world's humanitarian needs can best be met by the UN, with appropriate reforms' (i.e. not quite 'in its present form'). These are the words of an official SCF Position Paper on 'The United Nations and Humanitarian Assistance' of March 1994. But the position statement continues: 'the need for reform is urgent'. It is because of that urgency that it seems so worthwhile to put forward the ideas and analysis contained in this book, which draws on both scholarly and practical expertise. There is idealism in the chapters by Griffiths *et al.* and Taylor, in the sense that they rest on a belief in the possibility of realising principled, value-directed political action in international affairs. But they also advance concrete proposals. Readers must judge how far the principles and organisational reforms that are developed in these chapters promise to set up 'a UN equipped to deal with the sort of situation which we witnessed in Somalia in 1991' (Hinton, RSA speech), and to cope with the problems that are analysed in the chapters by Seaman, Slim and Emma Visman, and David Keen.

In keeping with the spirit of critical reflection which the project on which this book is based aimed to encourage, there are differences of view in these pages and they do not convey the official positions of either the Save the Children Fund or of the London School of Economics.

I should like, at last, to express my thanks to Larry Minear of Brown University for some helpful comments on the chapter on 'Sovereignty and

Suffering'; and to participants in a Forum organised by the Centre for the Study of Global Governance and run jointly with the Commission for Global Governance, in September 1993, for discussion of some of the work in the book. And I am grateful, above all, to Hugo Slim and to Mike Edwards for their unfailing, and unfailingly friendly support from the start of this project — and latterly for their patient responses to flurries of faxes from South Asia!

John Harriss

*SCF South Asia Regional Office, Kathmandu;
and London School of Economics*

Introduction:
a time of troubles — problems of international humanitarian assistance in the 1990s

John Harriss

Events and ideas in the 1990s have given greater prominence than ever before to the problems of international humanitarian assistance. In the immediate aftermath of the Cold War there were great expectations of a new era of international cooperation, of a 'New World Order', and of the United Nations Organisation as its foundation. The apparently definitive dissolution of the contest between the ideologies of the West and of the Soviet bloc seemed to show that democracy — understood essentially as parliamentary democracy — and the market economy had triumphed and should be the principles of the new international order. But the euphoria which many felt in 1989-90 was short-lived. It very soon became apparent that the divisions of the Cold War had only overlain social tensions which usually have much more to do with ethnicity, nationalism and the politics of identity than with the politics of class. The 1990s have seen the eruption of bloody conflicts which are only rarely between states. In the Human Development Report for 1994, the United Nations Development Programme counted only three wars between states in the period between 1989 and 1992, while it recorded seventy-nine instances of intra-state conflicts over the same period — many of which had already been under way for a decade or more (UNDP, 1994, 47). These wars, sometimes the outcome of structural crisis in the global economy, have contributed to the creation of 'complex emergencies', characterised by combinations of multiple causes: civil and ethnic conflict; famine; displacement of people; disputed sovereignty; and the breakdown of national government. Such emergencies give rise to immense human suffering, and to a corresponding sense of need for humanitarian assistance. But as the numbers and the intensity of complex emergencies have increased, the limitations of 'the international system', centred on the UN, have become all too apparent. Expectations that the UN could maintain international peace and security have led to increased demands being made upon it which have been unrealistic and, inevitably, have been disappointed. The sense of optimism about international relations has been crushed, by strife of ex-Yugoslavia, by the menace of the many conflicts within and around the borders of the former Soviet Union, and latterly — and most emphatically — by the evident paralysis of 'the international community' in the face of the bloodshed of Rwanda.

In this context of failed expectations it is the aim of this book to explore the experience of international humanitarian intervention in the 'watershed' cases of Somalia and of Iraqi Kurdistan, and to analyse the reasons for its failure. These particular cases are set in the context of a longer-run view of the development of humanitarian relief, and of a broader view both of reasons for the failure of the UN system and of the possibilities for its reform.

Contradictions: good government and human rights versus sovereignty; ideals and reality

The failures of the international system have been rendered all the more stark by the climate of ideas of the 1990s. There is a considerable degree of consensus (what some describe as 'the Washington consensus': see Archer, 1994) over a cluster of policy ideas concerning economic and political management. Within the cluster is the idea of 'good government' or 'good governance', which is synonymous, for the World Bank, with 'sound development management' (World Bank, 1992). Good government is vital for establishing the legal and regulatory framework which is necessary for markets to work efficiently, and in the provision of public goods. 'In order to play this role [governments] need revenues, and agents to collect revenues and produce the public goods. This in turn requires systems of accountability, adequate and reliable information, and efficiency in resource management and the delivery of public services' (World Bank, 1992, 1). In emphasising the importance of 'accountability' and of 'transparency' good government presupposes the existence of democratic civil society in which citizens can hold their governments to account. The 'good government' agenda thus marks an important shift from the neo-liberal views of the state of the 1980s:

> It recognises that markets are not the whole answer [to problems of development]. It rehabilitates the state, which is given central social and economic responsibilities. And it promotes human rights, democracy and the rule of law because these are seen to be requirements of a modern market economy and a well-managed state. (Archer, 1994, 7)

Arguments for 'good government' have thus lent further weight to the cause of universal human rights and have brought out the tension between concepts of individual rights and long-accepted ideas concerning national sovereignty.

The United Nations Organisation was itself created by, and is accountable to, states. Its Charter rules out the threat or use of force against the territorial integrity or political independence of a state (except in particular circumstances of 'Threats to the Peace', laid out in Chapter VII). The Organisation itself is not authorised 'to intervene in matters which are essentially within the domestic jurisdiction of any state'. Yet the Charter also begins with a declaration of human rights; and the recognition of human rights is implicitly in conflict with the traditional doctrine of non-intervention in the affairs of sovereign states. As Martin Griffiths and his co-authors explain in their chapter in this book, the building up of international law on sovereignty has been carried on by the governments of states. Not surprisingly, therefore, there has been a shift over time in the definition of the object to be protected from outside interference from 'the will of the people in any state' (the wording of an early resolution of the General Assembly of the UN) to the abstraction of 'the state'. But in the more recent past the privileging of this abstraction has increasingly come into question. Now, the authors suggest, 'the absurd argument that the abstract concept of the state can render immune from international action a government or authority which exterminates those whose corporate identity constitutes the state' is hardly tenable. The rights of states are no longer assumed to have priority over the rights of individuals. Oxfam has taken a position based on this argument: 'We do not accept that the principle of sovereignty should block the protection of basic rights, including the right to emergency relief and safety.'

States were reluctant to countenance intervention for humanitarian reasons because of fears about their deployment as a justification for the use of force; and until recently legal judgments fell short of advocating the use of force as a remedy for the violation of human rights. Now the view is increasingly being taken that there is a legal obligation on the part of government authorities to admit humanitarian aid, while there have also been four major cases in the recent past — those of Liberia, Iraq, ex-Yugoslavia, and Somalia — in which humanitarian action has taken place in the absence of government consent (though, as Slim and Visman show in their chapter on Somalia, concerns about sovereignty were allowed, fatally, to delay action in that case and to impede the adoption of a more appropriate style of intervention). There has been a fairly consistent trend towards the recognition of the legitimacy of humanitarian intervention. It has been justified, however — though appropriately in Paul Taylor's view, put in his chapter in this book — particularly by reference to the implications of problems internal to a particular state for peace and stability outside its borders.

There is a powerful set of arguments, reflected in the 'good government' agenda, which justifies international intervention, along a scale which ranges from the imposition of various conditionalities attaching to the provision of assistance, or access to markets, to armed action. Yet, just as these arguments have acquired force, the effectiveness of intervention by 'the international community' in the increasing number of cases where states have failed (and nothing remotely resembling 'good government' exists), and where the rights of individuals are clearly not respected, has apparently diminished. The UNDP's Human Development Report 1994 argues that 'Four situations would appear to warrant international intervention: (1) mass slaughter of the population by the state; (2) decimation through starvation or the withholding of health or other services, (3) forced exodus and (4) occupation and the denial of the right to self-determination ...' (UNDP, 1994, 57). Such conditions applied in Rwanda in early 1994, yet international collective action failed utterly.

Information and power: Somalia and Iraq

John Seaman argues that the international system of humanitarian relief which failed in Rwanda is not really a 'system' at all. It is more like an arena in which a large number of different sorts of organisations operate, though organised by both the quantity of resources flowing into it and the way in which they are controlled. These in turn are influenced notably by the quantity and quality of information available to the public (particularly in the West) — so that the media play an extremely important role; by the foreign policy interests of donor countries; and by the extent of financial and political independence of recipient countries. In practice the specialised UN agencies — like UNHCR and UNICEF — as well as NGOs like ICRC, Oxfam and the Save the Children Fund, are constrained to work in particular ways to the extent that their income is tied to donor contributions. 'For all practical purposes the UN is financed by its member nations, and is wholly dependent on a small number of Western governments to finance specific relief operations.'

Media visibility and donor interest have tended to encourage the 'emergency' model of relief, involving the quasi-military provision of medical personnel, blankets, shelter (etc.) for the supposedly passive population of 'victims' who are dependent for their survival on international relief efforts. There may be times when this view is justified — perhaps in the Rwandan crisis in July 1994. But there is another view, which is that 'although disaster certainly has physical effects and there is often a clear need to provide material assistance, and sometimes to provide this quickly, other factors must be taken into account if resources are to be used in the most efficient way'. The first of these 'other factors' is the recognition that the populations affected by complex emergencies are usually positive, practical actors and not passive 'victims'. Seaman points out that in the aftermath of earthquakes, for example, 'search and rescue and medical activities are usually completed before international assistance arrives ... the many survivors will engage, often selflessly, in rescue'. The positive agency of those affected by disasters is the main theme of the World Disaster Report for 1994, produced by the International Federation of Red Cross and Red Crescent Societies: 'Rather than disintegrating amid disaster, people seek to restore social and cultural order, even at the risk of death' (IFRC, 1994, 44). This recognition should encourage a 'development' approach to relief, in which the effort is made to listen to the affected people, to enter into dialogue with them, and to support local efforts. Experience has shown that international relief can then be more relevant and effective (see IFRC, 1994, Section 1). But it is in the nature of this approach 'that it is less visible to the media' which encourages the dramatic view of external agencies 'coming to the rescue' of the disaster 'victims'. And the media view stimulates, in turn, an 'emergency' response on the part of donors. Beyond this, it may be suggested, 'relief systems are a symptom of disengagement with the South. Overseas development assistance is either stagnant or declining while humanitarian aid is rising' (Mark Duffield, quoted in the *Guardian*, 7 May 1994).

These arguments are strikingly exemplified in the case of Somalia. Slim and Visman argue that

> Throughout the first two years of the Somalia crisis [after the fall of Siad Barre] ... the overwhelming tendency [of the media] was to condemn Somalia to that select group of 'basket case' nations whose problems seem to lie far beyond the pale of assistance and solution, and in the face of which the international community can only wring its hands.

There was a coincidence of interest between the western political establishment and the media which kept the spotlight off Somalia. In this period the UN not only failed to respond to 'early warning' signals, but even withdrew for an extended period because of concerns about security which flourished at least in part because of continuing respect for the 'sovereignty' of Somalia. A small number of NGOs remained in the country, undertaking humanitarian operations, while the UN and its agencies missed a crucial opportunity of working with surviving local institutions and structures, and even, simply,of learning about the country. By the time that the UN returned the chance had gone.

For Slim and Visman it is from the failures of the international system in this early phase of the Somalia imbroglio that the 'greatest lessons' are to be learnt: they are lessons about the vital importance of information, and of not allowing decisions to be based only on media exposure; about the importance of engaging as early and as intensively as possible with local institutions and structures, seeking to listen to, to learn from and to support the people involved. This might involve, in a country like Somalia, 're-empowering traditional community leaders' (as Ioan Lewis, the leading anthropological authority on Somalia, has argued: see Lewis, 1993; and also IFRC, 1994, pp 56–8, showing how the application of the same ideas in Somaliland has borne fruit). The 'strong and unilateral UN political and military action' which subsequently was the way in which the international community sought to handle the problems of Somalia is simply 'no substitute for the more intricate process of mediation'. As it turned out 'the UN became a player not a broker' and the whole operation ended in ignominious retreat. The general conclusion is that 'Military intervention and peace enforcement is no substitute for political negotiation actively combined with timely and well-planned humanitarian assistance' — such as Ambassador Sahnoun had been attempting to bring about in Somalia in 1992, but was prevented from pursuing.

Historically the UN has generally played a subordinate role in relief operations. It was the aftermath of the Gulf War in 1991, and the handling of the Kurdish problem, which gave the UN unprecedented prominence and encouraged expectations of humanitarian intervention. The sustained media coverage of the Kurdish refugee crisis led to a call for new international arrangements for disaster relief and to the bold initiative of the creation of 'safe havens'. Security Council Resolution 688, condemning Iraq for its treatment of the civilian population and setting up the safe havens and an air-exclusion zone, was a watershed in the politics of international humanitarian assistance, as Griffiths *et al.* show in their chapter. The four years since the passing of Resolution 688 have been a period of experimentation in which the international community has explored new models of humanitarian action.

As David Keen's analysis of subsequent developments in Iraqi Kurdistan shows, the trouble has been that protection has not been sustained. The UN has not tackled obstruction by the government of Iraq and has even played down problems with its own operations. At the same time inadequate developmental assistance has been provided, which has compelled continuing reliance upon emergency relief and has created a Catch-22 situation in which, partly because of the inadequacy of international assistance, corruption has been allowed to flourish, and this in turn has been used as a justification for low levels of assistance!

Keen argues that it has been the failure to understand the Kurdish problem which has encouraged an inappropriate response by the international community. Yet this would seem a generous proposition when he also refers to the loose but powerful coalition of international interests which seems anxious precisely to avoid 'self-sufficiency' in Iraqi Kurdistan — especially because of deference to Turkish fears about the creation of a 'Kurdish National Home'. What would have been desirable would have been for the international community to have found ways of working with the Kurdish administration, and to have been ready to reward 'good government', in the Kurdish experiment with democracy: 'This means providing aid that helps people to carve out economic and political security for themselves, rather than simply feeding people in high profile relief operations.' The argument echoes that put forward also by Slim and Visman, and Seaman's more general points concerning the 'development model' as opposed to the 'emergency model' of relief. But the example of Iraqi Kurdistan also illustrates very clearly the dominance of what are thought of as diplomatic and 'security' considerations over longer-run humanitarian interests, once the TV cameras of the international media have gone away in search of new dramas.

John Seaman suggests that it is already apparent that the high point of UN activism — roughly between Security Council Resolutions 688 on Iraq and 794 which authorised UN troops to use 'all necessary means' in Somalia to secure the distribution of aid — has probably passed: 'the UN is now and seems set to be increasingly marginalised by direct donor action and ... often bypassed by operational links between donors, NGOs and governments.' He believes that the failure of 'the international community' which became so clearly apparent in 1994 in Rwanda is a reflection of 'the breakdown of the structures, intellectual, philosophical and material, of the old global order'. The UN is compromised by its reliance on the resources of the major western powers, and by the fact that it is seen as a vehicle for western interests. At the same time the will of these same powers to commit their military forces — their own citizens — to the pursuit of political objectives which do not have to do with their own immediate interests is plainly lacking; and the nature of military power is itself undergoing change. The technology that won the Gulf War, of 'armies designed for nuclear war and formal conflict', 'may be ineffective against tribal armies' — or Serbian irregulars.

There is thus a kind of power vacuum in the international system, or perhaps more accurately an uncertainty of power which means that there is a degree of randomness in the way in which events unfold, and that priorities are confused. This might make it seem that it is rather pointless to continue to worry about the reform of the UN. But the authors of this book rather take the opposite view: it is precisely because of the uncertainty of power in the post-Cold War world that it is so important to work to create a better system for the management of international humanitarian problems — to work, indeed, towards 'global governance'.

Reforming international humanitarian action

In order to minimise political inconsistencies, and in an effort to arrest the perceived erosion of the credibility of the UN, in the context which I have described as that of 'the uncertainty of power', Griffiths, Levine and Weller argue for the formulation of clear principles to guide the action of the UN, and for governing humanitarian intervention in defence of the well-being of individuals. These principles must be grounded above all in the doctrine of humanitarian neutrality, embodied in the past notably in the role of the ICRC: the doctrine that assistance is given to those who need it without discrimination, except in their favour. In summary the principles proposed are:

1. Humanitarian aid must be given according to considerations of human need alone.
2. Impartiality and neutrality do not mean that two or more sides in a conflict should necessarily be treated equally in terms of levels of aid. These should depend on whose population is suffering most.
3. The only constraints in responding to humanitarian need should be those of resources and practicality.
4. Those rendering humanitarian aid have a right and, indeed, a duty to ensure its appropriate end use.
5. If armed obstruction to humanitarian aid requires that enforcement action be taken against one or more of the parties on the ground, such action does not violate the principle of humanitarian neutrality.

These proposals may be compared with the UN General Assembly Resolution 46/182 of 1991, which is the UN's clearest policy statement on the principles and practice of humanitarian assistance. It commits the international community to observing that 'humanitarian assistance must be provided in accordance with principles of humanity, neutrality and impartiality'. The Resolution authorised specific practical measures, focused on the creation of the Department of Humanitarian Affairs. Comparison may also be made with the 'Code of Conduct for the International Red Cross and Red Crescent Movement and NGOs in Disaster Relief' (see IFRC, 1994, pp. 26–9), which emphasises that 'The right to receive humanitarian assistance, and to offer it, is a fundamental humanitarian principle which should be enjoyed by all citizens of all countries'. The stress in this Code of Conduct is on neutrality and the primacy of need (exactly as in the proposals of Griffiths *et al.*), and upon the rights, and the capacities of those involved in disasters. Thus Article 9 of the Code states: 'We hold ourselves accountable to both those we seek to assist and those from whom we accept resources.' Griffiths *et al.* also, later in their chapter, draw attention to the same point about accountability: 'The failure to consult with and involve nationals, particularly the victims of humanitarian catastrophes, demeans them further and leads to less efficient operations' — which recalls the argument put forward with some poignancy by Slim and Visman about the failure of the UN system in Somalia.

What is problematical in the five points proposed by Griffiths, Levine and Weller is the argument in the last, that 'enforcement action ... does not violate the principle of humanitarian neutrality'. One might accept the principle but still be doubtful about the practice, bearing in mind the conclusion drawn by Slim and Visman that 'Military intervention ... is no substitute for political negotiation combined with ... well-planned humanitarian assistance'. 'Enforcement action' is rather likely to take a form 'suggestive of a threat of armed intervention' with the sorts of consequences which were observed in Somalia. Since the time indeed, in mid-1993, when the chapter on 'Sovereignty and Suffering' was first written, the central issue facing the UN and international NGOs has become that 'of whether force should be used to ensure delivery of aid in an emergency situation, or whether military convoys so compromise a mission as to make it unsustainable in a conflict zone' (*Guardian*, 7 May 1994). On the one hand Lord Owen, as one of the international mediators in Bosnia, raised the question as to whether the UN should not revert to its former 'hands-off stance', while on the other events in Rwanda in 1994 led the ICRC, for the first time, to drop its neutral stance and to call for military intervention.

The question then arises as to 'What triggers — or should trigger — humanitarian action?' As I noted above, the conventional doctrine of sovereignty should not be, and increasingly is not being, permitted to stand ahead of individual human rights. As Griffiths *et al.* suggest: 'The loss of a claim to international representation of a population or segments thereof [permits] international action in line with the implied or expressed desires of [that] population.' Once this principle is granted there is then unquestionably a need for improving the information base on which decisions about intervention can be made, or the system will continue to creak into action mainly in response to problems which are given prominence in the western media (which is another factor undermining the credibility and legitimacy of the UN). Paul Taylor, in his chapter, addressing this problem, advocates an information system which would adapt existing procedures and operate under existing mandates, and which, basically, would draw information systematically from the regular development agencies, with the UNDP Resident Representative in each country performing a coordinating role in supplying information to the Department of Humanitarian Affairs-UNDRO. This would help, no doubt, but it may ignore local perceptions and local knowledge because of the kind of instruments for obtaining information which regular development agencies employ. There is an important role here for agencies, like some NGOs, which work closely with local people and are engaged in dialogue with them.

The other factor which Paul Taylor's proposals ignore is that regarding what finally triggers intervention. The experience of famine early warning systems is salutary. A study conducted by the Institute of Development Studies, University of Sussex and the Save the Children Fund has shown that

> Improved capacity to predict drought-induced famines has not led to a con-
> comitant improvement in famine prevention ... It is often negotiation over con-
> flicting interests betwen donors and governments of recipient countries which
> determines the timing and level of famine response; the role of information
> becomes peripheral to much of the decision-making process (Buchanan-Smith *et
> al.*, 1994, abstract)

Information is likely often to be peripheral to decision-making over
humanitarian intervention more broadly, though the active involvement of
journalists by humanitarian agencies (such as Taylor suggests) should help
to improve the present erratic development of media interest.

If the question of 'triggers' remains one of the most difficult aspects of
the whole problem, the possibilities for action to improve the mechanisms
of intervention seem more clear-cut. Taylor refers to proposals put to the
Select Committee on Foreign Affairs of the House of Commons in the
United Kingdom by the Development Studies Association:

1. (An enlarged?) Security Council should agree that there is a massive and
   immediate threat to human life (based on advice from the Department
   of Humanitarian Affairs-UNDRO, obtained through a system such as
   that referred to above).
2. The decision of the Security Council should be approved by the General
   Assembly (by a two-thirds majority?)
3. The issues themselves, and the terms of the intervention (and the decisions of the Security Council in general), should be subject to jurisdiction of the International Court of Justice.

These are all arguments about the principles which should govern humanitarian intervention. But there are also many practical issues relating to
implementation and the operations of UN and other international agencies.

UN organisation and the practice of humanitarian action

There is a large set of questions concerning the operational capacity of
international humanitarian action, especially relating to the coordination of
the activities of different UN agencies and of other actors, such as NGOs,
and having to do with staffing and financing, which it has been sought to
address through the establishment of the Department of Humanitarian
Affairs, headed initially by Jan Eliasson, and subsequently by Peter Hansen.
Yet, at the moment, according to Griffiths *et al.*, 'There are few signs that
the fundamental coordination and management problems have been overcome'. Paul Taylor devotes much of his chapter precisely to these problems.

Taylor's proposals about the organisation and operation of the international humanitarian system have the great merit of starting with the world as it is rather than, as is all too often the case with policy advice, assuming a *tabula rasa*. His starting point is with the observation that the UN system is 'polycentric' (because of the constitutional independence of the Specialised Agencies from each other, and from the centre) within a multicentric system of states. In these circumstances 'though coordination is a vitally important function it cannot usually be about imposing a common framework of cooperation ... the agencies and other organisations simply cannot be induced to accept this, and it may not be desirable anyway'. The argument is illustrated with reference to past attempts to bring about coordination through the Economic and Social Council, and later through the Directorate-General for Development and International Economic Cooperation. These were obstructed by the characteristic bureaucratic pathologies of the UN: what Taylor describes as the 'reservation' and 'duplication' of functions, and tendencies of 'fragmentation'. The fate of these earlier efforts shows that the creation of a strong supra-national system for the management of disaster relief is a possibility which should be *excluded* because of the nature of international organisation. The approach has to be one which aims at establishing a facilitating, coordinating mechanism, not central management (capable, one might add, of implementing a 'process' rather than a 'blueprint' approach in management). Taylor concludes that what should be sought is a system of coordination which stresses the facilitation of the actions of a multiplicity of actors, while exerting some pressures upon them, so that a rational overall programme is more likely to emerge. What cannot be done is to impose a preconceived plan on all the actors in the system. A facilitating organisation should be more suited to the kind of listening and sensitivity to local conditions — and hence to the kind of mediation which is required in complex emergencies like that in Somalia — which are strongly advocated by Seaman, Slim and Visman, and by Keen.

More specifically Taylor advocates the reform of the system to distinguish 'two loops of functions with regard to crises, a reporting and disaster mitigation loop [the information system described earlier], and crisis management and operational loop'. The point is that the Department of Humanitarian Affairs can reasonably be expected to perform a central coordinating function in relation to information, but not in regard to operations, where it must function rather as a facilitator. Important elements in the second 'loop' are a stronger Inter-Agency Standing Committee (IASC) than exists at present, which would include the principal NGOs (which have, themselves, to improve their own coordination); and country coordination, in most cases undertaken by Special Representatives of the Secretary-General. A *sine qua non* of improvement is improved staffing within DHA-UNDRO, particularly by including many more people with knowledge and experience of field operations, and increased resources for them.

Conclusions

The post-Cold War world, partly because of the collapse of the balance of power between the United States and the Soviet Union, has seen the pro-liferation of complex emergencies. One measure of this is that whereas in 1990 UNICEF spent 4 per cent of its budget on emergencies, four years later in 1994 it spent nearly 30 per cent (*Economist*, 25 June 1994). The handling of these complex emergencies, in which enormous humanitarian demands are muddled up with political and military problems, has shown up as never before the weaknesses and limitations of the United Nations Organisation. The most fundamental of these are that the UN is an organ-isation of member states which pursue their own foreign policy and eco-nomic interests through their participation in the international body; and that it is, at the same time, constrained by the ability of the more powerful member states (notably the five permanent members of the Security Council) to influence its decisions, and by its very heavy dependence for resources upon the United States, which is often slow to pay. Indeed the United States now owes the UN more than $1 billion. Inevitably there are complex tensions arising over the political agendas of the states which make up the UN, and the extent to which the UN is dependent upon the United States complicates them still further.

Without US backing the UN has little clout. In mid-1994 the total fail-ure of the UN in relation to Rwanda had to be explained as being very sub-stantially the outcome of the unwillingness of the United States to become involved, since it was deemed not to fit President Clinton's criteria for US involvement (under PDD 25, the presidential decision directive on peace-keeping). The vacillation of Clinton's leadership in international affairs feeds and is fed by anti-peacekeeping sentiments in Congress, while the relationship between the Americans and the UN Secretary-General, Boutros Boutros-Ghali has deteriorated, perhaps irreparably. The UN's ability to respond firmly — difficult enough in any case when conflicting national interests are involved — is yet further compromised. But when the UN does have strong US backing it is easily represented as being merely a vehicle for American interests. There is an inescapable contradiction in these facts. One outcome is that there is selectivity in humanitarian inter-vention, which is heightened by the dependence of the international response to emergencies upon the media — the so-called 'CNN factor'. The case studies in this book on Somalia and Iraqi Kurdistan amply demonstrate the significance of the selective interest of the media in influ-encing outcomes.

The Economist argued that: 'Two omnipresent facts confront one another. First, there is no satisfactory alternative to collective action by the UN. Second, the UN is no longer equipped militarily or financially to deal with the world's explosions' (25 June 1994, 21). The first of these facts is the basic premise of this book. The authors also accept the truth of the second, but aim to confront it. We do this not by proposing new schemes for the funding of UN activity or ideas for the establishment of a UN military force — worthwhile though we believe the exploration of ideas on these themes to be — but rather by putting forward ideas on the principles which should govern UN action, and on its own organisational capacity in relation to humanitarian assistance. As Nicholas Hinton, Director-General of Save the Children (UK), put it in a speech made in February 1994:

> Clearly we have to face the resource implications of humanitarian or military intervention. We may have to face the fact that resource implications inevitably mean that intervention will be discretionary. What is unacceptable is that we have no way of regulating this discretion.(Hinton, 1994, 6)

A major part of the purpose of the key chapters in this book, by Griffiths his co-authors, and by Taylor, is to advocate and to lay out well-defined principles which should make for much greater consistency in humanitarian intervention, and (in Taylor's chapter) to propose mechanisms which should improve the whole process of decision-making. Greater consistency and a more transparent system of decision-making should make it possible, in turn, to bring about some prioritisation in intervention.

The further purpose of these chapters is to address organisational weaknesses which arise from the 'polycentric' character of the UN system and the way in which it is staffed. The new Department of Humanitarian Affairs has not yet realised the purposes for which it was set up — as *The Economist* said, '[DHA] is still groping for its role' (25 June 1994). Taylor's analysis of the nature of UN organisation shows how great the obstacles confronting the DHA are, yet firm commitment to principles of humanitarian action should help to make it possible for them to be overcome.

Three points, finally, should be stressed. The first is to emphasise that a further part of the reason for the increased importance of humanitarian assistance in the 1990s is precisely that such action has been substituted for economic and social action — as is shown, paradigmatically, in Keen's analysis of Iraqi Kurdistan. More generally complex emergencies in Africa have followed from the failures of development. The demand for selective humanitarian action mirrors, in fact, the failure of development; and it is possible that a self-defeating spiral is created as emergency 'relief' makes the achievement of development even harder. The second, related point is to underline the fact that those who suffer the consequences of complex emergencies are knowledgeable and resourceful, and can be active agents in the resolution of the difficulties which they confront, if they are not treated as 'victims' — hard though this may be to believe when one is confronted with television images of refugees from Rwanda in the camps of Goma. Putting these two points together, in emergency situations external agencies must work closely with local institutions and groups of people, for as long as possible, bearing in mind the evident implications of the failure to do this in Somalia. In terms of the distinction which Seaman makes, the effort must be made to pursue the 'development' rather than the 'emergency' model of relief.

An implication of these arguments is that humanitarian action should be accountable to those who are its subjects, or 'beneficiaries'. Beyond the suggestions made by Griffiths and his co-authors in their chapter here consideration should also be given to proposals made by Save the Children (UK):

> SCF believes that a permanent and independent body needs to be set up to act as guardian of humanitarian rights in emergencies, and to monitor the means undertaken to meet them. An independent commission on humanitarian assistance would be able to report on the needs of affected populations and on the conduct of all parties in responding to those needs. In so doing it could identify priorities and draw attention to abuses. Over time it could also make an important contribution to the consistent development of good and just practice in the field of humanitarian assistance. The nature of such a body remains open to ... discussion. (SCF, 1994, 11)

The final point concerns the difficult issue of the relations between peacekeeping and humanitarian intervention. Is it permissible for force to be used to ensure delivery of assistance? Martin Griffiths, Iain Levine and Mark Weller argue that 'enforcement action' may be justified. The Somalia case shows very clearly, however, that once the United Nations intervenes militarily in an emergency, its actions can all too easily become part of the problem. International forces can also withdraw having initiated a solution but leaving the consequences of that solution under-resourced and unsustainable, as happened in Iraqi Kurdistan. Hitherto, in complex emergencies, the mandates and identities of the three main aspects of the UN's role — humanitarian, political and military — have not been sufficiently distinct, and have compromised each other. Usually, as was the case in Somalia after the killings of the UN Pakistani troops on 5 June 1993, humanitarian operations have been marginalised. As Save the Children has argued:

> It is clear that a complete separation of humanitarian and politico-military operations is not feasible in many of today's complex emergencies. It is, however, equally necessary that the connection between these operations is one which

preserves the neutrality and enhances the effectiveness of humanitarian assistance within an appropriate security framework. (SCF, 1994, 11)

The realisation of this objective requires organisational structures which clearly distinguish humanitarian operations without marginalising them — such as would have made UNOSOM Humanitarian's symbolic shift of its headquarters in Mogadishu unnecessary. One possible structure, suggested in his chapter by Paul Taylor, would involve a special representative of the Secretary-General in each emergency to whom humanitarian and politico-military chiefs with equal status report (see also SCF, 1994, 11).

In the end all these arguments hinge around one basic contention: 'the overriding objective must be to work towards definitions of global security that are based not on security of territory, but on the security of people' (Hinton, 1994, 3).

Bibliography

Archer, R. (1994), 'Markets and good government', in; A. Clayton, ed., *Governance, Democracy and Conditionality: What Role for NGOs?* Oxford, INTRAC.

Buchanan-Smith, M., Davies, S. and Petty, C. (1994), 'Food security: let them eat information', *IDS Bulletin*, 25 2, April, 69–80.

Hinton, N. (1994), 'The UN in the 21st Century', Royal Society of Arts Lecture, 2 February 1994.

IFRC [International Federation of Red Cross and Red Crescent Societies] (1994), *World Disasters Report 1994,* Dordrecht: Martinus Nijhoff Publishers.

Lewis, I. (1993), Paper for the LSE Centre for the Study of Global Governance and Commission on Global Governance Forum, Chewton Glen, September.

Save the Children (1994), *Position Paper: The United Nations and Humanitarian Assistance.*

UNDP, (1994), *Human Development Report 1994,* New York: Oxford University Press.

World Bank (1992), *Governance and Development*, Washington, DC, The World Bank.

1

The international system of humanitarian relief in the 'New World Order'

John Seaman

In the last three years the international relief system has been fundamentally transformed. This system which, since the Second World War, had evolved gently under the stable conditions of the Cold War, saw such stability as it had achieved undermined by the double blow of the collapse of the Soviet Union and the events surrounding the Gulf War. Moreover, the reorganisation of the United Nations Secretariat, with peacemaking and humanitarian relief at the centre of the international political process; the creation of the UN Department of Humanitarian Affairs (DHA); and the demand from Western donor governments for effective action have caused the most fundamental shock to the system since the foundation of the UN.

This chapter examines these recent changes from the perspective of the historical evolution of the international relief system and speculates as to how the system may develop in future.

The international relief system

The international 'system' of humanitarian relief is not, in the ordinary sense of the word, a system at all. The term is applied to a large number of organisations and individuals which, although they declare similar objectives, operate within vastly different financial, political, organisational and technical constraints. The system extends from the bilateral (government-to-government) agencies and multilateral donors (the UN and the European Union), which are bound or influenced by domestic and international political agendas and international legislation, through organisations such as the International Committee of the Red Cross (ICRC) with special international status and functions, to the smaller international Non-Government Organisations (NGOs), and even, in some settings, to informal groupings and individuals engaging in relief entirely at their own initiative.

Nevertheless, the system may be regarded as a system to the extent that within it there are some basic drives torwards common action and cooperation, or competition and dissent; these drives are complex and interrelated. But it may be argued that the way in which the system functions at any time is the product of two main factors: the quantity of resources available to the system and the way in which they are controlled within it. These in turn depend in a complex way on several other factors of which the most important, as these are major determinants of the resource supply, are the quantity and quality of information available to the public — most directly through the visual media — and the wider foreign policy interests of the donor countries.

A further factor is the strength, financial and political, of the recipient country concerned. In the nature of international work in a sovereign developing country only the recipient government has the right to control or coordinate. Where, as is often the case in the poorer developing countries, the recipient government does not have the effective power to do this the individual components of the system, with the relative exception of the UN (which, strictly speaking, is subordinate to the recipient government), are free to act as they please. In the economically and politically stronger developing countries, such as India, China and Iran, where government and sometimes local NGOs have the resources to act independently and to control the actions of international relief agencies, the national policy tends to be dominant or even to exclude international relief agencies entirely. In the poorer developing countries, where government is often dependent on international assistance — or in cases such as Somalia where there has been no effective government at all — and local views can be overridden, the system behaves quite differently. It is in the latter situation that the new international policies have most force, and with which this chapter is largely concerned.

Resources

The resources used for international relief derive from two main sources, the governments of western countries and voluntary contributions from the general public. Each government has its own foreign policy reasons for giving or not giving relief aid, but they are all, even if only at a general level, responsive to the wishes of their electorates. For example, US policy towards Ethiopia during the period of Soviet involvement in that country was not to provide aid. In 1985 the policy was dramatically changed in the light of strong public feeling in reaction to images of mass starvation in Ethiopia, and the imminent presidential election. It might be argued that the provision of relief to the war in ex-Yugoslavia serves to satisfy, or at least to hold off, a western public demand for effective action and to balance this with the foreign policy interest of avoiding western military intervention.

The main flows of donor resources within the system are to the UN and in recent years increasingly to the larger western 'International' NGOs (INGOs) such as Oxfam and SCF (and often through them to local NGOs). Western public donations flow essentially through the international NGOs although money may also pass directly from the public to the site of need. Direct donations vary enormously, but where there are close connections between affluent fund-raising constituencies, such as *émigré* groups, and an affected population (as, for example, in Bosnia) the sums involved may be very large. Rough calculations suggest that in some instances the amounts may rival or exceed the official aid flows.

The dependence of each part of the system on resources from any particular source is the major factor determining levels of control by one part of the system of another. In general, government donors tend to have greater control over the agencies which they support. Government contributions are more or less tied to specific actions. Thus an NGO may obtain a grant for an agreed set of actions over an agreed period of time. This reflects both the nature of government aid, which is ultimately accountable to a national legislature, and the interest of the donor concerned. At least historically, US assistance has been more, and European assistance less closely tied. Public contributions may also be tied although more loosely as, for example, to 'drought in Africa', but they may often be used as the recipient thinks fit.

In practice an NGO or UN body is constrained to work in a particular way to the extent that its income is tied to donor contributions. For all practical purposes the UN is financed by its member nations and is wholly dependent on a small number of western Governments to finance specific relief operations. For example, the UNHCR currently receives only 5 per cent of its income from contributions to the UN Regular Budget (Loescher, 1993).

The media

In the modern world the western public obtains information on overseas emergencies chiefly from the visual 'media' coverage of events, a fact which conditions both the public willingness to support action and government views with regard to the relative importance of any specific emergency. Of the many distortions in media coverage, perhaps the most important is that only a minority of all emergencies receive mention, much less significant coverage, on the main television channels. For example, the mass killing and exodus from Rwanda in May 1994 attracted much media interest (and a substantial financial response from both government and people);

whereas the famines and food crises of Northern Sudan and Ethiopia which were taking place at the same time received no coverage at all. In the absence of publicity for the latter cases donor response was measured, short of a perceived risk of mass starvation (and therefore of media coverage and public interest) largely in terms of foreign policy interests.

To summarise, the system is a system to the extent that its component parts are linked by public information and opinion, and the resources generated by information. To the extent that any one part of the system can dominate information and resources its interests will be disproportionately represented. As international relief has become more costly and the resources required for effective action much larger — major food relief operations may involve resources in the hundreds of millions — this balance has become the central determinant of the interests and objectives reflected in relief action Whether a particular emergency receives international relief and, if so, how much and how quickly, and of what quality, is at best only partly correlated with the needs of the victims.

Competence: approaches to relief work

The actual work done by any agency in any case, the types and usefulness of the work actually done, which for brevity may be called its 'competence', depends as already noted upon the financial possibility of action and the freedom to deploy resources in an effective way. If a donor places constraints on funding this may preclude the efficient use of resources. For example, if the donor is anxious to support work with a high media profile and directs the agencies which it supports, this might argue for expatriate medical workers with a high visibility and a short period of involvement; considerations of efficiency might argue for the use of local people and for a lower-key public health approach or for longer-term work. Competence also depends on a much neglected area, that of the practical usefulness and efficiency of different approaches to relief work and the organisational ability to deploy the practical skills to implement them.

Opinions on what constitutes an emergency and an appropriate response vary widely. At one extreme is the view that the effects of disaster and relief needs are most easily defined purely in material terms — the number of trauma cases, the numbers of people who are thin or who need immunisations, etc. As a corollary to this view the role of international relief is to plan and act in a quasi-military way to meet these needs, through the provision of medical personnel, blankets, shelter or whatever seems appropriate. This view tends to be associated with the beliefs that the effectiveness of international disaster relief depends crucially on the speed of response and formalised planning (e.g., 'coordination'), and with the idea of a politically 'neutral' humanitarian response. The view is

implicitly (sometimes still explicitly) based on the 'model' that a population affected by an emergency is essentially passive and entirely dependent
on international relief for its survival and well-being and that the business
of relief is the narrow one of saving of life.

The competing, if less popular view is that although disaster certainly
has physical effects and there is often a clear need to provide material assistance, and sometimes to provide this quickly, other factors must be taken
into account if resources are to be used in the most efficient way. This view
begins with the consistent observation that the stereotype of an affected
population ineffectually waiting for relief is both an oversimplification and
routinely confounded in practice. To take a simple case, search and rescue
and medical activities after earthquakes in developing countries are usually
completed before international assistance arrives or could in practice arrive
from abroad: the many survivors will engage, often selflessly, in rescue;
even in poorer countries medical supplies will be found by using existing
stocks; and in any case the injured cannot wait the days or weeks it takes
for outsiders to arrive and become operational. With very rare exceptions
— no more than ten to twelve clear instances in Africa in twenty years —
the reality of famine is not of mass starvation demanding an emergency
response. The remarkable feature of famine-prone areas has been the
extent to which people have been able to avoid starvation from drought
and other calamities by adapting their economies, for example through the
diversification of sources of income. The effects of a famine in modern
Africa may be starvation for a few but are fundamentally economic — the
loss of livestock, land and the means to secure future survival. The need for
external intervention is often a modest but timely intervention before the
crisis occurs.

From an operational perspective the difference in these two positions is
profound. The first tends to a standardised and short-term response — typically medical teams — and has regularly led to actions which vary from
the inefficient to the absurd. After some disasters large numbers of international medical personnel have found themselves with no work to do, or
they have found work by treating, at phenomenal expense and for an arbitrary period of a few weeks, diseases which predated the emergency. The
latter view, sometimes called a 'development' approach to relief, which
takes as given that the greater part of the work will be done by the population of the country concerned, tends to seek synergy between international relief and local efforts and to be more relevant, efficient and effective. The practical difference in the two approaches is between the provision of a surgical team to assist the wounded in Mogadishu — an expensive approach which cannot by definition treat many cases — and the provision of material and organisational support for Somali surgeons who
without support could not effectively work; or the provision or sale of
building materials with which people can rehouse themselves, rather than

the supply of unsuitable prefabricated housing. A more complex example would be the attempts in some locations to prevent and relieve famine by market intervention and support rather than only by the free distribution of food. In short the approach looks for whatever action will make the local system work more effectively and efficiently. It is in the nature of this approach that it tends to have a longer-term effect and to be a more efficient use of resources; it is also in the nature of this approach that it is less visible to the media.

Media reports of emergencies tend to reinforce the simplistic view of disasters — of 'external' forces coming to the rescue — and to ignore the second. As has been noted, media coverage is necessary to the 'profile' of any part of the system, which is critical to the success of public fund-raising. The most successful relief work in terms of fund-raising may be the least successful from the perspective of the recipient.

Coordination

Coordination — the bringing together of the several organisations and interests which contribute to any relief operation into a coherent working whole — is possible only in circumstances in which all parties have a common objective and a common view as to how this might be reached when coordination comes about by agreement, or, alternatively, when one party can enforce a common pattern of activity on others. The former situation has been a very common one between NGOs in lower-key (low media profile) operations, where the tendency has been for fewer larger organisations to be involved; cases of the latter have been rare. Only the government of the affected country has had the legal right to coordinate; and few poor states have had the skills or power to impose their will on external agencies. An exception would be the government of Somalia in the early 1980s which effectively coordinated many external organisations within a common set of technical guidelines. The UN has not in general sought to coordinate except in some instances through informal meetings. In some cases, like that of Sudan through most of the 1980s, the UN actively avoided the role, presumably because the government did not wish coordination to occur.

The recent evolution of the international relief system

At the risk of slightly arbitrary division and some simplification, it could be said that the international relief system has been through three major periods since the Second World War. The first was the period of relief and reconstruction after the war, a period in which much current international legislation was written or reformed. During this period relief in the now developing countries was a largely domestic (albeit often colonial) matter. The point which marks the start of the second period is a matter of debate, but it can be fairly placed at the outset of the Biafran war of independence (1967), although this had clear precedents in international involvement in the relief operations which followed the Bihar drought and the conflict in the ex-Belgian Congo. The third, which has a less definite start, can be placed in the early 1980s, although it was firmly consolidated by the Ethiopian crisis of 1984–85. The first is not discussed here, although as the 'New World Order' of its day it has some interesting parallels and contrasts with aspects of the current changes in the system.

Biafra to the early 1980s

With hindsight, the period from the Biafran War to the mid-1980s, rather than the changes since the Gulf War, may be regarded as anomalous. During this period the international relief system enjoyed the luxury of regular and sustained support from both western governments and the western public. A large part of a generally affluent public found the persistence of extreme poverty and particularly starvation in poor countries repugnant and contributed to its relief and broadly supported government international aid.

This coincided happily with the policy objectives of western governments, which had good reasons of their own to give aid, if no other than that it provided one weapon in the proxy battles fought between East and West in the developing countries, and within the UN. In parallel with the stasis of the Cold War was a broadly secure and often largely untied income for both the UN and the international NGOs, the former from government donors, the latter largely directly from the public or on relatively untied terms from donors. Whatever the reasons, from the 1960s to the early 1980s it was possible for the international system to take its financial underpinning and, moreover, its growth largely for granted. The roles, structures and abilities of the different actors in the system evolved accordingly.

The UN served as a vehicle for a complex international political agenda, the objectives of which did not require and, indeed, often precluded the possibility of a high standard of practical performance. The UN, operating in the context of an international rhetoric of sovereign and equal states and the practical reality of constant conflict between two major power blocs with fundamentally opposite philosophies and each with its own 'camp' of developing countries, took of necessity — the UN is its collective membership — the line of least resistance.

In international relief, and from the perspective of many field operations, the UN developed the habit of avoiding conflict with member nations even to the extent of avoiding comment on gross breaches of human rights. For example, the crisis in the Uganda 'Luwero triangle', an area adjacent to Kampala, where part of the Ugandan army was out of control for a period of three years from 1983, where several hundred thousand people died of disease, starvation and violence and where the UN was fully represented, went virtually unremarked. The UN system appears to have developed within itself the internal systems of balance and control necessary to its survival, of absolute subordination to the views of member states, and of international political invisibility.

In keeping with its role of subordination to government, UN emergency 'assessments' were often little more than a basic economic description of the place, some statistics on the disaster event and a disconnected list of material needs. That this was apparently satisfactory to the donors, necessary to the survival of the agency, and probably unavoidable, does not alter the fact that the UN and its internal structures were formed and rehearsed in a context where their practical usefulness was not at a premium. A corollary to the relationship with government is that UN performance has been (and to a large extent still is) measured only by the volume of resources used. The effect of these resources on the recipients is not generally measured. The UNHCR, for example, does not report to donors on the welfare of refugees, as it is irrelevant to the UN position. Responsibility is with the government of the state concerned, no matter how weak this may be.

The practical result during this period was that each part of the system was assured of its income and its place in the action. A pattern developed in which the UN worked subordinate to the government of the affected country, and acted as a conduit for the larger material assistance, typically food and logistics, shelter, and bulk drug supply. The NGOs in their various forms and to varying levels of competence provided field-level skills mostly in health and other social areas. As the tag had it, 'the UN had all the money and no skills, the NGOs the reverse'.

Changes prior to the Gulf War

In the early to mid-1980s a perceptible shift occurred in the internal balance of the system. The early 1980s marked the beginning of a change in the Cold War, at least as this was pursued in the developing countries. By the early 1980s the economic decline which began with the oil price shocks had for many developing countries developed to the point of real economic crisis: in the economic war, western rather than Soviet aid had become necessary to the survival of some developing country governments. It is perhaps no coincidence that the same period marks the start of an increasing government and public disenchantment with the UN and with development aid. Western governments and particularly the United States were contributing financially to and often embattled in a process from which they gained no advantage and which, with the shift in relative economic and therefore political power in the developing countries, they did not need.

In the same period the INGOs began a phase of unprecedented growth. Donor governments had generally no reason to want a bilateral operational involvement in relief. Where it was politically advantageous relief could generally be satisfied by bilateral grants or, rarely, by the use of the military (for example, the Royal Navy in the Caribbean); and in the many situations where these means could not be used (notably the 'communist' countries), it was easier and often practically more satisfactory to provide support through the INGOs. As already noted, public support was at a high level.

Anti-UN sentiment was fuelled by a succession of highly publicised UN operational failures, for example: in the Karamoja famine (1981), the Ethiopian famine (1985), in provision for refugee populations in Malawi, Somalia and Ethiopia, as an increasing operational mismatch developed between the UN and the better-funded and more ambitious INGOs. The economic collapse and loss of effectiveness of the governments of many developing countries had led to greater expectations of the UN, expectations which it was practically and constitutionally incompetent to meet. For example, SCF (UK) was involved in a succession of disputes with the UNHCR over the material conditions of refugees, largely related to the repeated problems of the starvation of refugees and epidemics of vitamin deficiency diseases. The UNHCR was prominent in such disputes partly because of the enormous numbers of refugees escaping from wars and economic disaster, but also because it was the only prominent operational UN agency. Of the UN technical agencies with potential relevance to emergency relief only UNHCR and (in bulk food supply and transport) the WFP have a direct operational capacity. UNICEF is occasionally operational; FAO and WHO for all practical purposes are uninvolved.

It was also increasingly apparent that these problems reflected the constitutional limitations of the UN, compounded by those of the mandates of the UN agencies, drafted for an earlier and very different world. The refugee conventions were not designed to meet the needs of thousands of poor refugees displaced from one poor country to another. No matter how much an organisation like SCF felt that in the absence of any national government capacity to provide for a camp of refugees the UNHCR should take responsibility, the *legal* fact was that they had no responsibility for the matter. The ICRC also found that the Geneva Convention, a code drawn up to meet the needs of formal war between states, had increasing limitations when applied to civil wars in developing countries where even the distinction between civilian and combatant was blurred.

In the run up to the Gulf War the relief order established in the 1960s and 1970s was already disintegrating. NGOs were handling more money, material and influence than ever before: the UN was relatively weaker, poorly geared for an operational role and increasingly and publicly criticised; and the mandates of its technical organisations or their interpretation increasingly irrelevant to practical reality. By the late 1980s the NGOs were often filling roles formerly reserved for government and the UN. NGOs were running major relief operations on large budgets, were handling large quantities of food aid and were sometimes doing this in direct collaboration with governments, effectively marginalising the UN.

Changes since the Gulf War

It is tempting to see the recent changes in the international relief system as little more than the product of some astute but expedient decisions taken to manage the political difficulties generated by the Kurdish refugee crisis after the Gulf War. Hundreds of thousands of Kurdish refugees had moved to the Turkish border as a direct consequence of western involvement in Iraq: the movement was unanticipated and unplanned for. The refugees had been refused admittance to Turkey, an ally in the war, where there was flatter, more suitable land, and thus were confined to steep hillsides without access to water. People were living and visibly dying in appalling conditions; relief was in the form of a confusion of agencies of often questionable competency operating entirely without coordination and punctuated by Turkish military brutality. The whole was the subject of sustained, although from a political perspective mercifully uncritical, media coverage. The situation quite clearly contained the makings of a major political problem.

The steps taken by western politicians to deal with this crisis — the shifting of the blame to the UN for both the immediate chaos of the Kurdish relief operation and the fundamental failings of the system; and the call for new international arrangements for disaster relief and the creation of the 'safe havens' — were politically astute and a reasonable short-term line of action. Yet they can hardly be considered a rational basis for the total overhaul of the UN system, much less as the building blocks of the new world order.

It is not clear whether those who made the decisions on the 'New World Order' of humanitarian relief knew that the Turkish case was an atypical example. It seems unlikely that they had any profound knowledge of the system which they were setting out to reform. Such extreme relief chaos had not previously occurred since 1980, in the relief operation for Cambodian refugees on the Thai border. For instruction on the components of a well-managed relief operation and from it the components of a reformed relief system — essentially those of good intelligence, forward planning and clear objective — western governments need have looked no further than Iran, where a Kurdish population of near identical size and composition had been admitted and settled in a largely systematic and effective way, for all practical purposes without international assistance and without any dramatic increase in mortality.

It seems more likely that the steps that were taken never really amounted to a policy 'decision' at all, if a policy is taken as a set of principles which can be used to direct action; or if it was a policy 'decision' then it was one constructed at such speed and with so little thought that the limitations and contradictions were not taken into account. There seems little doubt that the later US intervention in Somalia was driven more by domestic policy interests — an idea put forward at the end of the Bush presidency which got out of hand because it was driven by the media and subsequently directed by the military — than by deeper policy considerations. But whatever the reasons, the weaknesses in the new international arrangements for disaster relief were manifest. Evidence of the chief contradiction, that only the West was placed to determine which countries were in sufficient breach of their obligations to their citizens to force intervention, and that in most circumstances only the West had the power to intervene may be found in the selective nature of the interventions. Bluster over Bosnia apart, there have been no moves to engage seriously in the many other local wars currently in progress.

Two recent events — the UN default during the slaughter in Rwanda and the protracted televised shelling of Gorazde in ex-Yugoslavia — leave little room for doubt about the realities of the new position. The events in Rwanda were wholly predictable in principle if not in detail, and yet it appears that the UN with all its new machinery of coordination was caught entirely unawares; in the latter, it was weeks before there was even a token threat of military retaliation. The UN position, that it cannot act more widely without greater commitment from member states to the supply of troops and other resources is certainly true, but where such supplies have been forthcoming there is an equally evident unwillingness by the UN (that is, its member states) to support any policy other than that which appears to support national interests.

The situation is, however, hardly one of a simple failure to press a weak policy with sufficient vigour or material. A stronger case is that it is merely a symptom of a deeper disease — the breakdown of the structures, intellectual, philosophical and material, of the old global order. It can no longer be assumed that the West is the global centre of military and economic power. Indeed there are now doubts about the nature of global power itself. During the Cold War other realities were subordinated to membership of one power bloc or the other. With the end of the Cold War it must be accepted that both the nature and balance of power have definitively changed. There is now not one dominant centre of world economic power but, with the growth of East Asia, two, and the probability that Latin America and South Asia must also soon be included.

The old measures of military power are now increasingly meaningless. Although the West, and particularly the United States, remains the nominal centre of military power this is measured in terms which are irrelevant to the current reality of war. The end of big-power proxy wars has merely confirmed the understanding, begun in Vietnam and perhaps completed in Somalia, that armies designed for nuclear war and formal conflict may be ineffective against tribal armies. It must also be accepted that Galbraith's 'contented class' of the West — educated, well off and informed by the media — can see no merit in going to war in pursuit of any ordinary political objective (Galbraith, 1992).

Since the Cold War the foreign policy interests of western states have also changed. Domestic policy is consumed by the problem of under- and unemployment. The competition from developing countries in the old industries and the displacement even of skilled employment by the new technologies is a problem sufficient to threaten the order of the modern state, in which paid employment is the basis of the social order. Foreign policy is dominated by the new priorities, and often contradictory objectives, of the maintenance of trade, the global environment and population and nuclear non-proliferation. The basis of the new global conflict is to be found between these interests and those of the emerging nations, for whom a cruder industrial development and prosperity is the aim, with population and environment as largely subordinate matters. Ironically, given the recent discussion of changes in the nature of sovereignty, the new reality is of an absolute economic interdependence through a mutual need for access to the global market, a severe curtailment of the power of any state, and for the richer world no possibility for differences between the affluent states to be settled by war.

Against this must be set a multilateral order founded at the end of the Second World War and maintained by big-power rivalry until the collapse of the Soviet bloc. The UN was founded by only fifty-one states — there are now over 150; veto power is effectively confined to the victors of a fifty-year-old war; its founding articles spring from the legal and moral traditions and the practical interests of the West; and it largely now continues to exist only because of western financial support. It is perhaps no great surprise that with the end of Cold War the UN does not enjoy universal support. The UN is now widely viewed as no more than a proxy for western interests,; and its legal norms are increasingly outdated, irrelevant and ignored by its member states. The Islamic States widely regard UN actions in Bosnia as openly partisan, and in Somalia and widely in the developing countries the UN is regarded and attacked as a western proxy organisation. It is perhaps evidence enough that the UN organisation which has been at the centre of events in Bosnia, the UNHCR, operating the largest general relief operation of modern times, does this with the limited mandate of the protection of refugees, themselves narrowly defined in international law. Even the ICRC, normally the most reticent of organisations, has been forced to protest the politicisation of the role of UNHCR and its relationship to UNPROFOR, which is compromising the work and mandate of the ICRC (*Guardian*, 1994).

The future

As the initial enthusiasm for the new relief system gives way and accommodates to practical reality it is already possible to see a new balance emerging in the working of the international system. The chief features of this are perhaps no more than a formalisation and consolidation of the trends already well established in the 1980s.

Donor governments now have and will probably continue to have good reasons to be involved directly in relief or to have their contribution to relief acknowledged by the western public. In a few situations, where engagement in relief fulfils a strategic or tactical need for western governments which they cannot pursue by historically more conventional means, relief will be used as a central instrument of state policy. As David Howell, Chairman of the Foreign Affairs Select Committee has put it, 'Humanitarian relief is now at the cutting edge of foreign policy' (Personal communication, H. Slim). Given the extreme constraints on government freedom of action one might almost say, to paraphrase Clausewitz, that relief has become 'the continuation of politics by other means'.

The importance attached to such cases may be estimated from the scale of expenditure, which is reckoned in terms formerly only associated with full-scale war. A few months of militarily-supported relief on the Turkish border after the Gulf War may be roughly estimated to have cost as much as the support of all refugees in Africa in the same year; and between 1990/1 and 1992/3, the proportion of the entire UK aid budget devoted to relief rose from 8 per cent to 13 per cent of total aid disbursements, a rise largely accounted for by additional provision for the costs of relief in the former Yugoslavia (*British Aid Statistics*, 1993).

More often, and involving donors less openly, there will be cases which involve the disproportionate allocation of resources where there is a substantial western interest. Current examples include Operation Lifeline Sudan (OLS), a massive airlift to Southern Sudan, and the airlift to UNITA-held areas of Angola. Both, but particularly the former, may be seen to have a primarily political and only secondarily humanitarian purpose — indeed some NGOs operating outside OLS but partly funded by the same donor sources are directly supporting rebel forces. OLS is estimated to cost approximately US$200 million each year. It is likely that as the outstanding business of the Cold War gradually comes to an end such operations will become increasingly rare.

The most common, and for the future most representative, situation will be in emergencies with high media profile, where donors can now take direct credit or advantage for their actions, which during the Cold War they were often denied. Here a trend to greater donor control over the practicality of relief is already evident and is likely to continue. Donors such as the EU are now regularly fielding their own staff to oversee relief work and the work of NGOs which they support. As many NGOs are now wholly dependent on donor funds to work at all, 'chequebook coordination', as it is known, is a reality. In the larger relief operations it is increasingly the case that the nature of the work is essentially determined by a few donor organisations. This may not always be in conflict with the interests of victims: given the confusion of some past relief operations, it is sometimes perhaps better to have donor coordination than no coordination at all. The chief negative effect may be to encourage and reinforce the worst tendencies of short term-relief.

On current trends the UN, both operationally as individual technical agencies and through the DHA, will remain prominent only in situations where there is substantial western interest in it being so (as in Angola at present). Elsewhere the UN is now and seems set to be increasingly marginalised by direct donor action and, as in the 1980s, often bypassed by operational links between donors, NGOs and governments.

The greatest change will perhaps be for the larger NGOs. There is already a sense of increased competition between NGOs for access to donor funds as donor systems of disbursement become more formalised. A tension is also developing between those NGOs which are prepared to take direction from donors and effectively become their proxies, and those which feel that to work effectively they must retain a degree of independence. The fear may be overstated. In the confusion of recent events and the open politicisation of relief it has sometimes seemed as if NGOs might increasingly be taking the role of missionaries for the new colonial order — in Somalia interference with an INGO could bring military retaliation. A more likely reality, as events develop, is that now as in past decades the greater number of emergencies will be out of the public eye. The availability of donor resources will be driven by foreign policy rather than domestic concerns and the relationships will remain much as before. Donors will continue to need politically neutral conduits for funds.

Bibliography

British Aid Statistics 1988/89–1992/93 (1993), Government Statistical Service, ODA, East Kilbride.

Galbraith, J. K. (1992), *The Culture of Contentment,* London, Sinclair Stevenson Ltd.

Guardian, London, 18 April 1994.

Loescher, G. 1993, *Beyond Charity: International Cooperation and the Global Refugee Crisis,* New York, Oxford University Press.

2

Sovereignty and suffering

Martin Griffiths, Iain Levine and Mark Weller[1]

In February 1992, shortly after he had taken up the position of Secretary-General of the United Nations, Dr Boutros Boutros-Ghali told a meeting of NGO representatives in Geneva that his period in office would be dominated by the incidence and consequences of internal conflicts. New nations will emerge from the ashes of these conflicts, he said, and the United Nations will be judged by the humanity with which they are treated.

Since then, events have borne out the Secretary-General's words. Internal conflicts, dire humanitarian crises, and political and military disputes over sovereignty have all dominated the international agenda. The United Nations, acting in concert with major donor nations, has been obliged to react to events in circumstances where consensus over proper international practice has frequently been absent. The disputes and disagreements arising from that lack of consensus have damaged the credibility of the United Nations, at a time when the organisation has been the focus of intense popular hopes for a more humane world. It is with many of these difficulties and hopes in mind that this paper has been written.

The complexity of the political and humanitarian crises faced by the international community has been of a new and daunting order. The dispiriting certainties of the Cold War have given way to a turbulent instability which has produced crises of a dimension not seen in thirty years. The scale of response, though often belated, has perforce been commensurate. We have witnessed the emergence of humanitarian and security operations each now costing well over $1 billion per annum. Great strains have been placed upon the international purse and upon the operational capacity of the United Nations itself. Naturally resources on such a scale can come only from the wealthiest nations, and in particular from the United States. This leads in turn to a perception that, in these complex operations, the United Nations is acting more at the behest of its paymasters than is appropriate for an international organisation. Again, it is the credibility of the United Nations that suffers.

The ending of the Cold War set in train a series of changes in international relations, only the outline of which is yet clear. One persistent theme, however, has been the growing emphasis on universality of values – most forcefully expressed within the context of human rights. The proponents of universality argue that the rights of peoples and of individuals largely supersede the rights of institutions, even those which govern them. This notion, of a world agreed upon certain minimum social and political conditions, where those who transgress may be brought to book by the international community, is undeniably attractive. Many governments and international institutions grow more willing to make their economic and political relations with states conditional upon a recognition of this universality.

The dangers of such an approach have also been recognised. The Vienna Conference on Human Rights (1993) saw this debate at its most open. Behind the anxiety of some governments about the growth of conditionality resides the deeper fear of a new and more formidable colonialism, its power expressed through the United Nations, promoting the values and aspirations of western governments.

This debate is central to the development of more effective humanitarian action by the international community, for at the heart of it lies the authority of sovereignty. The parody of sovereignty allows governments to do – or refrain from – pretty well what they please without let or hindrance from any external power. Critics argue that this never was the case – and certainly not since the writing of the UN Charter – and, in any event, that it is increasingly inappropriate in a world made smaller by technology and ambition.

We shall argue that, despite the absence of any declared international consensus on the limits to sovereignty, there is nevertheless a consistent trend emerging from the crises of recent years. This trend, prompted originally by more elastic definitions of the way in which internal problems may cause threats to peace and security beyond state boundaries, has begun to point the way to a more defined legal framework for humanitarian action even where sovereign approval is absent.

This encouraging development will, we believe, provide the Secretary-General with greater clarity about the circumstances and processes which legitimise UN humanitarian action – which in turn will begin to restore the credibility of the UN as an independent international institution, for it will be seen to act according to agreed criteria rather than at the apparent whim of politically dominant states.

This chapter examines the operational framework within which humanitarian action is taken, with a particular focus on the United Nations agencies. The examination reveals a selective and patchy response to humanitarian crises, partly as a result of the moral and legal vacuum already described, but also due to the scale and complexity of the operational task. We see that much needs to be done to enable humanitarian agencies to meet the responsibilities we have so glibly entrusted to them.

We are aware from first-hand experience of the often dismal record of response to crises in the recent past. But we remain optimistic about the potential for significant improvements in the legal and operational framework. It is less easy to be optimistic about the political context.

The dominance of security concerns over humanitarian concerns is not surprising. But it is alarming. The traditional – and underexamined – notion of the neutrality of humanitarian action is severely at risk. It is ironic that at a time when universality of values, based on a shared view of human rights, is receiving greater attention than ever before the fundamental principle of humanitarian work is in jeopardy, namely, that assistance is given to those who need it without discrimination except in their favour. This is the doctrine of humanitarian neutrality and it is the very premise of this paper. In the search for lucidity in regard to the law and improvements in practice the objective is to establish a clear space for humanitarian action impermeable to political demands. This is not to say that humanitarian crises do not also require political solutions – invariably they do. But such political processes need to run alongside, rather than across, or counter to the humanitarian process. What is required is constraint on the part of the dominant states and unimpeded leadership from the United Nations.

Sovereignty and suffering: the legal framework

Background

Sovereignty, in its traditional sense, denotes the supreme authority of the organs of a state over all persons and objects within its territory.[2] In relations between states, sovereignty signifies independence, or the right to exercise within a portion of the globe and to the exclusion of any other state the functions of a state, and to represent these functions externally.[3] As the Permanent Court of International Justice put it in the *Lotus* case:[4]

> The first and foremost restriction imposed by international law upon a state is that – failing the existence of a permissible rule to the contrary – it may not exercise its power in any form in the territory of another state. In this sense jurisdiction is certainly territorial; it cannot be exercised by a state outside its territory except by virtue of a permissive rule derived from international custom or from a convention.

Traditionally, the right to the exclusive exercise of internal and external public authority has been jealously guarded by governments. According to classical doctrine, the population of a state could only engage in international, legally relevant acts through the medium of its government. Whether the government was actually representative of the population whose interests it purported to embody was, at the international level, regarded as irrelevant. The decisive criterion was the effectiveness of state power.

Part of the doctrine of sovereign authority exercised by governments was the principle of consent in the establishment of obligations binding upon a state or, as the Permanent Court of International Justice put it, 'restrictions upon the sovereignty of a state cannot lightly be presumed'.[5] However, it is uncontroversial that an obligation, once it is established by treaty, custom or general principle of law, is indeed binding and cannot be revoked unilaterally.[6]

If a state is subject to an international obligation, the matter regulated by that obligation is no longer considered to warrant the claim to exclusivity of national jurisdiction. As the landmark decision of the Permanent Court of International Justice established in the *Nationalities Decrees* case, the protection of the sovereign decision-making authority of a state, extending to matters solely or essentially within its jurisdiction, concerns 'matters which, though they may very closely concern the interests of more than one state, are not, in principle, regulated by international law. As regards such matters, each state is sole judge'.[7]

Of course, human rights are part and parcel of both conventional and customary international law. Human rights can aim to protect individuals, groups, minorities, or entire peoples. Some human rights are regarded as part of international *jus cogens*, i.e., part of the body of peremptory international law from which no derogations are permitted. This body of essential rules includes, in particular, the right of a people to self-determination.

With the disappearance of the violent competition between two dominant ideologies of global aspiration it is now safe to assert that there also exists a common core of individual human rights of universal application which qualify as *jus cogens* (rules from which no derogation is permitted). The recent discussion at the Vienna Conference on Human Rights has not undermined the value of this proposition, as virtually all states have subscribed to the essential minimum standard of human rights in some form. These core rights, such as the right to life, to physical integrity and the absence of torture or degrading treatment, to freedom of conscience, religion and thought, to equality before the law and to fair treatment by the law, non-discrimination, etc., are applicable in times of peace, during public emergencies and even in cases of internal or international armed conflicts. They are enshrined in general human rights conventions (e.g. the 1966 Covenants) and other documents (e.g. the Universal Declaration of Human Rights), in specific conventions concerning certain issues (i.e. genocide, torture, apartheid, slavery, etc.), and in the laws of armed conflict, most notably the Geneva Conventions and Protocols. In addition, there is now emerging a consensus about the principle of solidarity in the face of natural or man-made disasters within states. This principle implies a duty to assist and applies to all governments capable of rendering aid. On the part of the target state, a corresponding obligation is emerging to ensure the efficient use of such assistance or to permit the distribution thereof, if the local government or authority is unable to effect this.

There exists already a wide range of mechanisms which permit individuals to vindicate their human rights through international organisations. It has been proposed to create a procedure similar to that established in ECOSOC Resolution 1503, granting individuals and groups, or perhaps more realistically, NGOs acting on their behalf, a right of complaint in cases of gross and persistent violations of their rights in humanitarian emergencies which have not been adequately addressed by their own governments, or indeed by international humanitarian agencies. This procedure might be administered by the UN Commission on Human Rights or, perhaps, by the Office of the Director of Humanitarian Affairs, with the assistance of its representatives on the ground.

Fulfilment of human rights and related humanitarian obligations is not only owed to the individual or to groups of individuals for whose protection they have been created. Human rights and elementary principles of humanity are obligations *erga omnes*, i.e. all states have a legitimate interest in their implementation.[8] Hence, most governments will no longer dispute that all states now enjoy the right to complain publicly or through diplomatic channels of human rights violations in other states. In some cases, international human rights agreements will provide for implementation mechanisms which may include the positive right of states formally to institute complaints against each other. Such mechanisms may result in formal condemnations of individual states. Another response might be the offer of good offices or mediation. Non-governmental organisations, in particular the International Committee of the Red Cross, as well as governments enjoy a positive right of initiative. However, it is a matter of controversy to what extent human rights violations or a denial of humanitarian assistance can trigger lawful responses beyond verbal condemnation or offers of good offices. Most developed states argue that acts of retorsion, i.e. unfriendly acts which do not breach international law, may be taken in response. The withholding of voluntary development aid, or the conditional granting of such aid, might be one such response (strictly humanitarian emergency relief, of course, must never be made conditional on political considerations).

Some governments and scholars go even further, asserting a right of states to take reprisals when faced with serious and consistent human rights abuses in other states. Reprisals are acts which are, in principle, unlawful, but which are legally justified by the prior violation of international law on the part of the target state which the act of reprisal seeks to terminate. Such acts of reprisal may, for example, include the unilateral suspension of trade arrangements.

It is a matter of even greater controversy whether armed action may be taken to put an end to violations of human rights or humanitarian principles so severe that they amount to an international crime or a threat to international peace and security.[9] According to the traditional view such actions might conflict with the doctrine of non-intervention.

The doctrine of non-intervention

International law, as it has developed since 1945, positively protects the power of a state represented by its government to rule its sphere of jurisdiction without foreign intervention.[10] The precise scope of the prohibition of intervention is highly contested in general international law, in particular where 'economic intervention' is concerned. However, few doubts arise with respect to intervention involving the threat or use of force. The International Court of Justice held in the *Nicaragua* decision:[11]

> A prohibited intervention must accordingly be one bearing on matters in which each state is permitted, by the principle of state sovereignty, to decide freely. One of these is the choice of a political, economic, social and cultural system, and the formulation of foreign policy. The element of coercion, which defines, and indeed forms the very essence of, prohibited intervention, is particularly obvious in the case of an intervention which uses force, either in the direct form of military action, or in the indirect form of support for subversive or terrorist armed activities within another state.

The prohibition of state-sponsored interference directed against an established government is based on various grounds. To some, it is inherent in the general principles which define the international system, such as the doctrines of sovereignty and the sovereign equality of states and of self-determination of peoples. Others have attempted to elevate non-intervention to the status of a positive, and perhaps independent 'fundamental right' of states.[12] And while the duty to refrain from intervention in matters essentially within the domestic jurisdiction of a state is only to be derived from the UN Charter by analogy,[13] the obligation not to resort to *armed* subversion can be extrapolated directly from it.

It is Article 2(4) of the Charter which rules out the threat or use of force against the *territorial integrity* or *political independence* of a state.[14] During the preparatory work of the Charter, there had been proposals to condemn specific acts of aggression, such as 'support given to armed bands for the purpose of invasion' and 'intervention in another state's internal or foreign affairs,' or the 'interference with the internal affairs of another nation by supplying arms, ammunition, money or other forms of aid to any armed band, faction or group, or by establishing agencies in that nation to conduce propaganda subversive to the institutions of that nation.'[15] The impermissibility of such acts was not doubted, but it was decided to leave the terms of the Charter as general as possible, in order to allow the Security Council the greatest flexibility when dealing with threats to the peace, breaches of the peace or acts of aggression.[16] In practice, the wording of Article 2(4) protecting *'territorial integrity and political independence'* has been broadly interpreted to cover all armed interference with the operation of the governmental structure of a state.[17] The precise scope and nature of the prohibition has been developed over the years in a number of subsidiary, standard-setting documents.

Although the direct legal effect of UN General Assembly resolutions remains contested, it is clear that consistent and uniform support for such standards, as expressed in the votes of a large majority of states, or unanimous adoption of resolutions, constitutes a valuable indication of the *opinio juris* of states and, in particular, of how they interpret the provisions of the Charter.[18]

Early standards pertaining to non-intervention sought to protect 'the will of the people in any state' from outside interference.[19] However, in a subsequent General Assembly resolution it was no longer 'the people', but the abstraction of the state, or its social and political system, which became the object of protection from outside interference. Thus, the *Declaration on the Inadmissibility of Intervention* recognised that 'armed intervention is synonymous with aggression'[20] and provided that:

No state has the right to intervene, directly or indirectly, for any reason whatever, in the internal or external affairs of any other state. Consequently, armed intervention and all other forms of interference or attempted threats against the personality of the state, or against its political, economic and cultural elements, are condemned.

A similar formula was adopted in the *Friendly Relations* Declaration which reaffirmed that 'no state may use or encourage the use of economic, political or any other type of measures to coerce another state in order to obtain from it the subordination of the exercise of its sovereign rights and to secure from it advantages of any kind'.[21] The most detailed formulation of the principle of non-intervention was achieved in the more controversial Resolution 36/103, which established a detailed catalogue of prohibited acts.[22]

Another instrument of interest is the *Declaration on the Enhancement of the Effectiveness of the Principle of Refraining from the Threat or Use of Force in International Relations*, adopted by consensus in 1987.[23] While this text adds little to the previous definition, one aspect of its negotiating history remains noteworthy. The initial draft included a section on justifiable exceptions to the prohibition of the use of force. However, neither the United States, which was at the time facing challenges in the Security Council to its policy on Nicaragua, nor any other delegation put forward a proposal that the failure to adopt a particular political system, or even the gross mistreatment by a state of its population, could justify intervention. On the contrary, the prohibition of intervention without exception for 'any reason whatever' was intended to rule out such a proposition definitively. This consistently hostile attitude towards armed intervention is mirrored in regional arrangements, including the OAS, the OAU, the Arab League and the CSCE.

In summary, a number of developments can be identified. First, the prohibition of intervention inherent, but not explicit, in the UN Charter, has clearly been reaffirmed as a positive rule of international law. There is a considerable broadening of its scope to cover a wide range of activities directed against a foreign state. While the admissibility of hostile measures at the lower end of the range, such as economic coercion or unfriendly propaganda, remains disputed, activities involving the threat or use of armed force are clearly prohibited. Secondly, the definition of the object to be protected from foreign intervention (initially 'the people', subsequently the state) has changed over the years, while states have taken pains to avoid any notion of legal equality between their rights and those claimed by an armed opposition. International law is, of course, made by states through the agency of their governments. That the framing of the obligation of non-intervention should privilege the concept of the state is thus no surprise.

Non-intervention and humanitarian action

As we have seen, intervention describes the exercise of public authority within a foreign jurisdiction in the absence of consent of the local sovereign. In the case of 'humanitarian intervention', such activity would have the aim of assisting significant segments of a population, or a people, in circumstances of grave humanitarian emergency. Such an emergency may be the result of a natural disaster or of deliberate policy (starvation as a means of internal warfare), or of the inability of a government to meet the basic needs of its population effectively.

Legally, only acts attributable to a state or a governmental organisation can qualify as 'intervention'. If individuals or groups conduct humanitarian activities within a foreign jurisdiction, and without the consent of the local sovereign, they are, according to traditional doctrine, simply in violation of local law.

Scholars have for decades attempted to legitimise 'humanitarian intervention', whether by government, international organisations or NGOs.

Some scholars have catalogued criteria for instances of lawful intervention. Most recently, Richard Lillich, who has been writing on the subject over the past three decades, has proposed the following standards in an as yet unpublished paper:

1. Humanitarian intervention must be based on the actual existence or impending likelihood of gross and persistent human rights violations that shock the world's conscience. (Such violations occur, *inter alia*, from systematic and indiscriminate attacks on civilians by a central government, or a system breakdown in law and order producing the dislocation and starvation of the civilian population.)
2. The intervention should be authorised, except in rare cases, only after all reasonable diplomatic efforts on the international and regional level have been exhausted and have failed to bring about the cessation of such human rights violations.
3. The intervention must be strictly limited in scope to actions necessary and proportionate to bring about the cessation of such human rights violations.
4. The intervening forces must begin their withdrawal as soon as reasonably possible, and in any event complete such withdrawal within a reasonable period after the cessation of such human rights violations. (If a lengthy presence is necessary, the intervening forces, if possible, should be under the direct command and control of the United Nations.)
5. The intervention should preserve the territorial integrity of the target state, by which is meant that the state's boundaries, except in rare cases, should not be redrawn.
6. The intervention should not interfere with the authority structure of the target state, except where the cessation of human rights violations clearly is dependent upon the removal of the central government. (In the case of 'failed states', e.g. Somalia, the intervening authorities should seek through UN auspices a national reconciliation based on the will of the people.)

Hitherto, the vast majority of academics have rejected such doctrines, emphasising the supervening importance of the prohibition of the threat or use of force in international law and the likelihood of abuse of a proposed humanitarian justification for the use of force.[24] This scepticism appeared well justified, in the light of the virtual absence of any state practice which would support the existence of a doctrine of humanitarian intervention. Although some scholars have invoked instances of nineteenth-century Great Power intervention at the periphery of their empires, the relevance of these alleged precedents from an imperialist age which was unfamiliar with the prohibition of the use of force is questionable. And, until very recently, states have shown a marked reluctance to justify armed intervention in humanitarian terms. Tanzania and Vietnam claimed that their military operations against Uganda and Cambodia respectively were covered by self-defence. India initially appeared to justify its intervention in East Pakistan (Bangladesh) on humanitarian grounds, but then changed the record of its submission to the UN Security Council, again relying on self-defence. In other instances, states may have advanced humanitarian considerations in the political domain, while justifying their actions in legal terms by relying on a mixture of treaty rights, self-defence and alleged invitations from governments to cover the intervention (Cyprus, Grenada, Panama). This practice revealed a strong desire on the part of states to avoid precedents which would undermine the prohibition of the threat or use of force, despite the fact that on occasion humanitarian motives may have partially inspired their armed actions.

Nevertheless, in 1986, the International Court of Justice appeared to encourage those in favour of humanitarian action. In the *Nicaragua* case, the Court held that 'there can be no doubt that the provision of strictly humanitarian aid to persons or forces in another country, whatever their political affiliations or objectives, cannot be regarded as unlawful intervention, or as in any other way contrary to international law'.[25] However, it is not clear whether this view did, in fact, reflect international law. Ironically, such doubt is derived from attempts by some states and organisations to enshrine a right to humanitarian assistance in international law. One such attempt was made when a diplomatic conference was called to negotiate the Protocols Additional to the Geneva Conventions. Initially, the sponsors of the project had hoped to include a paragraph which would have clarified that humanitarian relief may, under certain circumstances, be granted in the absence of state consent. However, after prolonged governmental negotiations, Article 18(2) of Protocol II provides that:

> If the civilian population is suffering undue hardships owing to a lack of supplies essential for its survival, such as foodstuffs and medical supplies, relief actions for the civilian population which are of an exclusively humanitarian and impartial nature and which are conducted without any adverse distinction shall be undertaken *subject to the consent of the High Contracting Party concerned.* (Emphasis added.)

The Institut de Droit International, a non-governmental drafting body of highest authority, considered the relationship between human rights and intervention throughout the 1980s. The resulting resolution confirms the right of states to take diplomatic and economic counter-measures in cases of grave and persistent violations of human rights, but specifically rules out the use of force as a remedy. With respect to humanitarian assistance, the resolution stipulates:

An offer by a state, a group of states, an international organisation or an impartial humanitarian body such as the International Committee of the Red Cross, of food or medical supplies to another state in whose territory the life or health of the population is seriously threatened, cannot be considered an unlawful intervention in the internal affairs of that state. However, such offers of assistance shall not, particularly by virtue of the means used to implement them, take a form suggestive of a threat of armed intervention or any other measure of intimidation; assistance shall be granted and distributed without discrimination. States in whose territories these emergency situations exist should not arbitrarily reject such offers of humanitarian assistance.

The delicate balance between moral exhortations directed at governments to accept offers of humanitarian assistance and the partial retention of their sovereign right to decline such offers has also been kept to some extent in recent resolutions adopted by the General Assembly. In 1988, the General Assembly stated that the 'abandonment of the victims of natural disasters and similar emergency situations without humanitarian assistance constitutes a threat to human life and an offence to human dignity'.[26] While the resolution affirms the principle of the sovereignty of affected states, it refers to their 'primary' role, i.e. not their exclusive role, in providing for humanitarian assistance within their territory, appealing to them actively to support outside humanitarian agencies. In a report of the Secretary-General of 24 October 1990, it was stated that 'Governments should permit unfettered access to all areas of a country where relief assistance is required, or is being distributed, for the accredited representatives of donor governments and recognised relief agencies'.[27] In Resolution 45/100, these principles were restated and, following upon a report of the Secretary-General on the subject, the Assembly embraced the proposal of establishing 'on a temporary basis, where needed, and by means of concerted action by affected Governments and the Governments and intergovernmental, governmental and non-governmental organisations concerned, relief corridors for the distribution of emergency medical and food aid'. Finally, in 1992, the Assembly adopted a comprehensive text on the *Strengthening of the Coordination of Humanitarian Emergency Assistance of the United Nations*. The resolution, like so many other drafting attempts before it, appears at first sight to take one step forward and two steps back. While establishing a comprehensive organisational mechanism for the provision of disaster relief, the resolution, in its guiding principles, confirms that the 'sovereignty, territorial integrity and national unity of states must be fully respected in accordance with the Charter of the United Nations'.[28] Still, in an important nuance, the resolution continues to state that humanitarian assistance 'should', rather than 'shall', be provided with the consent of the affected country and 'in principle' on the basis of an appeal by the affected country.

The slight ambiguity of standard-setting attempts among governments indicates that codification is not necessarily the best approach towards resolving the apparent tension between the principles of humanity and sovereignty. Recent practice, on the other hand, is characterised by the progressive creation of legally protected expectations which reflect the emerging consensus on international solidarity in the face of grave human suffering.

Humanitarian action: recent practice

All international governmental activity must be conducted in accordance with the UN Charter, which embodies the supreme law in the international sphere. As noted above, the Charter protects a state from the threat or use of force and from unlawful interference in its domestic jurisdiction. UN peacekeeping operations are therefore always conducted with the consent of the government exercising control over the area of deployment and, if the government has lost control over some of that territory, also with the consent of the effective authorities. Similarly, humanitarian agencies will also generally seek the consent of governmental or effective authorities.

If, despite the principles of humanitarian cooperation outlined in the General Assembly resolutions cited already, a government refuses to consent to humanitarian operations conducted on its territory, or if there is no government left which could do so, then the international community can pierce the armour of state sovereignty. There can be various phases in this process.

Fact finding

At the lowest level of initiative, there is the authoritative gathering of facts. Detailed proposals and initiatives relating to early warning and coordination of humanitarian intelligence gathering and analysis will be considered later in this chapter. However, from a legal standpoint, it is noteworthy that the Security Council, when deliberating the Secretary-General's *Agenda for Peace*, has recently recognised the importance of humanitarian concerns in conflict situations and recommended that the humanitarian dimension should be incorporated in the planning and dispatching of fact-finding missions. The Council noted 'with concern the incidence of humanitarian crises, including mass displacements of populations, becoming or aggravating threats to international peace and security. In this connection, it is important to include humanitarian considerations and indicators within the context of early warning information capacities as referred to in paragraphs 26 and 27 of *An Agenda for Peace*'.[29] The invocation of the concept of a 'threat to international peace and security' indicates that states can indeed be obliged to cooperate in humanitarian fact-finding.[30]

Humanitarian initiatives and consent

The right to offer humanitarian aid is unquestioned. All governments, international organisations with a humanitarian mandate and relevant NGOs enjoy this privilege. The ICRC even has a formal 'right of initiative' enshrined in the Geneva Conventions and Protocols. Those Conventions and Protocols also provide for an obligation of states during times of international armed conflict to facilitate humanitarian operations, especially with respect to occupied territories.[31]

However, most difficulties arise with respect to internal armed conflicts and it is here that the ambiguity observed in the General Assembly resolutions cited above comes into play. Governments will generally require humanitarian aid agencies to obtain their consent, even if the agencies seek to operate in areas which are not actually controlled by the government. UN agencies have mostly followed this requirement.[32] For example, in the case of Iraq, the UN awaited the negotiation of a memorandum of understanding with the Baghdad government before launching a campaign to assist the displaced population in Kurdish-controlled northern Iraq in 1991. In 1989, the UN engaged in negotiations with the authorities in Khartoum to avoid repetition of the mass starvation which had occurred in (rebel-held) southern Sudan during the rainy season in 1988, when no agreement on humanitarian aid had been forthcoming. The 1989 agreement provided for pre-positioning and delivery of supplies in the affected areas, including those not controlled by the government. It was implemented under the leadership of the Executive Director of UNICEF (acting as the Special Representative of the Secretary-General) and led to the establishment of 'corridors of tranquillity'.

Practice among NGOs varies in this respect. Some will always await governmental consent, while others have found it sufficient to obtain the agreement of whatever authorities effectively control the area of operation. Even the ICRC, which is generally reluctant to prejudice its relations with governments, has on occasion conducted operations in so-called rebel-held areas without having obtained the consent of the central authorities.

More importantly, UN organs are now confirming that both governments and opposition groups are required to cooperate in the delivery of humanitarian aid, whatever the subtleties of the abstract drafting work which went into Resolution 46/182 and similar texts. For example, with respect to Sudan, the General Assembly called on 'all parties' to permit international agencies and donor governments to deliver humanitarian aid to the civilian population and to cooperate with the recent initiatives of the

UN Department of Humanitarian Affairs.[33] More significantly the Security Council has also shown evidence of this tendency, for example when appealing to the parties in Angola, 'strictly to abide by applicable rules of international humanitarian law, including to guarantee unimpeded access for humanitarian assistance to the civilian population in need' and commending the UN Secretariat's efforts to establish agreed humanitarian relief corridors.[34] In short, practice in UN organs has now clarified that there exists a positive legal obligation on the part of governments and authorities to admit humanitarian aid. In addition, the existence of international legal protection for humanitarian aid workers has recently been confirmed in a whole series of Security Council resolutions. With respect to Somalia, the Council established criminal responsibility for those who obstructed relief work or attacked relief workers. And, of course, the Security Council has used its enforcement powers to achieve compliance with the obligation to permit relief.

Humanitarian action in the absence of consent

It is obviously preferable that humanitarian operations be conducted on the basis of consent and the active cooperation of all parties involved. However, it may be necessary to derogate from the principle of consent either when there is no government or authority left within a state which could consent, or when there is active obstruction of humanitarian action by a government or one or more authorities.

There are now four major cases of humanitarian action in the absence of governmental consent (Liberia, Iraq, former Yugoslavia, Somalia). The following section will seek to extrapolate some general trends from these cases, as they relate to:

1. The threshold of international action: threats to international peace and security
2. Authorising agency
3. Extent of authority
4. Control of operations

1. THE THRESHOLD OF INTERNATIONAL ACTION: THREATS TO INTERNATIONAL PEACE AND SECURITY

The refusal of governments and authorities to admit humanitarian deliveries to the territories they control or claim may amount to a threat to international peace and security. A determination that such a threat exists has two principal functions. In terms of general international law, it confirms that a specific situation does not fall within the exclusive jurisdiction of the state in which it arises. In UN procedural terms, it is required under Article

39 of the Charter to bring into action Chapter VII on enforcement measures. And enforcement powers override any national claim of sovereign authority. In this latter sense, an Article 39 determination is the passport to action under Chapter VII.

The semantic conversion of what is primarily an internal situation into one which threatens international peace and security is not a new phenomenon. During the 1960s and 1970s the Security Council found that the internal political situation in Southern Rhodesia and South Africa threatened international peace and security.[35] In the former case, the United Kingdom was even authorised to apply limited military enforcement measures.[36] These resolutions were specifically related to the problem of political systems based upon racial segregation. Since 1990, however, the international community has moved hesitantly towards the adoption of possible precedents of wider relevance.

(a) Liberia. Civil strife in Liberia had led to the displacement of some 500,000 individuals – a fifth of the population of that state. Action was taken by the Economic Community of West African States (ECOWAS) to restore peace in Liberia. Despite certain legal and operational imperfections in ECOWAS, the UN Security Council adopted a Statement commending the ECOWAS effort.[37] On the occasion of that Council meeting, a delegate appearing for Liberia (i.e. the interim government created by ECOWAS) asserted:[38]

> That a response is now being made ... raises, in my opinion, the imperative need to review, and perhaps re-interpret, the Charter, particularly its provision which calls for non-interference in the internal affairs of member states.

The Nigerian delegate, speaking in his function as alternate Chairman of the group of ambassadors of ECOWAS member states, reiterated the neutrality of ECOMOG's operations in Liberia. He added:[39]

> ECOWAS should be commended for acting in ways that promote the principles of the United Nations Charter by stepping in to prevent the situation in Liberia from degenerating into a situation likely to constitute a real threat to international peace and security.

The admission that the situation did not yet constitute a 'real threat' to international peace and security at the time of ECOWAS action is perhaps surprising, implying as it does that an organisation may intervene even in the absence of the requirements which have to be fulfilled in the case of Security Council action.[40]

On 30 October 1991, all parties to the conflict concluded the Yamoussoukro IV Accord relating to a peaceful settlement of the situation.

However, violence continued and ECOWAS forces came under increased military pressure. In response, ECOWAS embarked upon what it termed an enforcement operation against the Charles Taylor faction which was held principally responsible for obstructing the peace process.[41]

The Security Council met on 19 November to consider the situation in Liberia, in response to a request for an emergency meeting from the delegation of Benin, acting in its capacity of Chairman of ECOWAS.[42] At the Council meeting, the Minister for Foreign Affairs of the interim government of National Unity of Liberia fully endorsed the ECOWAS operation, praising its initiative at a time when international opinion on Liberia was divided between the imperatives for humanitarian intervention on the one hand, and the value of reaffirming classical conceptions of sovereignty, 'however anachronistic', on the other.[43] ECOWAS members addressing the Council again stressed the humanitarian motive of the operation, the desire to restore democracy in Liberia and the need to prevent a spread of hostilities. Not a single speaker during the debate which followed challenged the ECOWAS operation, although some states emphasised that the case had important external ramifications, since fighting had threatened to spill over from Liberia into neighbouring states. India emphasised that the Foreign Minister of Liberia himself had requested UN action. The Council memorialised these points in the preambular paragraphs of Resolution 788 (1992), which was adopted unanimously. In particular, it determined that 'the deterioration of the situation in Liberia constitutes a threat to international peace and security, particularly in West Africa as a whole'. Acting formally under Chapter VII of the Charter, the Council established a general and complete embargo on all deliveries of weapons and military equipment to Liberia. In a subsequent resolution, adopted in March 1993, the Council declared its readiness to consider appropriate measures in support of ECOWAS if any party were unwilling to cooperate in implementing the provisions of the Yamoussoukro Accords, in particular the encampment and disarmament provisions. The Council also demanded that the parties concerned refrain from any action that would impede or obstruct the delivery of humanitarian aid supplies. Nevertheless, ECOWAS initially prohibited the delivery of humanitarian aid outside of Monrovia. Later, it established what it called a corridor of tranquillity. However, rather than opening up additional safe routes for the delivery of aid, this corridor scheme represents an attempt to control all humanitarian access via that one corridor.

(b) Iraq. Indiscriminate attacks against civilians, and especially minority populations in northern and southern Iraq, resulted in the creation of some 500,000 Kurdish refugees from northern Iraq who flowed into the border region with Turkey and well over a million Kurdish and Shi'ite refugees who sought shelter in Iran. At the same time, large numbers of internally

displaced persons were threatened by harsh conditions and military attack in the mainly Kurdish-populated areas of northern Iraq. Although this developing situation was well known to the members of the Security Council, no provision relating to the atrocities was included in the definite cease-fire terms imposed upon Iraq in Resolution 687 (1991). However, the day after the adoption of that resolution, the Council did receive formal complaints about the situation from Turkey and Iran as well as other states.[44] Turkey called for 'urgent and forceful action to secure an immediate cessation of the repression'.[45] Other delegations placed more emphasis on the doctrine of non-interference when addressing the Council, although few disputed that the situation within Iraq had created circumstances threatening the stability of the region. After stressing the importance of Article 2(7) of the Charter relating to non-intervention, Romania pointed out that 'the armed repression of the Iraqi population can be a legitimate concern of the international community. Our action in this field should be guided by the principles of non-selectivity, by impartiality and objectivity'.[46] Yemen, on the other hand, considered that the 'Security Council is mandated only to safeguard international peace and security. In our view, the draft resolution sets a dangerous precedent that could open the way to diverting the Council away from its basic functions and responsibilities for safeguarding international peace and security and towards addressing the internal affairs of countries'.[47] After a prolonged discussion, the Council adopted Resolution 688 (1991) by ten votes to three, with two abstentions.[48] The resolution recalled Article 2(7) and expressed grave concern at the repression of the Iraqi population in many parts of Iraq, including most recently in Kurdish populated areas which led to a massive flow of refugees towards and across international frontiers and to cross-border incursions, 'which threaten international peace and security in the region'. It condemned these acts of repression and demanded that Iraq, as a contribution to removing the threat to international peace and security in the region, immediately end this repression and expressed the hope in the same context that an open dialogue would take place to ensure that the human and political rights of all Iraqi citizens were respected. The Council insisted that Iraq allow immediate access by international humanitarian organisations to all those in need of assistance in all parts of Iraq and to make available all necessary facilities for their operations.[49]

The resolution was couched in mandatory language and adopted after a formal finding that there existed a threat to international peace and security. That threat, however, was not to be found directly in the slaughter of segments of the Iraqi population by its own government, but rather indirectly, in the resulting refugee flow and its consequences for the region. Still, despite what appeared to be an Article 39 finding, bringing into play the enforcement provisions of the Charter, the resolution did not formally invoke Chapter VII. By way of a political compromise necessary to allow its adoption, the resolution was declared to have been adopted outside of Chapter VII. Nevertheless, its provisions reflected obligations incumbent upon Iraq under general international law, i.e. the obligation not to exterminate its population and to permit humanitarian assistance to those in overwhelming distress.

In the light of Iraq's stated refusal to implement the resolution, the UK prime minister announced on 8 April the commencement of humanitarian air drops in northern Iraq, conducted without the consent of the Iraqi government.[50] In addition, the idea of creating humanitarian islands, or safe havens, was proposed. On 16 April, the US president announced:[51]

> Consistent with United Nations Security Council Resolution 688 and working closely with the United Nations and other international relief organisations and our European partners, I have directed the US military to begin immediately to establish several encampments in northern Iraq where relief supplies for these refugees will be made available in large quantities and distributed in an orderly way.

The United Kingdom, too, justified the measure as one consistent with Resolution 688 (1991), adding that it was an immediate measure designed to save lives.[52] Two days after this announcement, Iraq agreed to a Memorandum of Understanding providing for a UN presence within Iraq and for the delivery of humanitarian aid throughout the territory.[53] The coalition forces which had been introduced into northern Iraq to protect the distribution of aid and refugee centres were later replaced by a lightly armed UN guard force. The coalition powers maintained in place, however, an aerial exclusion zone covering northern Iraq.

When, in the summer of 1992, the UN Special Rapporteur on Human Rights in Iraq submitted an emergency report to the Security Council, predicting an imminent attack of Iraqi forces against mostly Shiite civilians in southern Iraq, the coalition powers announced an aerial exclusion zone south of the 32nd parallel. The zone was justified with reference to 'extreme humanitarian need' and portrayed as an operation designed merely to monitor Iraqi compliance with Resolution 688 (1991).[54] After aerial confrontations in the zone late in December of 1992, the United States, France and the United Kingdom issued an ultimatum, requiring Iraq to withdraw anti-air defences from the no-fly zone. When this requirement was not met, the three states launched air attacks against defence installations, first in the southern zone and subsequently in the northern zone.[55] These operations were justified by a combination of considerations relating to humanitarian action and self-defence. If the presence of coalition planes in the exclusion zones was lawful to pursue a humanitarian mission, it was argued, then it must also be lawful for those aircraft to exercise the right to self-defence when threatened by Iraqi anti-air forces.[56]

(c) Somalia. In January 1991, the single-party rule of Major-General Mohammed Siad Barre over Somalia was terminated by a coalition of rebel factions. Hostilities continued in what remained of Somalia, resulting in the death of 300,000 individuals. The UN estimated that some 1.5 million lives, out of a population of 4.5 million, were at immediate risk from famine and warfare. About 1 million Somalis were reported to have sought refuge in neighbouring states.[57] Attempts by the United Nations and others to relieve the humanitarian situation, were hampered by a general climate of anarchy. On the initiative of the UN Secretary-General, reconciliation efforts were begun among the various factions.

The Security Council met to discuss the situation in Somalia at the request of the Somali delegation which urged international action to address the 'deteriorating human dilemma prevailing in Somalia'.[58] Although it was doubtful that the Somali delegation was indeed representing any government, it is interesting to note that the Council considered it necessary to have such a request submitted to it before taking action. The Council responded by adopting, without a debate, Resolution 733 (1992), which expressed grave alarm at the heavy loss of human life and widespread material damage resulting from the conflict and an awareness of the consequences for regional stability. The Council found that the persistence of this situation constituted a threat to international peace and security and made a number of requests to the Secretary-General with a view to securing a cease-fire, the passage of humanitarian relief and the safety of agency personnel. Only one provision of the resolution was adopted under Chapter VII, however. That provision imposed, for the purposes of establishing peace and stability in Somalia, a general and complete embargo on all deliveries of weapons and military equipment to Somalia.

Subsequently, in response to the deteriorating situation on the ground, the Security Council threatened to invoke Chapter VII of the Charter, in Resolution 775 (1992), reaffirming 'that the provision of humanitarian assistance in Somalia is an important element in the effort of the Council to restore international peace and security in the area'. In addition, the Secretary-General made clear that, although the UN troops were deployed under a peace-keeping mandate, they would, in accordance with standard practice, be entitled to use force in self-defence. In a very extensive interpretation of the concept of self-defence, the Secretary-General indicated that this included a situation 'in which armed persons attempt by force to prevent it [UNOSOM] from carrying out its mandate.' With no discernible improvement in the situation, the UN Secretary-General concluded that:[59]

the Council has now no alternative but to decide to adopt more forceful measures to secure humanitarian operations in Somalia. ... At present no government exists in Somalia that could request and allow such use of force. It would therefore be necessary for the Security Council to make a determination under Article 39 of the Charter that a threat to the peace exists, as a result of the repercussions of the Somali conflict on the entire region, and to decide what measures should be taken to maintain international peace and security. The Council would also have to determine that non-military measures as referred to in Chapter VII were not capable of giving effect to the Council's decisions.

At a meeting of the Council on 3 December, a number of delegations objected to giving too much freedom of action to the United States, which, it transpired, was willing to offer some 30,000 troops, provided these were not restricted by a UN command and control mechanism.

At the beginning of the Council meeting, Resolution 794 (1992) was adopted unanimously. The resolution emphasised the exceptional nature of the step taken by the Council but, in a breathtaking development, determined that the magnitude of the human tragedy caused by the conflict in Somalia in itself, further exacerbated by the obstacles to the distribution of humanitarian assistance, constituted a threat to international peace and security. Acting under Chapter VII, the Council authorised the Secretary-General to implement the offer of troops and to use all necessary means to establish as soon as possible a secure environment for humanitarian relief operations in Somalia, under a unified command and control mechanism reflecting that offer. Also acting under Chapter VII, the Council called upon states to use necessary measures to ensure strict implementation of the arms embargo.

By the end of January 1993, the Secretary-General could report on the signing of a set of agreements relating to a cease-fire, the disarming of factions and political negotiations. In addition, some 40,000 tons of humanitarian relief had been delivered since the deployment of the US-led force and a programme to repair essential elements of the local infrastructure was under way. In early March it was reported that 'all areas are stable or relatively stable' and the Secretary-General proposed that UNOSOM, which had continued to exist in the shadow of the forces authorised by Resolution 794 (1992), take over the enforcement mandate contained in that resolution.[60] This proposal was adopted in Resolution 814 (1993). The resolution, adopted under Chapter VII, provided for an enforcement contingent of some 28,000 UNOSOM II troops with a mandate to take armed action against parties precipitating a resumption of violence in Somalia. This mandate was implemented, possibly with excessive force which led to questions concerning the UN's control over its own operations.

(d) Former Yugoslavia/Bosnia. The initial Security Council response to the crisis within what was Yugoslavia was hesitant. It took the Council a full three months following upon the outbreak of the crisis to call for a meet-

ing. Even then, several delegations to the Council apparently felt it necessary to obtain a formal request for such a meeting from the Belgrade authorities.[61] This reluctance has, of course, to do with the discomfort of many governments when addressing issues of self-determination and secession outside a colonial context.

Despite the fact that the former central authorities had requested a Council meeting and had, indeed, formally argued in favour of a comprehensive arms embargo directed against the territory they purported to control, it was again felt necessary by a significant number of delegations to stress that it was not the humanitarian suffering within former Yugoslavia, but rather the resulting consequences for the region which allowed for Council action. As the Indian delegate explained:[62]

> [A] formal request by the state concerned is an essential requirement in such cases before the Council can take up the matter. At the same time, we must not forget [Article 2(7)] of the time-tested Charter of the United Nations ... Let us therefore note here today in unmistakable terms that the Council's consideration of the matter relates not to Yugoslavia's internal situation as such, but specifically to its implication for peace and security in the region.

The meeting resulted in the adoption of Resolution 713 (1991), which recorded the Yugoslav request for Council action and expressed deep concern about the fighting in (former) Yugoslavia and its consequences for the countries of the region, adding that the 'continuation of this situation constitutes a threat to international peace and security'. Acting expressly under Chapter VII of the Charter, the Council imposed a general and complete arms embargo.

The Republic of Bosnia and Hercegovina had been recognised by the EC and its member states on 6 April and soon found itself under military pressure from elements of its Serb population, which were assisted by the armed forces of the Belgrade authorities. On 15 May 1992, the Council demanded a cease-fire and the cessation of outside interference. It also called for the establishment of conditions for unhindered delivery of humanitarian aid. When this initiative met with no success, the Council adopted Resolution 757 (1992), imposing comprehensive economic sanctions against the Federal Republic of Yugoslavia (Serbia and Montenegro) and demanding a withdrawal of Serb forces and a cessation of hostilities. The resolution, adopted under Chapter VII, also demanded, *inter alia*, that all parties create immediately the necessary conditions for unimpeded delivery of humanitarian supplies to Sarajevo and to other destinations in the Republic of Bosnia and Hercegovina.

On 8 June the Council noted the agreement of the parties to reopen Sarajevo airport and authorised the deployment of additional elements of the United Nations force (UNPROFOR) to ensure the security and functioning of the airport in accordance with that agreement. In light of a steadily worsening humanitarian situation and the refusal of local Serb elements to permit unhindered relief action, the Council adopted Resolution 770 (1992). Acting under Chapter VII, the Council called upon states to take all measures necessary to facilitate, in coordination with the United Nations, the delivery of humanitarian assistance to Sarajevo and other parts of the Republic. This decision would, in principle, have allowed for armed actions by individual states acting only loosely within the framework of the UN operation in Bosnia. UNPROFOR itself was authorised to use force in self-defence which, according to a report of the Secretary-General endorsed by the Council, 'is deemed to include situations in which armed persons attempt by force to prevent United Nations troops from carrying out their mandate'. However, this authority was never transformed into instructions for the forces on the ground, or these instructions, if they ever existed, were disregarded. UNPROFOR commenced armed escorts of relief convoys, but it yielded to the slightest pressure exerted by the parties and only some six months later started to return fire. Indeed, in January 1993, Deputy Prime Minister Hakija Turajlic was dragged out of an UNPROFOR armoured personnel carrier and killed while UN forces stood by. UNPROFOR has always hesitated to use force, or the threat of force to ensure humanitarian aid deliveries, despite the explicit authorisation to do so.

To overcome the obstacles in moving aid on the ground, the Council adopted a statement, dated 25 February, strongly supporting the use, in full coordination with the UN, of humanitarian air drops in critical and isolated areas of the Republic. A month later, member states were authorised, in Resolution 816, to take all necessary measures to enforce a ban on fixed and rotary wing aircraft imposed by the Council the previous year.

This modest action did little to restrain Serb advances against Muslim enclaves. In April, the Council expressed shock at the developing situation in Srebrenica. On 16 April it adopted Resolution 819, purporting to establish a 'safe haven' in Srebrenica. The Council did, however, only authorise a monitoring presence in that area. In the meantime, other Muslim-held pockets had come under Serb attack, including Bihac in the north west of the Republic. On 27 April, UNPROFOR General Lars Eric Wahlgren ordered his forces in Bihac 'to prevent violations of human rights according to the Geneva conventions' and sent an additional 300 troops to the area. He added: 'They will be empowered to use force if they are prevented by force from carrying out their task.' This view was countermanded the same day by the UN deputy civilian representative on the ground, Cedric Thornberry. Soon afterwards, General Wahlgren was replaced.

In early May the Council, acting again under Chapter VII, declared five more so-called safe areas, including Sarajevo. A month elapsed, however, before UNPROFOR was authorised to take the necessary measures, including the use of force, to protect these areas and the passage of human-itarian aid in or around them. Resolution 836 (1993) also authorised mem-ber states, acting nationally or through regional organisations or arrange-ments, to use air power in and around the so-called safe areas in support of this mandate.

2. AUTHORISING AGENCY

In all of the cases under review the determination of the existence of a sit-uation requiring or permitting international action in the absence of gov-ernmental consent was taken by an international agency. In most instances, the determination was made directly by the UN Security Council. In the case of Liberia, ECOWAS made such a determination. When the United Kingdom, the United States and France imposed a no-fly zone in southern Iraq, they relied upon the findings of the UN Special Rapporteur on Human Rights in Iraq as an objective agency to confirm the existence of an overwhelming humanitarian need.

With respect to international action as a result of such a determination, four kinds of cases can be distinguished. There can be:

— direct UN action (UNOSOM II);
— authorisation granted to states to act under the aegis of the UN (Resolution 794 (1992) on Somalia); authorisation of states to use air power to protect safe havens (Republic of Bosnia and Hercegovina); authorisation to take necessary measures to protect aid deliveries (ibid.);
— authorisation granted by a regional organisation, with subsequent endorsement by the Security Council (Liberia);
— action by individual states or groups of states in pursuit of aims identi-fied by an objective international agency.

3. EXTENT OF AUTHORITY

The aim of the respective operations under consideration obviously differs according to circumstances. In two cases, the aim defined by the UN (and in the case of Liberia also by ECOWAS) has been the restoration of civil authority within a state, based upon internationally supervised elections. In the Republic of Bosnia and Hercegovina the aim of armed action was restricted to the supply of humanitarian aid and the protection of so-called safe havens only, although the wider political aim was, initially, the restora-tion of the territorial integrity of the state. In the case of Iraq, the coalition powers committed themselves to the protection of segments of a popula-tion.

The United Nations, when authorising the use of force, almost invari-ably utilises the somewhat flexible wording of authorising 'all necessary means' for the achievement of certain aims. With respect to forces under its direct control, the UN has, however, been quite specific in identifying the extent of permissible force. This highly cautious approach is most clearly discernible in the case of former Yugoslavia, where the right of self-defence was broadened to include armed action in response to the hindering of humanitarian activities and was gradually extended to the protection of the so-called safe areas. The mandate of UNOSOM II was also defined with some care, although the events of June and July 1993 indicate that the interpretation of proportionality of armed action appears to be highly flexible.

Regional action undertaken by ECOWAS has, perhaps, exhibited the greatest flexibility. The 'vigorous defensive measures' adopted by the organisation in November 1992 appear to imply the possibility of full-scale war, or rather regional enforcement action, against an authority controlling some 90 per cent of a territory. So far, of course, no such comprehensive military campaign has been launched.

The use of force by individual states or groups of states is limited by the requirements of general international law, which also apply to the activities of international organisations; there must be no other means available to achieve an internationally validated aim; the use of force must be minimal and proportionate to the aim, and it must not violate principles of humanitarian law.

4. Control of operations

UN enforcement operations are conducted under the direct control of the Security Council which operates through the medium of the Secretary-General. In the case of Somalia, the UN Secretariat has involved itself not only in the day-to-day direction of operations, but in hour-by-hour management. However, the offensive use of force by UNOSOM II has raised the issue of the UN's accountability. The Security Council appears reluctant to criticise operations it has authorised and the Secretariat may not always exhibit the greatest zeal when it comes to investigations of its own practices, especially by means of independent, outside inquiry (as, for example, when the attempt was made to prevent the results of a commission of enquiry being made public in March 1994: see the chapter by Slim and Visman).

The intolerably loose practice of UN supervision over enforcement action carried out on its behalf by individual states in the Gulf crisis was, in theory, addressed in Resolution 794 (1992). In practice, the coordination mechanism established for the management of mostly US forces on the ground has, at times, been operated more in the way of retrospective information-gathering. However, this defect was remedied in the latter stages of the large-scale US deployments in Somalia.

Very loose coordination procedures were provided for in the case of 'necessary means' authorised with respect to the enforcement of UN sanctions by individual states in the cases of Somalia and former Yugoslavia.

The same is true of procedures relating to the application of force by states, rather than UN troops, to protect humanitarian aid which was apparently authorised under Resolution 770 and subsequent resolutions concerning Bosnia. However, the lack of hard restrictions and of viable coordination mechanisms can perhaps be explained by the Council's well-founded anticipation that no force would be used outside the context of UNPRO-FOR operations.

The UN has been fairly indulgent in supervising the activities of ECOWAS. According to Chapter VII of the Charter, regional organisations require UN authorisation in advance of engaging in enforcement action. This requirement was somewhat undermined by the practice of the OAS in the 1950s and 1960s, and the ECOWAS experience may well have put an end to it. The unwillingness of the UN to become significantly involved in Liberia may have contributed to the uncritical attitude with which it has endorsed ECOWAS decisions, some of which may stretch the law.

Individual states, or groups of states acting outside international control, must always expect to be held to account by the UN Security Council. However, the principle of accountability has been undermined by the reluctance of Council members to criticise operations involving the only remaining superpower. The failure of the Council even to consider condemning the US cruise missile attack against Baghdad in June 1993 bears this out.

The issue of humanitarian neutrality

According to the General Assembly standards on humanitarian action, which reflect the ICRC's operating principles, neutrality and impartiality must be guiding principles in the rendering of assistance across borders. These concepts have a clearly defined meaning only in the context of the operations of the ICRC, which is mandated to provide humanitarian services to any and all parties to a conflict, irrespective of their legitimacy or conduct. The cases of former Yugoslavia and now Somalia have highlighted considerable confusion over the meaning of the concepts of neutrality and impartiality.

We therefore wish to propose a set of principles which might establish the legal basis of humanitarian neutrality:

1. Humanitarian aid must be given according to considerations of human need alone. Its granting, or its acceptance must not be made dependent on political factors, but instead be made available wherever humanitarian need is greatest.
2. Impartiality and neutrality does not mean that two or more sides in a conflict must be treated equally in terms of levels of aid granted. Emergency aid given preferentially to the side in an armed conflict

whose population is suffering most does not amount to intervention on the side of that party.

3. The only constraints on responding to humanitarian need should be those of resources and practicality.
4. Those rendering humanitarian aid have a right and, indeed, a duty to ensure its appropriate end use. This includes a right to monitor or conduct the distribution of humanitarian aid on the ground.
5. If armed obstruction to humanitarian aid requires that enforcement action be taken against one or more of the parties on the ground, such action does not violate the principle of humanitarian neutrality. Indeed, under such circumstances, further action may be required to protect humanitarian aid agencies and the continuation of their operations.[63]

Summary of the legal framework

The cases surveyed here indicated an expansion of the concept of lawful international action relating to humanitarian crises within states. In the case of Iraq, a segment of the population was threatened in its very survival by a genocidal campaign of its own government. In the case of the Republic of Bosnia and Hercegovina, a government was unable to protect its citizens from the armed onslaught mounted by segments of its population and supported and directed from outside. The action of ECOWAS, later endorsed by the Security Council, concerned an incident of breakdown of authority, followed by the threat of the taking of power by one faction in the ensuing conflict. Finally, in the case of Somalia, long-time anarchy and stalemate were to be replaced by a disempowerment of all political factions and a reconstruction of political structures.

In more formal terms, this trend which is whittling away at the abstract concept of state sovereignty can best be traced by following the continued expansion of the concept of international peace and security. In the Security Council, it was initially the element of state consent which had to be evidenced (Yugoslavia arms embargo) or artificially manufactured (Somalia arms embargo, Liberia arms embargo) before action relating to apparently internal situations was widely acceptable. Still even in those cases, and in the case of Iraq, it was the external consequences of a predominantly internal situation which were emphasised. In the cases of the first Yugoslavia resolution, the first Somalia resolution and the Liberia resolutions there was a genuine security threat to neighbouring states which could be invoked. In the cases of Iraq, the first Yugoslav resolution, the first Liberian resolution and the first Somalia resolution, there was the additional regional destabilisation caused by significant refugee flows.

This carefully restrained approach was progressively undermined in the development of the Yugoslav and the Somalia episodes. In the case of

Bosnia, the obstruction of Sarajevo airport was considered a threat to international peace and security; likewise the preclusion of humanitarian aid and later the threat to UN personnel and to 'safe areas' established by the Security Council. Resolution 792 (1992) crowned this development by finding that the grave humanitarian circumstances in Somalia in themselves threatened international peace and security.

It may well be possible to consolidate this practice into cases which permit certain international responses to certain types of grave and persistent violations of human rights. However, this approach seems unsatisfactory. The UN Commission on Human Rights routinely identifies a number of states as persistent and gross violators of human rights. Hardly ever would there be a suggestion that armed action should ensue as a consequence. It is preferable to view this practice concerning humanitarian action as part of a wider trend in international law relating to legitimacy and representation of peoples and groups.

There are already a number of circumstances in which international law disregards the claims of governments to represent peoples or groups, the most obvious being unlawful occupation. Since the adoption of General Assembly Resolution 1514, it has been established that a colonial government does not internationally represent the population it controls. In the case of Namibia, the UN even established an administrative Council which, although it exercised no effective authority whatever in the territory, was regarded as being its legitimate international representative.

The possibility of dissociating all or part of a population from an effective government has recently been confirmed in Haiti where the international community has refused to recognise the military regime which ousted the democratically elected president. In June 1993, the Council found that the situation in Haiti amounted to a threat to international peace and security and imposed sanctions against the regime.

In the examples given here, sovereignty reverts to the people, whether or not effective government exists. In the preamble of Resolution 794 (1992), the Security Council confirmed that ultimate responsibility for reconstruction and authority lay with the Somali people, rather than with any one or all of the factions. The NPFL's claim to authority in Liberia was simply disregarded, even though it controlled some 90 per cent of the country. When addressing the humanitarian catastrophe in the Republic of Bosnia and Hercegovina, the UN also superimposed its humanitarian demands over the claims of authority put forward by all groups directing armed forces within the territory. And the claim of the Baghdad government to exercise exclusive control over the segments of its population it was about to exterminate was pushed aside by the Security Council and, to a greater extent, by members of the international coalition.

The loss of a claim to international representation of a population or segments thereof thus appears to permit international action in line with the implied or expressed desires of a population. Genuine international humanitarian action, and even armed action, can never be considered intervention in a legal sense precisely because it is based upon the actual or anticipated consent of the sovereign, i.e. the people. This view would negate the absurd argument that the abstract concept of the state can render immune from international action a government or authority which exterminates those whose corporate identity constitutes the state.

Instability is bound to result if it is left to individual states to determine when international action may be taken in the absence of consent and to implement their decisions unilaterally. However, it has been demonstrated that there are objective structures for the identification of circumstances permitting international action, for the determination of the extent of authority which may be exercised on behalf of peoples. It must be said, however, that with respect to international control of, and accountability for, humanitarian action, a strengthening of international mechanisms would be most welcome.

Operational and political considerations

This section will look at some of the main political and operational considerations pertinent to the provision of humanitarian assistance to victims of conflict in zones of contested sovereignty. Following on from the previous section which looked at legal issues, the three main stages of humanitarian action will be analysed:[64]

(a) The decision-making process: what triggers humanitarian action?
(b) The implementation of operations: what are the issues which determine the efficiency and effectiveness of operations?
(c) The accountability of relief operations.

Based on an analysis of the cases considered earlier (Liberia, Iraq, Somalia and ex-Yugoslavia), this section will identify some of the key political and operational constraints to successful humanitarian action in failed states and in countries where governments are in effective control of only part of their sovereign territory. Building upon the analysis of the legal problems of meeting the needs of civilians in humanitarian disasters, it will argue that humanitarian neutrality is being compromised by the political complexities of such situations and that the United Nations has been unable to respond to this problem adequately. Lack of UN leadership, the strategic interests of the major powers and poor operational performance are just some of the factors which contribute to an unacceptable failure to meet human needs in many areas of the world.

What triggers humanitarian action?

According to the United Nations Department for Humanitarian Affairs[65] there were, in December 1992, approximately 35 million people in humanitarian crisis as a consequence of the eighteen civil wars then being waged. These victims of war are, by and large, living in what have been called 'failed states' (Yugoslavia, Liberia, Angola, Somalia, Sudan, etc.) where governments cannot meet their needs, or may only control limited areas of sovereign territories or are, for various political and economic reasons, in retreat, cutting back on the provision of basic services to their populations.

It is clear that the degree of need created by these conflicts far outweighs the resources available at national or international level and that the criteria which are used by the international community to decide where humanitarian action may or may not take place are neither clear nor objective. Until now, decisions taken about action and assistance have been *ad hoc*, tending to reflect the political interests of the major powers. We argue that without clearly defined criteria within a more accountable international system, humanitarian actions will continue to be less than adequately effective in operational terms and of dubious political credibility.

1. RIGHTS OF PEOPLE AND RIGHTS OF STATES

The legal argument giving precedence to the humanitarian needs of civilians over those of the nation-state has already been reviewed. The more extreme interventionists such as Bernard Kouchner[66] argue that:

> Humanitarian intervention, backed by UN resolutions, has become our duty. And little by little, under the impetus of war, catastrophe and the awakening of the world's conscience, this duty should become our right; to intervene wherever victims are calling out for help, where human beings are suffering and dying, regardless of borders.

Though this position is far from becoming common practice, there is little doubt that international opinion is moving in that direction. Perez de Cuellar[67] articulated the predicament in a speech at the University of Bordeaux in 1991,

> Has not a balance been established between the rights of states as confirmed by the UN charter and the rights of the individual, as confirmed by the UN Declaration of Human Rights? We are clearly witnessing what is an irresistible shift in public attitudes towards the belief that the defence of the oppressed in the name of morality should prevail over frontiers and legal documents.

Though much of the debate regarding intervention in the defence of human rights has previously centred upon first-generation rights, or civil and political liberties, we would argue that a framework of rights should be extended to include basic human needs such as food, health care, shelter and other essentials required to sustain life and physical integrity. Such a position is backed up by a series of internationally recognised conventions including the Universal Declaration of Human Rights, the Convention on Economic, Social and Cultural Rights and the Convention on the Rights of the Child.

As Simone Weil[68] pointed out, 'a right is not effectual by itself but only in relation to the obligation to which it responds, the effective exercise of a right springing not from the individual who possesses it, but from other men who consider themselves as being under a certain obligation towards him ... it is an eternal obligation to the human being not to let him suffer from hunger when one has occasion to come to his assistance'. However, while the right to food has been endorsed more often than other human rights, it has also been violated more comprehensively than almost any other right. In practice, there is little opportunity for the victims of famines and conflicts to demand that the obligations of their own governments, still less those of the international community and its agencies, be fulfilled. In other words, we are not dealing here with rights that correspond to accountable obligations but rather with mere declarations of moral principles or manifesto rights.

Since the moral obligation to honour the right to food, for example, can never be more than a non-enforceable obligation — it is denied to roughly one billion people every day — it is clearly impractical and unrealistic to talk of a legal obligation to act. It is far more useful to think in terms of the creation of moral expectations which the international community feels duty-bound to act upon with international law permitting rather than obliging action in these circumstances, even at the expense of sovereignty.

2. STRATEGIC INTERESTS OF THE UN AND THE INDUSTRIALISED COUNTRIES

When the UN launched Operation Restore Hope in Somalia in December 1992, the reaction of much of the developing world was swift and highly critical. The Fraternité Matin of the Ivory Coast claimed that the credibility of the African continent was at risk while the opposition Al-Shaab paper of Egypt said 'the Somali commanders have handed their country over to the Americans on a golden platter'. Although the intervention was justified as being an initiative to save life in the face of the complete collapse of the Somali government, and effectively of the state, it was seen by many, though not all, developing countries as the last stage in a continuum of intervention and interference by western countries in the developing world.

Beyond the obvious cases of armed intervention such as the US invasions of Grenada and Panama during the 1980s, developing countries face what they consider to be continuous control and interference by the powerful western nations and international institutions such as the World Bank, the IMF and the UN which are seen to be promoting western political and economic interests. Such control includes the economic conditionalities of the Structural Adjustment Programmes and the new political conditionalities of the good governance debate.

Those in favour of conditionalities argue that the inefficient and corrupt nature of most Third World governments warrants conditionality, if only to ensure that aid to the developing countries reaches the poorest and most disadvantaged. For critics, this approach is simply a form of neo-imperialism which helps to sustain the international financial system at the expense of the poor and by undermining the legitimacy and competence of governments. There appears, in any case, to be a fundamental contradiction in the nature of interventions which claim to benefit the people of developing countries but do so by undermining the very legitimacy of the state which is authorised to meet their needs.

The legal position which has not to date allowed non-consensual humanitarian intervention except under Chapter VII — on the grounds of a threat to regional peace and security — leads critics to conclude that the majority of interventions are decided on in an *ad hoc* manner, in keeping with the strategic and political interests of the western powers.

Any decision to intervene in a failed state or a zone of contested sovereignty will inevitably be closely scrutinised for ulterior political motives and protestations of purely humanitarian concern will often meet with profound scepticism.

For the more cynically minded, the creation of safe havens for the Kurds under Resolution 688 was simply an attempt to humiliate Saddam Hussein; ECOMOG's presence in Liberia is a defence of Nigerian economic interests and Operation Restore Hope was a sign, in the words of Yemen's *Al Jamaheer* newspaper, that 'The USA are preparing to dominate the Horn of Africa'. The UN cannot afford politically or morally to be seen to continue acting only when in the ostensible interests of its most powerful member states.

For this reason, the establishment of objective criteria justifying intervention as discussed in the earlier part of this chapter would not only be vital for the victims of humanitarian disaster but might also help to re-establish the credibility and legitimacy of the UN in its provision of humanitarian assistance in such zones.

3. Information available

Accurate and timely information is a *sine qua non* of effective and appropriate decision-making in emergency relief operations of any kind. At present there is still a need for much improved international information gathering and intelligence to ensure better decision-making. The major sources of information for the international relief network are:

(a) The media and particularly TV;
(b) Official information from the international relief network;
(c) Early warning systems.

(a) Media. Decisions taken at a political or policy-making level to launch a major international appeal or to provide international humanitarian assistance – non-consensual or otherwise – depend to a large degree on information available and public and political pressure. In this sense the role of the media is vital and no one should doubt the importance of public opinion on both major international leaders and the international relief network in determining what gets done and where. Ever since President Johnson, watching pictures of the Biafran War, told his advisers to 'get those nigger babies off my TV screen' the response to a humanitarian crisis has too often been in proportion to the media coverage rather than the degree of need.

April 1993 provided a stark illustration of the importance of the role of the media in creating the impetus for political and humanitarian action. While Srebrenica in Bosnia fell to the Serbs in the full glare of the (mostly western) media, Huambo in Angola was captured by UNITA with equal if not greater loss of life and suffering but scant media attention. Anguished appeals for humanitarian intervention in Srebrenica were made from all sides of the political spectrum with calls for the UN to intervene to protect lives. Yet for the civilians caught up in UNITA's siege of Huambo there was no such publicity and no such support.

The former Yugoslavia is clearly of greater political interest to western audiences accessible to camera crews and journalists from Europe and North America than distant (and politically peripheral) Angola. What is worrying is that the UN, which should be adopting a universalist and objective approach to the suffering generated by armed conflicts, is tending to prioritise those crises of more political concern to the West because of the greater coverage which they receive.

The impact of a widely covered story on high-level decision-making is illustrated by Kurt Jansson's memoirs[69] of his time as United Nations Special Coordinator for Emergency Operations in Ethiopia during 1985–6. He recalls that he was asked to take on the job only after the transmission of Michael Buerk's now famous BBC film which first revealed the extent of the famine. But, as Peter Gill showed in his book, *A Year in the Death of Africa*,[70] the Ethiopian government and agencies on the ground had been predicting a massive famine for months.

Media pressure may work in a variety of ways. The media, particularly TV, require photogenic famines to make a good story. A less obvious tragedy without good strong pictures of starving babies (who may in fact be close by but in an insecure or inaccessible zone) may be given little if any coverage even if the degree of suffering is high. On the other hand, the

Cambodian crisis of 1979–80 and the Khartoum floods of 1988 provided examples of exaggerated predictions of doom. Often visiting journalists lack an understanding of normal life in a country and find it difficult to assess the real extent of a crisis. In addition, journalists may arrive in a country with very strong and negative perceptions of the government, leading them to seek to confirm the old adage that 'news is the difference between what the government says is happening and what is in fact happening' rather than reporting objectively.

African Rights'[71] recent evaluation of Operation Restore Hope in Somalia claims that exaggerated press reports of the degree of looting and anarchy gave a false justification for intervention and then allowed the UN to exaggerate the programme's success. The report claims that the worst of the humanitarian crisis had probably been overcome before Operation Restore Hope was launched. Given the dependence of the international relief network on the information provided by the media, this is a serious charge.

The UN and other agencies need to spend less time chasing after the latest emergency exposed by the international media. In other words they need to become more proactive rather than reactive in their relations with the media and particularly TV. There is a great need for increased mutual understanding through regular meetings at national and international levels and even the involvement of media representatives in inter-agency committees. Another possible tactic might be to use the media to publicise the plight of those caught up in 'forgotten' emergencies, appealing where necessary over the heads of donor governments — and recipient governments — to public opinion. Claudio Caratsch[72] of the ICRC has talked of using press releases as a negotiating tool when repeated discreet attempts have failed to bring any improvement to the situation of the victims. For the ICRC, such press releases are not so much information as a means of appealing to the collective responsibility of the parties concerned for ensuring respect for the Geneva Convention and their principles.

(b) Official information systems of the international relief network.

> Half the statistics come from village clerks who made them up and the other half are manipulated by the government for policy purposes ... When you discover that the official world does not correspond to the real world, you can either accept the official version or make your own judgement. It's always best to take the government figures. That way you save yourself work and don't tread on the toes of anyone who matters. We are here, after all, as guests.[73]

The above quotation reflects the reality of aid workers in many developing countries. The difficulty of obtaining accurate, timely data is even greater in failed and failing states in conflict where the areas of need will usually be the most insecure and poorly resourced. For example, in Mozambique, throughout the war, there were no statistical data at all on the Renamo-controlled areas and only the sketchiest anecdotal information. Even in government-controlled areas, often remote and with no communication with provincial centres, relief officials had little idea of the extent of needs.

Clearly more and better data are required to enable planners to decide at what point action is warranted. The data also need to be impartially assessed, though this rarely happens. Strategic interests often determine which countries are placed on the priority lists of the UN system with the political interests of the major donors paramount. The estimated million deaths caused by the Ethiopian famine of 1984–5 could have been significantly reduced if the UN and the major bilaterals had heeded Dr Kenneth King, the senior UN official in the country whose warnings were ignored because of western opposition to the socialist policies of the Ethiopian government.

In addition, countries may seek to manipulate figures for a number of different reasons. Some governments exaggerate success: in response to enormous pressure from UNICEF to achieve successes in the Universal Child Immunisation programmes, a number of countries are thought to have manipulated their figures in order to secure further funds. This may not be official policy but a strategy on the part of officials seeking to impress their bosses. Others overstate need. In the 1980s in Somalia, UNHCR routinely assumed that government estimates of refugee populations were doubled so as to gain extra food for the army. A different problem is the downplaying of potentially embarrassing problems, the existence of cholera, for example, because of its potential impact on tourism.

(c) Early warning systems. In recent years early warning systems have been seen as one way of identifying potential famines and ensuring a timely international response. Such systems tend to concentrate — using satellite imagery and other techniques — upon food production and food availability at national level. Other systems, particularly those promoted by NGOs in the Sahel and other regions, focus more upon household food security, grain and livestock prices in local markets, and other socio-economic indicators. However, as one study[74] of early warning systems found, the urgency of response by donors and others usually depends on evidence that a crisis is already under way. The benefit of early warning is thus lost since it does not lead to early action. One very senior UNHCR official[75] argued recently 'early warning is a big waste of time and resources. Reuters and CNN give us early warning. What we need is early response'.

As more and more of the humanitarian crises around the world are caused by refugee movements which are in turn caused by conflicts, any early warning system capable of predicting crisis needs to take account of potential political problems and wars. The United Nations established in

April 1991 an Ad Hoc Working Group on Early Warning Regarding New Flows of Refugees and Displaced Persons. This is supposed to alert the international community to impending mass exoduses. However, judging from the UN response to Liberia and Bosnia — to name but two examples — there is little evidence that the system has any real impact on decision-making. Greater success has been achieved in areas of prolonged conflict, particularly in Eritrea and Tigray where early warning and response systems were run by the humanitarian wings of their liberation movements. The effectiveness of these systems was entirely dependent upon international recognition and the provision of assistance by western donors.

What is now needed is a similar type of early warning system providing information on impending or ongoing conflicts that might allow the international relief network to foresee and prepare for potential displacement and loss of control of territory to rebel movements or neighbouring states (see the specific proposals made by Taylor in the following chapter). Such systems do exist within some university departments but could be more widely used with a more formal and perhaps even obligatory participation by all countries to ensure that the available information is of the highest quality.

Although grave doubts have been expressed at the idea of Boutros Boutros-Ghali[76] to establish UN embassies to provide a more coordinated and organised UN presence, such embassies might have an intelligence-gathering function that could feed into a central data bank located at the UN headquarters, possibly at the ECOSOC.

The ownership of such information is a significant point. Governments (or their substitutes) and donors need to work together if the information provided is to be credible and capable of triggering an effective response. And they need together to try to make the systems accountable to the real victims, an issue that will be discussed later in this section.

What makes humanitarian action effective?

1. CLARITY OF DEFINITION OF OBJECTIVES

Recent instances of humanitarian intervention in failing states — particularly Somalia and Liberia — suggest that many difficulties arise because of overambitious and unclear goals. Only a combination of coherent strategy, sufficient leverage and a keen sense of timing will allow third parties to offer peace, protection, food or any other form of assistance to the victims of humanitarian crises.

Some have argued that the provision of humanitarian aid may prolong war by feeding combatants on both sides and by consolidating both armies' hold over 'their' civilian populations. Stedman[77] has argued that most civil wars become amenable to settlement only after playing themselves out with ferocity and that meeting the short-term needs of civilians for food, health care, safe water, etc, may prejudice the fulfilment of the long-term objectives of peace and stability. This argument was favoured by the Mozambican government throughout its war with Renamo; it consistently asserted that the provision of aid to civilians under Renamo control would only prolong the war by feeding the Renamo soldiers.

It has to be recognised too that humanitarian aid is often required because of abject political failure. Bosnia is perhaps the best example of a situation where the major international players (the UN, Russia, the USA) have used humanitarianism as a fig leaf for the poverty and indifference of their policies. As a consequence they have probably prolonged the political and human agony of the country.

Yet despite these arguments, the withdrawal of humanitarian aid to achieve political goals strikes us as being morally untenable. It is obviously true that the provision of humanitarian assistance cannot be expected to break down the long-standing hatreds and bitterness which fuel war. It is also true that adversaries will, whenever possible, make great strategic use of food aid to force populations to move, to consolidate their hold over civilians or to feed their own armies. Despite these problems, humanitarian assistance needs to be seen as an imperative in its own right regardless of its perceived impact on political events. The only sure consequence of withholding food from civilians is to starve them.

This is not to say that relief agencies should accept the diversion of food or other relief supplies. Indeed NGOs and others have a duty, wherever possible, to monitor food aid to the beneficiary to ensure that it reaches those most in need; armed adversaries should be obliged to grant the necessary access to relief workers to ensure that such monitoring takes place. In cases where large quantities of food aid are being diverted to the military or other groups, relief agencies may be forced to withdraw food supplies. Such decisions depend upon local operational factors and it is not feasible under these circumstances to establish standard criteria for the withdrawal of aid.

For the same reason we reject the idea that humanitarian assistance should be withheld from civilians because of hostility to the political or moral behaviour of the government or occupying rebel force under whose control they live. Such arguments have often been used to deny aid to those living under the Khmer Rouge or Renamo since these movements would gain credibility along with a proportion of this aid. However, we do not believe that it is acceptable to make the poorest and most vulnerable pay for the crimes of their *de facto* leaders.

That is not to say that a humanitarian operation cannot and should not be used to promote long-term peace and security where possible. One can obviously hope that the goodwill created and the presence of international relief personnel in an insecure zone might create a basis for negotiation and conflict resolution. In its early days, Operation Lifeline Sudan was able to achieve this and was seen as providing some form of prelude to a political *rapprochement* between the two sides, though this hope has now faded. It does seem that, in political terms, the passage of a relief convoy is no more significant than a game of football played in no man's land by soldiers on opposing sides of a conflict: a sign of humanity maybe but no guarantee of anything more.

Another feature of the potential incompatibility between long-term and short-term objectives relates to the provision of humanitarian assistance to those who have been ethnically cleansed, displaced or otherwise affected by conflict or by the abuse of power. In such cases, humanitarian assistance may be perceived as worse than inadequate. As a recent letter to the *Guardian* from seventeen British Labour Members of Parliament put it: 'military intervention which is confined to humanitarian aid borders on hypocrisy when the children we feed are subsequently decapitated by Serbian shells'.[78] In such circumstances, the provision of humanitarian assistance must be seen as essential but inadequate in and of itself and has to be linked to political and military operations.

The crucial point for non-consensual intervention is less the magnitude of need than the collapse of government legitimacy. Though international humanitarian assistance can save lives and meet basic human needs over the short term — possibly more effectively than a government — the long-term needs of the citizens of a country can only be met through effective, efficient, representative and accountable government. The more extreme interventionists can distinguish between humanitarian and political concerns but not between the fulfilment of short-term and long-term humanitarian needs. Intervention may well undermine the sovereignty and functioning of the nation-state whose very lack of legitimacy and ability to meet the needs of its citizens is the basis of the underlying humanitarian crisis.[79] Operation Restore Hope is a good case in point. While the US/UN intervention in the country has promoted the immediate humanitarian well-being of some Somali communities it has utterly failed to encourage a lasting settlement that will ensure their continued welfare.

So what are legitimate objectives for humanitarian intervention? They must be to create peace and security that allow aid to be delivered on the basis of true need; the provision of whatever aid is required within resource and logistical constraints; support to the re-establishment of national institutions which can deliver services to the people and the promotion of peace, reconciliation and a civil society that can demand accountability from those who rule them.

2. OPERATIONAL CAPACITY OF THE INTERNATIONAL RELIEF NETWORK

The international relief network has been evolving since 1863, with the founding of the International Red Cross. However, it was not until 1943 that a Convention was established to create a UN Relief and Rehabilitation Administration. Such an organisation, like many of the nascent agencies of the UN established in 1946 (UNICEF, International Refugee Organisation) was destined to ease the suffering of post-war Europe and was seen as temporary in character. Once post-war reconstruction had eliminated the need for emergency relief, the newly formed organisations had to search for a role and from the mid-1950s moved into Third World development work as this area became a growth industry. It was only in the 1960s that relief work returned to the international agenda. The Congo crisis helped create a recognition that disaster was to be a persistent phenomenon and from the early 1960s to the 1970s specialised relief bodies sprang up in governments, inter-governmental organisations and non-governmental organisations. The Biafran (1967–70) and Bangladesh (1970–1) crises demonstrated the need for better management and organisation of response.

The creation of the United Nations Disaster Relief Organisation (UNDRO) in 1972 raised hopes of an improved response but nothing more. Its mandate significantly outstripped its capacity and it never had the political clout to achieve its aims. Throughout the twenty years of its existence it was beset by many problems including an uncertain mandate, inadequate staffing and funding, lack of in-country capacity, lack of support from other UN agencies, a long-running dispute over whether or not it should be operational, and poor credibility within the donor community. The situation improved a little when UNDP Resident Representatives were made special coordinators for relief, when necessary, but at the beginning of the 1980s the UN Joint Inspection Unit produced a damning report of UNDRO's performance.

The Kampuchea crisis of 1979–82 reaffirmed the inadequacy of the UN system in both dealing with the mechanics of a major disaster response and, more importantly, in coping with the complexities of an enormously difficult political situation. The Sahel famine of 1984–5 caught the UN system napping once again despite endless warnings of impending disaster from the Ethiopian government and others.

With the arrival of Boutros Boutros-Ghali and the 'new world order' emerging out of the ashes of the Cold War, it was clear that new possibilities meant new challenges and new responsibilities for the UN and that a significant reorganisation of its disaster relief capacity was necessary. The performance of the UN agencies involved in the provision and coordination of relief during the Kurdish operation of 1990 and 1991 led some Western governments to make an unprecedented call at the G7 Heads of Government Meeting in London in July 1991 for improvements in the system.

> We should like to see moves to strengthen the coordination, and to accelerate the effective delivery of all UN relief for major disasters ... to include
> ... the designation of a high level official, answerable only to the United

Nations Secretary-General, who would be responsible for directing a prompt and well-integrated international response to emergencies, and for coordinating the relevant UN appeals'.[80]

The answer was the creation of the Department of Humanitarian Affairs and the nomination in December 1991 of Swedish diplomat Jan Eliasson as Under-Secretary-General. The DHA absorbed UNDRO and is in fact split between New York and Geneva in the former UNDRO offices.

The same resolution which created DHA also established a Central Emergency Revolving Fund (CERF) of $50 million to facilitate a rapid and coordinated response to emergencies.

Three of the priority issues which Mr Eliasson said that he wished to address are[81]:

(i)   the need to balance accepted principles of national sovereignty with the demands of solidarity with those in severe distress;
(ii) the urgent necessity to create more effective preventive, early-warning and quick-response systems to head off disasters;
(iii) the need to build in the development dimension at a very early stage of relief planning and operations.

Jan Eliasson and the newly formed DHA had a torrid time coping with wars and conflict-induced famines in Bosnia, Somalia, Angola, Liberia, Southern Sudan, Armenia/Azerbaijan, Mozambique and others. There are few signs that the fundamental coordination and management problems have been overcome. Somalia presents an example of what was clearly an inadequate and tardy response (see the chapter by Slim and Visman) and there have been some damning critiques of DHA's caution and lack of decisive response.

The UN has been most successful, according to some analysts,[82] in some of its *ad hoc* operations, particularly the Office for Emergency Operations in Africa (OEOA). This success is attributed to strong, experienced leadership; effective coordinating groups at headquarters and field level; collaboration with governments and NGOs; the use of a wide range of sources for assessing relief needs and well-conducted relations with the media.

Of course the UN alone does not constitute the international relief network in its entirety even if it provides a central role. Affected governments remain important if neglected players, whose role has sometimes been obscured by the recent debate on sovereignty versus suffering. However, General Assembly Resolution 46/182 was clear that ultimate responsibility for relief programmes lies with the affected government. Bilateral donors are also enormously important for their financial contribution — increasingly through non-governmental organisations, as we shall see. The major powers have always been aware that the provision of aid confers legitimacy on recipients and have used the political influence that emergency aid can provide. As Henry Kissinger claimed in 1976,[83] 'disaster relief is becoming increasingly a major instrument of foreign policy. The assistance we can provide to various nations may have a long-term impact on US relations with those nations and their friends'.

Non-governmental organisations (NGOs):

NGOs have always had an important role to play in relief programmes. During the Cold War, when the work of UN agencies was limited because of political considerations, the ICRC and the NGOs were often the only available channel for relief to suffering populations. Although the ICRC's often very strict rules on neutrality and impartiality have sometimes constrained its activities, particularly in areas where it was not possible to obtain the agreements of all parties, NGOs have been more flexible — if less impartial — able to deliver to one or other side of a political conflict. In fact the rise of NGOs in disaster relief throughout the 1980s has been spectacular. In 1991, 450,000 tonnes of food aid were channelled through European NGOs to Africa as compared to 180,000 tonnes in 1989.[84] Twenty-eight per cent of the British Government Overseas Development Administration's disaster and refugee budgets was channelled through NGOs from 1988–9 to 1991–2 compared to just 0.5 per cent from 1977–8 to 1980–1.[85]

The reasons for this success are easy to see. The great strengths of NGOs — flexibility, speed of reaction, comparative lack of bureaucracy, operational and implementational capacity, commitment and dedication of the usually young staff — are particular advantages in emergency work. In addition, the political independence of the NGOs, not bound by the rules of the UN Charter, gives them a strong comparative advantage in increasingly complex internal conflicts. Not that all NGO relief operations are professionally competent. Accounts of relief operations from Cambodia,[86] Sudan and Ethiopia[87] and Mozambique[88] showed that NGOs run programmes as incompetent as the worst UN programmes.

There is of course a price to pay: some critics suggest that NGOs are becoming victims of their own success. As they become larger and more professional, a creeping bureaucratisation is inevitable. A yet more dangerous phenomenon is the increasing use of NGOs by bilateral donors as an alternative channel for funds. USAID in Mozambique used to refer to the American NGOs whose programmes it largely funded as 'our NGOs'. Some European NGOs are almost entirely government-funded. It is difficult to see how NGOs can maintain political independence unless they enforce strict limits on the amount of government funding which they are prepared to accept.

Based on an analysis of recent experiences in the management of humanitarian operations, some of the most serious operational problems identified are as follows:

(a) Uncertain and overlapping mandates and responsibilities. Though each UN agency is supposed to have clear operational responsibilities, these are increasingly becoming blurred. Within the family of UN agencies, only UNICEF has a recognised mandate to assist in civil war settings. That mandate is largely a *de facto* one based upon involvement in such civil wars. This means that UNICEF can provide humanitarian assistance to civilians without conveying recognition of the insurgency. This is one of the reasons why UNICEF was chosen to be the lead agency for Operation Lifeline Sudan when WFP might have been a more obvious choice. WFP must await an invitation by the Secretary-General or by the recognised government to work in a particular region.

These problems are often exacerbated in operational situations particularly when one of the agencies is nominated lead agency, creating confusion and competition for power, prestige and money. Bosnia is an example of such blurring of mandates with UNHCR acting as lead agency in a crisis where the victims are not refugees in international law since they are defined as internally displaced.

These overlapping mandates and competition for resources are exacerbated by the fact that the different agencies are often competing for the same bilateral funds. The pressure is often on to outshine a fellow agency rather than to cooperate with it.

(b) Organisational behaviour of UN agencies. UN agencies are frequently over-centralised with slow decision-making procedures and excessively bureaucratic systems. Of course, these are also strategies to ensure organisational survival (see Taylor, below) in the face of so much uncertainty, ambiguity and lack of control but, more importantly, the UN is prone to deliberation by its very nature. That, after all, is the essence of a large bureaucracy that purports to represent all peoples of the world. A confusion of demands, the need for consensus in decision-making and the tendency towards incremental action rob the UN of coherent strategy when approaching intervention.

(c) Inter-agency relations and coordination. By early 1980, there were, in addition to all the UN agencies and the ICRC, ninety-five NGOs working on the Cambodian crisis in Thailand. In Mozambique by the late 1980s there were close to 150 NGOs. The task of coordinating so many organisations is enormous. It is often made more difficult by the hostility which exists between the host government and the relief community; between the different UN agencies; between the different NGOs; and between the UN

and NGO 'communities'. Some of the problems were summed up in one recent newspaper article which quoted a UN official as saying: 'sometimes I think that we've got two enemies in Mogadishu, General Aideed and Save the Children. And the General is easier to deal with'.[89] Though shockingly brutal, this statement came as no surprise to those who have been close to relief programmes in recent years and illustrates the extraordinary degree of bitterness which can often be found in inter-agency relations.

To overcome the problems of running large humanitarian operations with so many participants requires coordination, which Minear[90] defines as the systematic utilisation of policy instruments to deliver humanitarian assistance in a cohesive and effective manner. As he points out, coordination is a mixed blessing at the best of times since everybody believes in coordination but few wish to be coordinated. While some reject coordination for self-serving reasons, there is no question that poor coordination may increase costs, delay actions, centralise decision-making and politicise aid.

Few question the need for information-gathering and sharing, appeal coordination, and the setting of some key policy guidelines on ration levels, public health policies and the like. Coordination on matters such as standardisation of vehicles is frequently difficult particularly with bilaterals who will usually insist on donating cars and trucks produced by their own national companies. The real problem arises with a definition of coordination which implies some kind of central control of humanitarian operations, negotiating a framework of action with the political authorities and providing leadership. This is particularly so for the more interventionist types of NGO who resent the constraints imposed by operating within a more structured and politically restricted operation.

Coordination is also necessary to identify comparative advantage amongst the different agencies. At different times in a humanitarian operation, different skills and capacities will assume greater and lesser importance. It is therefore vital to know who can respond to life-threatening suffering most quickly, who can move large amounts of relief material quickly, who can provide protection for humanitarian operations and who can negotiate best on behalf of humanitarian interests. On the basis of this identification of strengths amongst the various agencies involved, effective planning of operations can take place.

Though the DHA would seem to be the most logical body to provide the coordination role for all major emergencies, it has not shown, to date, any ability to assume such a role effectively. Nor, with just forty staff of its own and sixty from UNDRO, does it have the human resources at present to take on a more active coordination role — even with the support of the NGOs and the ICRC.[91]

Politically as well as practically, failure to coordinate can damage a programme. Operation Lifeline Sudan, for example, has been constrained by

NGOs which, impatient with its ponderous consultation procedures, have delivered food aid to SPLA areas without government approval. Under some circumstances, particularly in sensitive political programmes, coordination might well have to be mandatory. However, this will only be possible with a number of important changes, including:

(i) the professionalisation of DHA with more and better staff, a good data-base and better communication;

(ii) the involvement of a few of the major NGOs and ICRC in DHA planning via the Inter-Agency Standing Committee to ensure credibility with NGOs;

(iii) much clearer definition of the roles of the different agencies agreed by the most senior staff of UN agencies and NGOs at the start of an operation so that field staff know exactly where their limits lie;

(iv) the appointment of a field-experienced and respected figure as coordinator who can command the confidence of all agencies as well as of the host government;

(d) Financing. The United Nations is surprisingly cheap to run given its increasingly important role in world affairs. The 1990–1 annual budget was $2.1 billion for the UN secretariat and $15 billion for two years for the total system, including voluntary funds and peacekeeping operations. Although this represents a comparatively modest sum, particularly when seen against the defence budgets of some of the major world powers, it is proving difficult to force the member states to pay up on time. At the end of August 1991, nearly half the assessed regular budget was outstanding as well as nearly $5 billion from previous years. Nearly half the assessed contributions ($430 million) for the six current peacekeeping operations had not been paid. Principal debtors were the USA ($531 million), the Soviet Union ($46 million) and Japan ($61 million).

Budgetary strains are likely to increase with the rising costs of some of the major humanitarian and military operations such as Somalia, Bosnia, Mozambique and Cambodia. For every $1 spent in Somalia and Bosnia on humanitarian operations, $10 goes on security there. One point arising out of this conundrum is that early action, apart from saving lives, is much cheaper. Timely UN action in Somalia in 1991 would almost certainly have obviated the need for Operation Restore Hope. Similarly, a concerted political intervention in Bosnia in mid-1992 would have saved lives and money.

The Secretary-General is clearly preoccupied with the issue and reports that 'a chasm has developed between the tasks entrusted to this Organisation and the financial means provided to it'.[92] He describes the present financing system as 'myopic' and its failure as weakening the financial foundations of the Organisation. It is clear that if the member states wish the UN to be more effective, then they must be prepared to pay up. Unfortunately, it is difficult to see how member states can be convinced to finance the massively expensive operations except when their own strategic interests are involved, thus further compromising the credibility of the UN as an independent organisation.

(e) Staffing and professionalism. It has often been alleged that field workers in aid and development are either 'missionaries, mercenaries or misfits' and there is little doubt for anyone with disaster experience at field level that a high proportion of misfits make it into relief work. Indeed Kent[93] cites one senior UN official as alleging that relief work is the last bastion of the amateur.

William Shawcross[94] describes a characteristic scene from the Thai–Cambodian border in 1979:

> But, inevitably there was a MASH-type atmosphere in Aran; some [NGO] doctors and nurses strolled nonchalantly into Maxim's in full medical regalia, even though the hospitals in which they worked were over twenty miles away. As in many such humanitarian emergencies, rivalry between some agencies was intense. Some doctors competed for bodies the way gospellers fought for souls.

Given the generally poor recruiting standards of the UN and many NGOs and the often rushed nature of the selection process for humanitarian relief operations — though this is often due more to bad planning than the emergency itself — what is most surprising is just how competent and dedicated some relief workers are. Very often, the most experienced workers in a humanitarian disaster are local people though these may be marginalised by expatriate staff.

Consistently improved relief programmes will only be possible if the quality of staff at all levels is significantly improved. Effective humanitarian assistance in politically complex areas requires politically sensitive and mature staff with expertise in the more traditional disaster-related skills — nutrition, logistics, public health, etc. — and the political, diplomatic and human skills both to fight for the humanitarian imperative within a Machiavellian context of intrigue and to negotiate with unsympathetic belligerents.

At present, it is unclear what policies the DHA will pursue to ensure the selection and training of staff for both headquarters and field-level operations. The need to draft a proper policy for training programmes involving DHA and specialised agency staff is abundantly clear. Secondment of staff between UN agencies and the NGOs would also do much to attenuate the suspicions and hostilities which currently exist.

(f) Security. The deaths of aid workers in Cambodia, Bosnia, Somalia and

Afghanistan have illustrated the dangers facing field staff posted in these sensitive and unstable areas. Somalia was a watershed with, for the first time ever, the ICRC and NGOs recruiting armed guards to protect relief supplies and personnel.

Consistency is required in the determination of when it is and is not safe to work. Many were critical of the UN decision to pull out of Somalia in 1991, alleging that despite the hostilities there were safe areas in which work could have been done.[95] Better political intelligence and more consultation with the Somali communities might have obviated the need for a mass pull-out of staff. The subsequent lack of field staff in the country detracted greatly from the UN's performance. Ironically, more relief workers have died since Operation Restore Hope than before its launch.

We recommend that:

(i) greater attention be paid to non-military means of providing security through improved understanding of the political situation, more sophisticated negotiating skills and greater involvement of local people and institutions; if this step fails then

(ii) the UN stipulate that any attempt to obstruct the passage of humanitarian relief will be regarded as a breach of international law and that action will be taken against the perpetrators; current practice in this respect is inconsistent with the use of force in Somalia against parties threatening operations while in Bosnia no action has been taken against Serbs and Croats impeding the passage of aid;

(iii) in the last resort, armed guards for humanitarian workers (national or expatriate) may be envisaged.

3. Ensuring neutrality and impartiality

The very concept of humanitarian neutrality — an independent status for humanitarian work beyond political consideration — is under threat from the militarisation, the overt politicisation of humanitarian crises and an ever greater reliance on donors to underwrite the costs of humanitarian operations. Recent UN resolutions have demonstrated that international law has moved forward in recognising the imperative of humanitarian needs above the sovereignty of the nation-state. There is none the less scant evidence that this has allowed humanitarian agencies to pursue their mission without political interference. The enormous cost of providing military support to relief programmes — the US spent around $1.5 billion in Somalia in 1993 — means that major programmes will only be possible in zones which are of strategic interest to the major donors: Cambodia for the Japanese and Somalia for the USA.

Relief operations in any conflict — and particularly civil war — have to be impartial and neutral, if they are to have the cooperation of the warring parties. We define these terms as the following:

Impartiality: provision of relief solely on the basis of need
Neutrality: the refusal to take sides in a conflict

These are not new concepts; they have been endorsed for years by the International Committee of the Red Cross. But ICRC has argued recently that they are becoming harder to put into practice. Caratsch[96] has suggested that the lack of respect by belligerents for international humanitarian law is now the main obstacle to ICRC's work.

Humanitarian assistance will usually be seen by belligerents as secondary to military and strategic objectives and will only be permitted when it is deemed to benefit their political objectives. In such circumstances, it is common for humanitarian assistance to be denied by a government to communities under the control of the adversary. This has been the case with Operation Lifeline Sudan where, throughout its existence, the programme has suffered long periods of inertia due to a lack of consent. The same problem occurred in Mozambique in 1992, when after the signing of an agreement for the provision of aid to both Frelimo (government) and Renamo (rebels) controlled areas, the UN committee established to run such a programme failed to secure the agreement of both sides. Instances of manipulating food aid for military and political purposes have also occurred in Somalia, Bosnia, Ethiopia and Angola. In bitter internal conflicts, even children are seen as pawns in the struggle. As one Nigerian official stated when requested to allow relief to the secessionist Biafran state in 1968, 'the son of a snake is a snake'.[97]

4. SUMMARY: WHAT ARE EFFECTIVE PROGRAMMES

By what criteria can one judge the success or effectiveness of humanitarian programmes in situations of internal conflict? It may well be impractical to expect to target the most needy since in many situations almost everybody is needy — even the fighters and looters of donated food. Even if food is looted or sold off in markets it should have the effect of reducing prices, allowing people to eat more and therefore reducing tension. On the other hand, as pointed out in the recent African Rights'[98] evaluation of Operation Restore Hope, the arrival of too much food aid and indiscriminate distribution in Somalia has led to decreased agricultural production since local farmers have been unable to gain reasonable prices for their agricultural surpluses.

Humanitarian programmes must be judged not only on their short-term success in providing food but by their capacity to rebuild shattered economies and generate public health and other essential services run, wherever possible, by local institutions whether government or opposition (as in the case of Kurdish authorities in northern Iraq). Humanitarian programmes should not be judged by their ability to create peace and security or to end fighting or, more generally, to cover up for the inadequacy of political decision-making at either national or international level.

How to make humanitarian action accountable

This is the most understudied area of humanitarian action. Our own remarks should be understood as pointers, intended to open up the debate. Humanitarian work, while motivated by a concern for the victims of humanitarian disaster, rarely considers the question of accountability to those same people. Nor is sufficient recognition given to the conflicting demands of accountability — accountability to beneficiaries, to donors, to senior staff at headquarters levels — or to conflicts that this creates for staff in the field.

1. ACCOUNTABLE TO WHOM?
There are three major groups to account to in humanitarian operations: the victims, the host government and the donors who fund the programmes. In addition, aid workers in the field must obviously account for their actions to their superiors. It is no surprise to find that those with greatest reason to demand accountability — the victims — are those least likely to receive it. Theirs is a weak and powerless voice, rarely heard.

One reason for this is that early warning systems are not accountable to communities affected by potential or actual famines since those running the systems — usually expatriates or élite, urban nationals — are unlikely themselves to suffer food shortages. This discrepancy exists at all levels of an assistance programme: the decision-makers rarely share, or understand, the dilemmas and needs of the victims. Indeed the very word victim implies one passively suffering rather than one who could be given the opportunity to take more control over his fate.

Until UN agencies, NGOs and host governments find more systematic ways of genuinely answering to those whom they claim to serve, the problem will remain of accountability to those with power but not to those without.

2. EMPOWERMENT OF THE BENEFICIARIES
Relief culture is often a culture of paternalism, assured of its superiority and moral virtue,[99] and ready to marginalise the nationals of an affected country — be they government officials, representatives of rebel movements or the victims themselves, who are imprisoned in the degrading images produced by the media and the fund raisers for voluntary agencies.

The failure to consult with and involve nationals, particularly the victims of humanitarian catastrophes, demeans them further and leads to less efficient operations. It also contributes to a loss of agency legitimacy and inhibits the growth of indigenous service delivery institutions.

Much of the criticism of Operation Restore Hope has concerned its failure to involve Somalis in decision-making. Critics of the UN operation have argued that a greater involvement of Somali community leaders could have defused the situation.

3. ROLE OF THE MEDIA

As Sen[100] has shown, famines do not occur in countries with democratic governments, an adversarial political system and a free press. An active local press encourages accountable and responsive government.

In most of the humanitarian crises throughout the world, there are low levels of literacy and media technology and a shortage of local press organs calling for accountability of either government or international organisations on behalf of the victims. Coverage tends to come from the international press with its own priorities.

For the moment though, the international media can provide an assessment of relief operations and exert pressure at an international level on behalf of the victims of crises. Though some of the weaknesses of media reporting have already been noted, we believe that these may be best overcome by working more closely with journalists, not to compromise their objectivity but to ensure that their position is more informed. The media may often embarrass aid workers but they play a potentially vital role as a voice for the dispossessed.

4. MONITORING AND EVALUATION

Monitoring and evaluation remains a very weak area of humanitarian operations and a review of the literature produced — mostly by journalists and writers rather than relief agencies themselves — suggests an inability to learn some of the basic lessons of previous failures. Some of the major management problems of the 1970s and 1980s have been repeated in the 1990s in places as diverse as southern Sudan, Mozambique and Cambodia.

Given the rapid turnover of relief workers, this problem is in turn hampering the creation of effective institutional learning. All humanitarian programmes should be externally evaluated by independent experts with the results widely disseminated — however embarrassing for agencies and individuals concerned. Up to now, negative evaluations have been hidden by the agencies concerned. This is a practice that should not be allowed to continue.

We also strongly recommend that evaluations should consult beneficiaries and, even more importantly, those who did not, but should have benefited from a humanitarian operation. This would contribute not only to improved learning to but a greater accountability to the victims of disasters.

Sovereignty and suffering: conclusion

The end of the Cold War has seen a fundamental reordering of the relations between states and the rights of citizens. It is depressing, but not altogether surprising, that these changes are only dimly perceived by political leaders, who have been slow to redefine the role of international institutions accordingly. It is our view that with more visionary leadership at an international level much of the confusion and distress that have characterised the international response to crises in recent years could have been avoided.

The issue of sovereignty has been the most obvious area of failure. Three years ago, even to suggest that the traditional bulwark of sovereignty should be re-examined was deemed, in some quarters, to be politically naïve. In evidence to the House of Commons Foreign Affairs Select Committee, Sir David Hannay spoke of his 'surprise' at the way in which some members of the Security Council had greeted the call from non-aligned African states to send UN troops into Somalia.[101]

There is now an emerging consensus that clear criteria for humanitarian intervention are necessary.[102] This is progress. In this chapter we have put forward our own formulae. Others exist.[103] But the question of what authority might attach to such criteria remains unanswered. Some argue for an amendment to the UN Charter; others favour a General Assembly resolution. Our own view is that the criteria for humanitarian intervention should be allowed to develop through the common law process of international legislation. We argue this for two reasons. First, any attempt to secure the formal adoption of these criteria at the UN is likely to result in their dilution during the negotiation process. Secondly, it is probable that the criteria will, in any case, continue to evolve; it would be inappropriate at this stage to freeze the debate with a single statement. Meanwhile, voluntary treaty agreements between individual states or associations of states in specific cases of humanitarian action could in due course, through the evolution of customary law, become binding on others.[104]

As we have noted, we remain optimistic in view of the emerging clarity — albeit belated — about the criteria for intervention, which lay down an objective framework for humanitarian action. Much remains to be done, however, to improve the operational effectiveness of humanitarian agencies.

Our own examination reveals four main areas where improvements are necessary.

First, there is an urgent need for humanitarian agencies to establish complementarity of action. This in turn requires further steps towards better coordination, under the auspices of the UN's Department of Humanitarian Affairs. The DHA requires better resourcing and, perhaps more important, thorough professionalisation. Its central role will only be acceptable to other UN agencies and to NGOs if it can offer them tangible advantages. At present these have only been glimpsed, in terms of improvements in consolidated appeals and in the (admittedly faltering) use of the Central Emergency Revolving Fund (CERF).

It is not politically practicable at this stage to pursue the possibility of the DHA being granted a controlling sanction over the operations of other humanitarian agencies within the UN — let alone over NGOs. We believe that, in addition to the two areas cited above, the DHA should concentrate on the provision of operational intelligence, both early warning of crises and actual crisis monitoring.

Second, the question of resources — both financial and human — requires greater attention. Financial support for the UN must be assured. Humanitarian operations suffer from the fact that government contributions are usually voluntary rather than assessed. This renders planning uncertain and also delays action. A greater proportion of funds for humanitarian operations should, in future, come from assessed contributions. As regards human resources, the professionalisation of staff is crucial. A strategy for training, exchange and secondment between agencies needs urgently to be developed. This is a task that the DHA should assume.

Third, the improvement of security for humanitarian operations is essential. We have put forward proposals on this point. The UN should recognise the *policing* of humanitarian operations as a task to be carried out within a clear legal framework, with all the checks and balances that a judicial context provides.

Fourth, greater accountability in humanitarian operations is now imperative. We have suggested a number of ways to broaden a narrow fiscal conception towards a vision of greater accountability: to the international community as a whole and to individuals and communities within the operational area. One idea in particular which deserves further consideration is the availability to individuals of the ECOSOC Resolution 1503, enabling them to press claims of a humanitarian character over the heads of their governments.

We have identified a number of legal and operational improvements, all of which are eminently achievable and many of which already enjoy support from practitioners and scholars. All this, however, falls short of the real target. The success of humanitarian operations depends not only on the changes proposed in this chapter but, crucially, on the political will to accord humanitarian neutrality a primary place in the conduct of powerful states, in and beyond the context of the United Nations.

We fear that humanitarian operations are sometimes seen as substitute for political action, that they are prone to political and military hi-jack, that the doctrine of humanitarian neutrality is open to abuse, and that each abuse damages the credibility of humanitarian agents. To safeguard this neutrality is no easy task. It is understandable that international relations should be influenced by the political interests of dominant states. Nor is it surprising that those who contribute most to the resources and, more significantly, to the peacekeeping forces deployed in a given operation should insist on its congruence with their own interests.

It is essential that the principles referred to in the latter part of the chapter in the section on the issue of humanitarian neutrality (pp. 57–8) inform the conduct of humanitarian operations. Taken together they provide a powerful safeguard for the moral legitimacy of UN humanitarian action. We therefore believe that a formal restatement of these principles would be timely and valuable.

We have already observed that a failure of leadership has contributed significantly to the tragedies of recent years. The opportunity to lead the international community out of this valley is not yet lost. In the meantime, it is not acceptable to rely on the minimalist approaches usually defended as 'pragmatic'. This is a time for vision and for the kind of creative leadership which disdains difficulties. It is a time for the clear and energetic pursuit of an entente between nations, with humanitarian neutrality as the core of what would, indeed, become a new world order.

Notes

1   This chapter has been prepared under the auspices of ActionAid, although the views advanced here do not necessarily reflect those of that organisation.

2   Bodin, *Six Livres de la république* (1576).

3   *Island of Palmas*, 2 UNRIAA 838.

4   PCIJ, Series A, No.10, at 18.

5   *Lotus*, ibid.; see also *Free Zones*, PCIJ, Series A/B, No. 46, at 166.

6   *SS Wimbledon*, PCIJ, Series A, No. 1, at 24.

7   *Nationality Decrees in Tunis and Morocco*, PCIJ, Series B, No. 24, at 23.

8   *Barcelona Traction,* 1970 ICJ 32.

9   Cf. Article 19 of the ILC draft convention on state responsibility and the work of the ILC on Crimes against Peace and Security of Mankind.

10   *Nicaragua* case, 1986 ICJ, at 106; *Corfu Channel (Merits) case,* 1949 ICJ 4, 35; The Court affirmed that 'respect for territorial sovereignty is an essential foundation of international relations'. Thus, despite the dangers to international shipping caused by mines in the Corfu Channel, Britain was not empowered to sweep the territorial waters of Albania without the consent of the territorial sovereign. In the famous dictum of the Court: 'The Court can only regard the alleged right of intervention as the manifestation of a policy of force, such as has, in the past, given rise to most serious abuses and such as cannot, whatever be the present defects in international organisation, find a place in international law. Intervention is perhaps still less admissible in the particular form it would take here; for, from the nature of things, it would be reserved for the most powerful states, and might easily lead to perverting the administration of international justice itself.' The Court's view that Britain was entitled to assert its right of innocent passage, emphasised by some authors, need not be discussed in the context of subversive intervention, which is, prima facie, an act not based on a positive right.

11   1986 ICJ, op. cit., at 108.

12   E.g. on the Latin American practice in this respect, see Garcia-Amador, 1(1) *The Inter-American System,* (1983) 80ff.; UNCIO, *Selected Documents,* (1946) 102; Cuban *Declaration of the Rights and Duties of Nations*, para 2.

13   Article 2(7) applies to the relationship between the United Nations Organisation and its members, but in practice the terms employed in it are frequently used in inter-state relations as well. E.g. the *Nicaragua* case, supra note 10, at 106; Cot & Pellet, *La Charte des nations unies,* (1985) 146; Hambro, Rovine & Simmons, *Charter of*

the United Nations, (3rd edn. 1969) 63. But consider the exchange between the USSR and USA concerning the intervention in the Dominican Republic, SCOR 20th yr, 1196th mtg., from para 11, 1198th mtg, in particular the answer of the US representative, ibid., at para 154: 'The Soviet Union representative has bitterly attacked our action in the Dominican Republic. He says it was an open act of aggression. First of all, I note that in his haste to cite every possible provision that he might accuse us of violating, he has even dragged out Article 2, paragraph 7 of the Charter of the United Nations. But that Article deals only with limitations on the authority of the United Nations itself; it is in no way relevant to the situation before the Council.' Also see the discussion in the Council in the aftermath of the 1973 Coup in Chile, SCOR 28th yr, 1741st mtg., throughout. An eloquent exposition of the better view, by Ecuador, on the occasion of the Grenada intervention, S/PV.2491, states that Article 2(4) prohibits armed interference, adding, with respect to Article 2(7), the *a fortiori* argument: 'Moreover, Article 2, paragraph 7, of the Charter states that not even the United Nations is authorised to intervene in matters which are essentially within the domestic jurisdiction of any state.' A more scientific presentation of this view in GAOR, 21st Sess., 6th Cte., 935th mtg., para 6.

14 Article 2(4) of the UN Charter provides: 'All Members shall refrain in their international relations from the threat or use of force against the territorial integrity or political independence of any state, or in any other manner inconsistent with the Purposes of the United Nations.' Attempts by the Latin American States to include the obligation of states not to intervene in each other's internal affairs in Article 2 were unsuccessful. E.g. Brazilian proposed amendment to Chapter (Article) II (4), UNCIO, *Selected Documents,* (1946) 102; Cuban *Declaration of the Rights and Duties of Nations,* para 2, ibid., at 103; Ecuador draft, para 1, ibid., at 106; Mexico, para 3, ibid., at 107; Panama, para 1, ibid., at 108; also Iran, para 4, ibid, at 107; Netherlands, principles 2 & 3, ibid., at 238. These draft articles all cover acts of subversive intervention.

15 Philippines draft amendment (Chapter VIII, B), UNCIO, *Selected Documents,* (1946) 185; Bolivia, ibid., at 186.

16 Report of the Rapporteur of Committee III/3 to Commission III on Chapter VIII, Section B, UNCIO, *Selected Documents* (1946) 761, 763: 'The progress of the technique of modern warfare renders very difficult the definition of all cases of aggression. It may be noted that the list of such cases being necessarily incomplete, the Council would have a tendency to consider of less importance the acts not mentioned therein; these omissions would encourage the aggressor to distort the definition or might delay action by the Council.'

17   That formulation was, in fact, introduced into the Charter by smaller
      states as an added measure of protection, when the major powers
      resisted an explicit definition of aggression and the inclusion of a pro-
      vision on non-interference. 4 UNCIO 342ff.
18   The Court, in the *Nicaragua* case, supra note 10, at 100, went even
      further: 'The effect of consent to the text of such resolutions cannot
      be understood as merely that of "reiteration or elucidation" of the
      treaty commitment undertaken in the Charter. On the contrary, it
      may be understood as an acceptance of the validity of the rule or
      rules declared in the resolution by themselves.' In light of Article 103
      of the Charter, and the probable *jus cogens* character of the prohibi-
      tion of the use of force, it seems preferable to regard the standard set-
      ting instruments as a means of discovering the true meaning of the
      rather broad Charter provisions, instead of considering the resolu-
      tions as a source of independent obligations.
19   Resolution 290 (IV), para. 3.
20   Preamble, Resolution 2131 (XX). The United States regarded the res-
      olution as a statement of political intent, but not a formulation of
      law. GAOR, 20th Sess., 1st. Cte., A/C.1/SR.1423, at 436.
21   Res. 2625 (XXV).
22   (a) The duty of states to refrain in their international relations from
      the threat or use of force in any form ... [or] to disrupt the political,
      social or economic order of other states, to overthrow or change the
      political system of another state or its Government;
      (b) The duty of a state to ensure that its territory is not used in any
      manner which would violate the sovereignty, political independence,
      territorial integrity and national unity, or disrupt the political, eco-
      nomic, and social stability of another state;
      (c) The duty of a state to refrain from armed intervention, subver-
      sion, military occupation or any other form of intervention and inter-
      ference, overt or covert, directed at another state or group of states;
      (f) The duty of a state to refrain from the promotion, encouragement
      or support, direct or indirect, of rebellious or secessionist activities
      within other states, under any pretext whatsoever, or any action
      which seems to disrupt the unity or to undermine or subvert the polit-
      ical order of other states;
      (n) The duty of a state to refrain from organising, training, financing
      and arming political and ethnic groups on their territories or the ter-
      ritories of other states for the purpose of creating subversion, disor-
      der or unrest in other countries;
      (o) The duty of a state to refrain from any economic, political or mili-
      tary activity in the territory of another state without its consent.
23   Res. 42/22, Annex.
24   An extensive review of this debate, accompanied by bibliographical

footnotes, is presented by Malanczuk in *Humanitarian Intervention and the Legitimacy of the Use of Force* (1993).

25   1986 ICJ 124.
26   Resolution 43/131.
27   A/45/587, at 17. See also A/46/568, at 27.
28   Resolution 46/182.
29   S/25070/Add.8, 8 March 1993. On the Council's initiative on fact-finding, see S/24872, 30 November 1992.
30   Ibid., at 7.
31   E.g. Arts. 23, 55, 59, 60, 61, Fourth Geneva Convention. Protocol I concerning international armed conflicts also stipulates that relief operations 'shall' be undertaken on behalf of populations in territory under the control of a Party to the conflict other than occupied territories, although that requirement is somewhat undermined by the caveat 'subject to the agreement of the Parties concerned'.
32   UNICEF is considered an exception.
33   A/C.3/47/L.77, adopted by 102 votes to 8, 28 abstentions, at the 47th Sess., 58th plenary meeting. Sudan voted against that text.
34   Resolution 851 (1992).
35   E.g. Resolutions 221 (1965), 232 (1966), 253 (1968), 277 (1970), 288 (1970), 314 (1972), 318 (1972), 320 (1972), 333 (1973); Resolution 418 (1977).
36   Resolutions 217 (1966), 221 (1966).
37   S/22133, 22 January 1991.
38   S/PV.2974, at 3.
39   Ibid., at 7.
40   See main text below, section (b).
41   S/24812.
42   S/24735, 29 October 1992.
43   S/PV.3138, *passim*.
44   S/22435, 5 April 1991, S/22442, 4 April 1992, S/22443, 4 April 1991, S/22447, 4 April 1991. Reproduced in Weller, *Iraq and Kuwait: The Hostilities and Their Aftermath* (1993) (Weller hereinafter), 604f.
45   S/PV.2982, reproduced in Weller, 124.
46   Ibid., at 126.
47   Ibid., at 127. Zimbabwe stated that 'While we realise that the humanitarian dimensions affect neighbouring states, we do not believe that this in any way makes the internal conflict in Iraq an issue that the Council should be seized of'.' Ibid., 127, also Cuba, 129.
48   Cuba, Yemen and Zimbabwe voted against, China and India abstained. Ibid., 131.
49   Iraq formally protested against the adoption of the resolution.

S/22460, 8 April 1991.

50   Weller, 714.
51   Ibid., 717.
52   Ibid., 720.
53   Ibid., 615.
54   Ibid., 723ff.
55   A cruise missile raid on an alleged nuclear installation in southern Baghdad conducted only by the United States was not part of this operation. Although the UN Secretary-General appeared to justify this raid as being covered by the original mandate to use force against Iraq, granted in Resolution 678 (1990), this view is rightly treated as highly dubious.
56   Some doubt has been raised as to whether or not the coalition raids fulfilled the requirements of an immediate and overwhelming threat posed to coalition aircraft.
57   United Nations Reference Paper, *The United Nations and the Situation in Somalia*, April 1992.
58   S/23445.
59   S/24868, 3 December 1992.
60   S/25354, 3 March 1993.
61   The early response to the Yugoslav crisis has been described in Weller, 'The international response to the dissolution of the Socialist Federal Republic of Yugoslavia', *American Journal of International Law,* 86 (1992), 569.
62   S/PV.3009, at 25.
63   Editor's note: this is a highly controversial proposal. Readers should note that this suggestion is in conflict with the Resolution of the Institut de Droit International, cited earlier: 'offers of assistance shall not, particularly by virtue of the means used to implement them, take a form suggestive of a threat of armed intervention or any other measure of intimidation.' The consequences of action which was 'suggestive of armed intervention' in Somalia in 1993 are documented in their chapter by Slim and Visman in this book.
64   Editor's note: readers should compare the arguments here with those in Taylor's chapter below.
65   DHA (1992) cited by Salim Lone, *Enlarging the UN's Humanitarian Mandate*, New York, UN Department of Public Information.
66   B.Kouchner 'A call for humanitarian intervention', *Refugee* magazine, (December 1992), UNHCR.
67   J. Perez de Cuellar: speech made at the University of Bordeaux, April 1991.
68   Simone Weil (1949) cited by O.O'Neill, *Faces of Hunger: An Essay on Poverty, Justice and Development*, Helsinki, WIDER (1986).
69   K. Jansson, M. Harris and A. Penrose, *The Ethiopian Famine: The*

Story of the Emergency Relief Operation, London, Zed (1987).

70 Peter Gill, *A Year in the Death of Africa: Politics, Bureaucracy and the Famine,* London, Paladin (1986).

71 African Rights, *Somalia Operation Restore Hope: A Preliminary Assessment,* (1993).

72 C. Caratsch, Humanitarian design and political interference: Red Cross work in the post-Cold War period', *International Relations,* **XI**, 4 (April 1993).

73 Leonard Frank, *The Development Game,* Cambridge, Granta (1986).

74 M. Buchanan-Smith, S. Davies and C. Petty, *Famine Early Warning Systems and Responses: The Missing Link,* SCF/IDS (1992).

75 Letter from Deputy High Commissioner for Refugees, 24 June 1993.

76 T. Deen, 'The UN in transition', *Development Forum,* **20,** 5 (September–October 1992).

77 S. J. Stedman, 'The new interventionists', *Foreign Affairs,* **72** 1 (1993) 1–16.

78 Letter in *Guardian,* 17 April 1993.

79 M. Duffield, *War and Famine in Africa,* Oxford, Oxfam (1992).

80 *Declaration: Strengthening the International Order* by leaders of the Group of Seven countries at their July 1991 London summit.

81 Eliasson in Salim Lone, *op.cit.* (1992).

82 K. Eduards, G. Rosen and R. Rossborough, 'Responding to emergencies: the role of the UN in emergencies and ad hoc operations', in Nordic UN Project, *The United Nations: Issues and Options,* Stockholm, Nordic UN Project (1991).

83 H. Kissinger cited by R. Kent, *The Anatomy of Disaster Relief: The International Network in Action,* London, Pinter (1987).

84 Figures cited by M. Bowden, 'Food aid and famine: the NGO perspective', paper presented at a Conference on Food Aid and Famine, London, November 1992.

85 Figures cited by J. Borton, 'The enhanced role of NGOs in relief operations', *Development Research Insights,* IDS/ODI, (Autumn 1992).

86 W. Shawcross, *The Quality of Mercy: Cambodia, Holocaust and Modern Conscience,* London, Deutsch (1984).

87 See, for example, Gill *op.cit.* (1986), Graham Hancock, *Ethiopia: The Challenge of Hunger,* London, Gollancz (1985) and B. Harrell-Bond, *Imposing Aid: Emergency Assistance to Refugees,* Oxford, Oxford University Press (1986).

88 Joseph Hanlon, *Mozambique: Who Calls the Shots?* London, James Currey (1991).

89 Peter Hillmore, 'The peacemakers at odds', *Observer,* 27 June 1993.

90 L. Minear, 'Making the humanitarian system work better', in K. Cahill (ed.), *A Framework for Survival: Health, Human Rights and*

Humanitarian Assistance in Conflicts and Disasters, New York, Council on Foreign Relations and Basic Books (1993).

91 Editor's note: by January 1994, DHA-UNDRO had a staff of 150.
92 B. Boutros-Ghali, *Agenda for Peace,* New York, United Nations (1992).
93 R. Kent, op.cit. (1987).
94 W. Shawcross, op.cit. (1984).
95 See A. Penrose and A. Timpson, *The United Nations and Humanitarian Assistance: A Case Study of Somalia,* Save the Children Fund (UK) (1992).
96 Caratsch, op.cit. (1993).
97 D. Jacobs, *The Brutality of Nations,* New York, Alfred Knopf (1987), 15.
98 African Rights op.cit. (1993).
99 See Kent, op.cit. (1987) and Harrell-Bond, op.cit. (1986).
100 A. Sen, *Poverty and Famine,* Oxford, Oxford University Press, (1981).
101 Foreign Affairs Committee Report on 'The expanding role of the United Nations and its implications for UK policy' (1993), para. 99.
102 Ibid., para. 110.
103 See, for example, the Development Studies Association Memorandum to the Foreign Affairs Select Committee (1992) .
104 See the Cairo Declaration of the World Food Council, GAOR, 44th Session, Suppl. No. 19.

3

Options for the reform of the international system for humanitarian assistance

Paul Taylor[1]

Since the end of the Cold War the intergovernmental organisations which form the United Nations system (the central system and the agencies), and non-governmental organisations (NGOs), like the Save the Children Fund, Oxfam, Médecins sans Frontières, the International Committee of the Red Cross, Catholic Relief Services, and CARE, have been faced with an increasing range of demands on their scarce resources.[2] The UN has been stretched with regard to peacekeeping activities, but it has also found it necessary to deal with an increasing number of complex humanitarian emergencies, the main characteristic of which is an unacceptable level of human suffering: there are severe shortages of resources like food and medicine, an absence of security, often because of civil war, and the collapse of government and administration.[3]

Faced with such problems a large number of practical and conceptual problems have emerged which demand our attention. The UN's main difficulty, however, has been to steer a course between two imperatives: on the one hand to face the crises with efficient and effective international action, and on the other to protect the orderly conduct of relations between states, through respect for the UN's central principles, especially the sovereignty of its member states.

How can the international community respond more effectively to the increasing demands being made of it in the 1990s? The mechanisms are those of a polycentric system, made up of international organisations, both IGOs and NGOs, which have a high degree of constitutional independence which they are determined to protect; the setting is a multicentric structure, namely the society of states, which are sovereign and legally equal. The primary concerns here are: to identify the changing relationships between the IGOs and the NGOs; to examine the problems of coordinating and managing international action; and to evaluate the major changes in thinking about what kind of action is acceptable. They spring from a range of striking recent developments: NGOs have emerged as major players; there have been significant institutional innovations to provide better management; and the difficulties in the way of humanitarian intervention caused by the sovereignty of states are being re-examined.[4]

Similar issues arise both in the area of efforts to maintain international peace and security, such as peacekeeping, and in the area of intervention in complex crises to promote humanitarian assistance. Indeed both activities frequently occur at the same time, and, if they do, each has implications for the other.[5] But in this paper humanitarian assistance is the primary concern; the evidence is taken mainly from the interventions in Somalia, and other parts of the Horn of Africa, and from the Kurdish territories in Iraq.

The questions to be addressed relate to the three stages of the relationship between international organisations and a crisis.

First are issues which arise at the point when the organisations begin a programme of intervention, such as acquiring adequate information and resources, engaging the organisation's attention and defining its mandate, in addition to finding an acceptable justification for involvement, which raises issues concerning sovereignty.

Second are those which arise during its execution, such as coordinating and managing the activities of the operational organisations, including the non-governmental organisations; finding appropriate relationships between peacekeeping, and political and humanitarian operations, and between international organisations and governments and other authorities, within the host states, and finding ways of funding operations, and monitoring developments effectively.

A third set concerns the end phase, when the programme might be considered to be in some sense complete or, for other reasons, withdrawal has entered the agenda. These include such questions as the relationship between relief, rehabilitation and recovery. Discussion cannot be sharply compartmentalised: issues discussed in one context may also arise in another.

Involvement: starting a process of humanitarian intervention

Information-gathering

By this is meant the process by which the attention of international actors is drawn to the existence of the crisis, the ways in which information about the crisis is generated and received, and the initial response, including the definition of a mandate. In each of these areas faults may arise which lead to a failure to attract attention: a lack of relevant information, or a failure to understand it, or it may be a failure to provide an appropriate mandate.

It is not the purpose of this chapter to analyse the causes of humanitarian crises: they may be largely man-made, as in the case of war or even economic mismanagement, or they may be the result of natural phenomena, such as drought or earthquake.[6] Usually they are the product of a combination of the two. In January 1993 there were an estimated forty to fifty countries suffering man-made or natural disaster situations, ten of them classified by the United Nations as 'complex' as they involved multiple 'causes' with a breakdown of government and public security[7]. But in order for there to be an international response it is obviously necessary that information should be collected about the crisis with regard to its intensity, the territory where it is located, the variations in its dimensions in different parts of the territory, and the kinds of deficiencies which are involved, for instance with regard to food, shelter, clothing, medicine or public health. Information relating to the security of personnel is also essential.

It is also necessary to have available analysis of the ways in which the crisis is likely to unfold in a number of different circumstances: if nothing is done, or if certain forms of aid are given, but not others. There needs to be some indication of the chronological dimensions of the problem given various kinds of support. This is necessary in view of the great cost of disaster relief — in Mozambique ten times more was spent per capita on disaster relief in one year than was normally spent on development,[8] and organisations are often faced with the problem of having to decide upon the proportion of their budget to be spent on crisis intervention and that on longer-term development.[9] It was considered by UNICEF officials in 1993 that their organisation might need to restrict its spending on disasters to around 20 per cent of the overall budget.[10]

Such information may not be available for a number of reasons. Because of the complexity of crises, analysis means calculating the interaction between a number of different factors. It may also be the case that the crisis has a layered quality so that disturbances at one level conceal disturbances at another, as with the way in which the war in Ethiopia led to the partial concealment of the famine there for several months.[11] Governments may also for political reasons not wish to collect or provide information about crises which generate pressures for humanitarian intervention.

Sovereignty and information-gathering

Such difficulties raise issues which impinge upon the question of sovereignty. It is widely acknowledged that there could be improvements in the procedures for the generation and analysis of information concerning crises. One suggestion is to involve the affected people themselves in the collection of data and for international organisations to help by providing the technical assistance to do this. There are ways of measuring trends towards food deficiency, levels of malnutrition, and also the likely future availability of necessary foodstuffs, given probable local harvests and likely alternative provision. This would be part of a process of evaluating what have been called 'entitlements' to various provisions[12]. The point has been stressed that involving local responsible individuals in this is also helpful as a way of sustaining order and preserving a sense of self-reliance. Such direct links between international organisations and citizens might not, however, be welcomed by the national political authorities. They would expect to be involved in the system's establishment and management, thus reducing confidence in the information generated.

Another option is to use more 'high tech' procedures, such as satellite surveillance, which is now capable of mapping areas where there is a shortage of rainfall sufficient to damage crops or pasture. This should also involve what is called 'ground truthing', that is confirmation on the ground by direct inspection of the evidence provided by surveillance. Once again, however, the problem arises of states seeing such surveillance, and direct inspection, as an infringement of their sovereignty. It is not just that there is sensitivity to the presence of an external actor, and anxiety that it should comply with conditions on its presence imposed as expressions, not necessarily rational, of the states' sovereignty. It is also that so many developing states are concerned with the process of state building: the involvement of the governments in creating regimes which they control in as wide an area of activities as possible is part of the process of establishing the state and confirming its right to exist. There is, in other words, a delaying factor in the way of timely intervention in disaster relief which might be called 'sovereignty drag'.

The conclusion must be that until the attitudes of states towards the implications of sovereignty alter to the extent of accepting international observation as a matter of routine, there will be problems with regard to producing timely and accurate information of an impending or actual crisis. A further difficulty is that the main aid agencies, be they non-governmental or intergovernmental, often need to become involved on the basis of partial and uncertain information, yet they are the main repositories of the techniques for obtaining such information. But their presence in a vulnerable country outside a period of crisis may well be unacceptable to the governments and impractical for resource reasons. There is a 'Catch-22' situation here: difficulties in the way of giving aid agencies early access, so that they can get full information about a crisis, means that their intervention will almost always be too late.

This suggests that there are advantages from the point of view of information collection if agencies that are not concerned directly with humanitarian assistance, and which have a full-time presence in a country, such as the development agencies, or the resident coordinator of the UNDP, are given primary responsibility for monitoring on a longer-term basis on the ground.[13] The presence of development agencies over a period of time,

TAYLOR, in HARRISS (ed), 1995

when there is no significant crisis, or of agencies concerned with longer-term social programmes like UNICEF, is likely to be more acceptable to governments. The issue of their adequacy with regard to this function needs to be further examined.

It has been suggested that the procedures being set in place to produce 'UN country strategy' documents should be adapted to serve also as a crisis early warning system. In pursuing this strategy the responsible agency at the country level is the Resident Coordinator of the UNDP, who is responsible for establishing and convening Round Tables of representatives of the range of development agencies involved in a country. The Resident Coordinator is encouraged to establish good relations with the government. Involving a range of organisations, each with its specialised skills and understanding is important: specialists in one area, such as health, tend not to place enough stress on the holistic approach to disaster relief.

The idea that such a framework should also be involved in a kind of 'disaster watch' is new. It was only in the General Assembly Resolution 46/182 of April 1992 that it was proposed that:

> On the basis of existing mandates and drawing upon monitoring arrangements available within the system, the United Nations should intensify efforts, building upon the existing capacities of relevant organisations and entities of the United Nations, for the systematic pooling, analysis and dissemination of early-warning information on natural disasters and other emergencies. In this context, the United Nations should consider making use as appropriate of the early-warning capacities of Governments and intergovernmental and non-governmental organisations.[14]

What is stressed is the adaptation of existing procedures and operating under existing mandates. This would appear to be appropriate because, as already indicated, the constraints of national sovereignty suggest that a certain indirectness of approach could be prudent. This is another case where in order to serve the interests of individual people, even *in extremis,* it may be necessary to cope with the non-cooperative tendency of governments. Despite the constant references to the primary responsibility of governments, for coping with the disasters of people in their own states, the general pattern will be for the international community to have to bring pressure to bear on them to respond appropriately, or to circumvent their opposition, even with regard to collecting information.

Focusing attention

But the existence of accurate and sufficient information is not in itself enough to engage the attention of the international community. In Somalia the nature of the crisis was known by the non-governmental agencies in early 1991, yet there was no positive UN involvement until after the worsening of the military situation in December of that year, and no decision to act until April 1992. There were a number of reasons for this. One was that the UN system had rules regarding the security of its personnel which led to officials there, such as the resident coordinator, withdrawing to Nairobi. The point has been made by more cynical commentators that such a retreat could not have been much deterred by the payment of higher rates to officials who had been displaced.

There was, therefore, a situation in which information about the crisis got lost in disputes about whether the security situation would allow involvement for UN personnel. Non-governmental organisations felt particularly aggrieved by this as they were not so constrained and remained in Somalia during 1991, with their staff risking their lives.[15] On the other hand, however, it was argued by some diplomats that the NGOs contributed to the impasse regarding security and UN Agency involvement: they implied that significant deployment of security forces was not necessary, whilst simultaneously complaining that the UN was inadequately engaged.[16] One intergovernmental organisation, UNICEF, got round the problem by using only volunteer workers. The question was also naturally raised about how far the United Nations could generate its own security by introducing peacekeeping forces, and this became a nettle which governments hesitated to grasp because their attention was focused primarily upon the situation in Yugoslavia.

The Secretary-General himself made a major contribution to refocusing the world's attention on the Somalia crisis when he publicly complained after the first London Conference on the Yugoslavia crisis in July 1992 that Yugoslavia was taking up too large a share of the UN's resources, and that the Somalia crisis was being ignored because it was a Third World problem. He had complained bitterly about not having been consulted about the new commitments made on behalf of the UN at that conference, and that he had not been invited.[17] It has been suggested, however, that he had indeed been invited, but that he had ignored the invitation.[18] Is it possible that he deliberately generated the quarrel in order to focus world attention on Somalia? Clearly one of the duties of the Secretary-General is to ensure that the priorities attached to the work of the United Nations are not skewed in favour of one group of states or a particular area.

The issue here is that of bringing relevant information to the attention of an actor who is in a position to contribute something essential, in resources or skills. A further problem in getting attention in this sense is that links between the information holder and the actor whose attention is sought may be faulty. In relations between the intergovernmental UN system and the non-governmental organisations such as Save the Children Fund, there were serious failures of communication in the course of 1991 in Somalia.[19]

The UN did not seem to listen to the non-governmental organisations. When James Jonah went to Mogadishu in January 1992, he failed to seek the advice of the non-governmental organisations already there about whom he should see and the routes he should use. Routes were arranged for him that were known to be impossible for security reasons, and he refused to deal with the *de facto* authorities on the ground, such as General Aideed, of whom apparently he made an enemy. Some participants thought that Aideed would have been able to make positive contributions to the assistance programme, but the view taken was that the principle of not appearing to compromise the UN's neutrality should have precedence over the task of providing humanitarian assistance. Indeed in General Assembly Resolution 43/131 of 20 March 1989, which appealed for more to be done in the area of humanitarian assistance, it was ruled that the 'principles of humanity, neutrality and impartiality must be given utmost consideration by all those involved in providing humanitarian assistance',[20] without regard to the way in which the second principle might get in the way of the others if strictly interpreted. Political expediency prevailed over practical considerations.

Other officials, such as the representative of WHO and the Resident Coordinator, made very fleeting visits — they simply did not have the time to get information about the situation on the ground, and did not deal effectively with those organisations which did. Such were the failures in relations between those who had stayed in Somalia and the UN system that Ambassador Sahnoun, the Secretary-General's personal representative, resigned in October 1992. He had carefully cultivated local contacts to facilitate the programme, stressing above all else the job of helping people. But his work was constantly frustrated by the procedural failures in the UN system and its concern with a wider agenda in which political and bureaucratic considerations had prominence. The view was widely held that if the response had taken place in early 1991 the crisis could have been managed and the violence of December 1991 might not have occurred.

The media

A further problem concerns relations between the organisations and the media. The media can obviously be of very great importance in generating public pressure to act in a crisis, and can be regarded as one of the primary resources of the concerned organisations. There is evidence to suggest that at the moment not enough use is made of them by the non-governmental organisations: they are natural allies in attempts to put pressure upon governments.

There are numerous examples of the media making a difference. The world was galvanised by television pictures of famine from Ethiopia (in 1985) and later pictures from Somalia and the Sudan pricked the conscience of the publics in the developed states, so that charitable contributions by private citizens were much increased.

But there are occasions when media attention has to be handled with great care, and occasions when it might be damaging to the aid process. Two kinds of problem have been experienced. In a first case publicity might stimulate the scale or kind of response which makes the governments of target states more resistant to intervention. A 'softly, softly' approach may provide cover for the distribution of aid according to need so that the constraints of internal political division or civil war are evaded. Public attention reinforces the governments' inclinations to bar aid to the dissenting areas, or impose conditions on its distribution. In Cambodia, UNICEF and ICRC had established a presence during the Vietnamese occupation and were allowed to operate throughout the area in a low-key way. The publicity generated by reports of massive starvation there by the journalist John Pilger, who had the support of Oxfam, not only led to serious quarrels between Oxfam and the other participating organisations, but invited the Vietnamese government to restrict aid to the area it occupied. Eventually aid had to be delivered to the Khmer Rouge area in the north west of the country from Thailand.[21]

A second difficulty is the stimulation of a response which is out of proportion to the scale of the crisis and ill directed. Again in Cambodia, the argument of the Pilger reports was that there was massive famine in the country, but Oxfam's own officials concluded after research had been carried out by them that the reports were greatly exaggerated. The effect of media publicity may also be to attract the intervention of a vast array of agencies and organisations, some of which are unprepared to fit into a well-constructed programme, which see advantages for themselves in acting independently, and which get in each other's way. The risk also exists of stimulating the supply of massive quantities of goods, such as clothing or types of food, which are entirely inappropriate to local conditions and preferences.

But the media are nevertheless of great importance for the process of humanitarian assistance. It is important to find ways of maintaining an easy coexistence between them and the humanitarian organisations. The best way is probably not to produce special publicity materials, which are likely to be treated with scepticism, but rather to encourage reporters to deal with the organisations in the routines of their work — to let reporters see for themselves, and to listen to explanations as the work proceeds. But a further point is of importance: that the organisations should develop a much stronger collective media strategy, perhaps involving a system of correspondents through which others can be told of the position and problems of each organisation.

It is not just that communication between the media and organisations should be refined, but that a condition of success here is the improvement of communications between the organisations themselves. The Cambodian débâcle was an illustration of the failure of UNICEF and ICRC to talk to Oxfam, rather than of the television programme makers or of John Pilger. The problems of effective relations with the media, as with the gathering of information, and of attracting the attention of the competent agencies, impinge not only upon the sovereignty of governments but also upon the 'sovereignty' of organisations, each of which is too often tempted to work for itself.

Sovereignty and humanitarian intervention

Sovereignty has been regarded as central to the system of states. It implies that they are equally members of international society, and are each equal with regard to international law. Sovereignty also implies that states recognise no higher authority than themselves, and that there is no superior jurisdiction; the governments of states have exclusive jurisdiction within their own frontiers, a principle which is enshrined in Article 2(7) of the United Nations Charter.

The principle that sovereignty required that states should not intervene in each others' internal affairs was enunciated surprisingly late in the emergence of international society — the mid-eighteenth century[22]. But the United Nations Charter produced a hard version of the doctrine in Article 2(7) in implying that there was an absolute prohibition on intervention. In earlier periods states had indeed intervened in each others' business and thought they had a right to do so in a number of ways. American governments refused to accept any curtailment of their right to intervene in the internal affairs of other states in their hemisphere until 1933,[23] a position which was reminiscent of the Brezhnev doctrine of the 1970s, which held that the Soviet Union had the right to intervene in the member states of the socialist commonwealth to protect the principles of socialism.

Much earlier the British had insisted in their relations with other states on the abolition of slavery: they intervened to make sure that this had been done in that they stopped ships on the high seas and imposed it as a condition in treaties.[24] There have also been a number of occasions when states have tried to bind other states to respect principles on which they have insisted. A number of states in Eastern Europe were bound to respect the rights of minorities within their frontiers by the agreements made at the Berlin Conference of 1878 by the Great Powers. At the end of the First World War the settlements similarly imposed conditions on the new states to guarantee the rights of minorities within their frontiers.[25]

Indeed in the phase of the creation of the modern states' system, in the settlements at the end of the Thirty Years War, the Treaties of Westphalia, there was a form of intervention in that the states were bound to guarantee the religious freedoms of their subjects. This was the other side of the coin of the secularisation of the new regimes, and the downgrading of the power of the Catholic Church; within their frontiers individuals were now to be guaranteed, through international treaties, the right to practise the religion of their choice.

This was a kind of intervention: imposing restrictions upon the practice by states of their sovereignty within their frontiers. There is, of course, another kind of intervention which is relevant in this context about which there is far greater contention: that of following appropriate procedures to force states to comply with what are judged to be the correct principles, be they the upholding of the rights of minorities, or other circumstances within their frontiers. Such interventions could be military, or through other pressures operating on the decision-making structures within the target states to ensure their compliance.

This kind of intervention was relatively unusual. Indeed the main complaint of those who wished to sustain the international community was that the victor states after the First World War, having enshrined the rights of minorities in treaties, then did very little to ensure that they were respected. Most states disclaimed them; for instance the Polish government did this explicitly in 1934.[26] After the Second World War there were occasions when intervention took place, and usually there was appeal in the pronouncements of the intervening states to some higher principle, frequently echoing arguments of John Stuart Mill in his essay from the mid-nineteenth century about the right of the British to intervene in Hungary against the Russian invasion.

But the number of occasions when there was appeal to a principle involving the rights of individuals was very limited. Well-known interventions, such as that of India in East Pakistan in 1971, Tanzania in the Uganda of Idi Amin, or of the United States in Panama, were justified by reference to the need to protect the citizens of the invading states, and the right of self-defence, both of which are ancient justifications of intervention under international law. Indeed it is argued by a number of international lawyers that there is no need for any justification of intervention beyond that of the existence of a threat to international peace and security. As serious breaches of human rights almost always create such threats, through a flow of refugees for instance, intervention could be justified on those grounds, and this would be a safer way than seeking to justify intervention on strict humanitarian grounds.

What considerations were relevant in the early 1990s to the involvement of the international community within a country? A first response, and one which derives from a rather fundamentalist interpretation of Article 2(7) of the United Nations Charter, was that there could be no intervention within a state without the express consent of the government of that state: the implication appeared to be that no form of behaviour of a sovereign government within its own frontiers was a matter of concern to outsiders. This position was probably most frequently seen in the arguments favoured by the government of mainland China (as in the arguments at a conference at Kyung Hee University, Seoul, Korea, 21–2 September 1993).[27] This position might be compared with the other traditional view, namely that intervention within a country to promote human rights was only capable of justification on the basis of a threat to international peace and security. Evidence of this could be the appearance of significant numbers of refugees, or the judgement that in the circumstances of the emergency other states might intervene militarily. In the hands of liberal lawyers this condition appeared flexible enough to justify intervention to defend human rights whenever it seemed prudent. In the hardline view, however, it was a more difficult condition: although the Chinese did not dispute the general principle, and could not do so if they were to remain members of the United Nations, they saw it more as a way of defeating any proposal to intervene. The former saw it as a bridge to action, the latter as a way of creating barriers by denying there was a threat to international peace and security wherever possible.

In the late 1980s and early 1990s, however, other justifications for intervention, in the face of the opposition of a government, emerged, though they remained controversial. It was pointed out that the Charter had not merely asserted the rights of states, but also the rights of peoples, and that statehood could be interpreted as being conditional upon respecting the rights of peoples: for instance the Preamble held that the organisation was 'to reaffirm faith in fundamental human rights', and Article 1(3) asserted the obligation to 'achieve international cooperation ... in promoting and encouraging respect for human rights and fundamental freedoms for all ...'. There was ample evidence in the Charter to justify the view that the sovereignty of states was not unconditional and that the extreme transgression of human rights could itself be a justification for intervention by the international community.

There was in the early 1990s the increasingly expressed view that there should be a return, in a sense, to the earlier period, but this time with a greater determination and wider range of instruments, to protect generally accepted standards. Where there was a massive and immediate threat to human life and human rights, it was thought, there should be a right to what was called non-consensual intervention: that is, intervention even without the approval of the government of the target state. By 1993 it could be claimed that this question had been placed on the agenda and that there was some evidence of a move away from the hard model of state sovereignty towards a softer view under which non-consensual intervention could be sanctioned because of gross infringements of human rights or intolerable individual human suffering (see the chapter by Griffiths, Levine and Weller in this volume).[28] That there were fundamental rights for individuals which were to be upheld by states was clearly enunciated in the Charter. Hitherto, however, sovereignty and exclusive jurisdiction had priority.

The hard version of sovereignty, and what it involved, also had other debilitating implications for humanitarian intervention, some of which have been touched on in the previous section. The intergovernmental organisations of the UN system were constrained by the fear of appearing to be partial in the event of civil war within states, even at the expense of failing to provide humanitarian relief, because of their equation of sovereignty with neutrality regarding internal affairs. Their preference for working through governments, even those that were in disgrace, and their respect for security guidelines and information provided by governments ahead of that from non-governmental organisations, was a response to the same constraints. These hesitations are aspects of the hard version of sovereignty and exclusive domestic jurisdiction (see the analysis of UN hesitation in Somalia by Slim and Visman in this book).

The most striking example of non-consensual intervention hitherto was the decision of the Security Council in Resolution 688 in 1991 when it was agreed that there should be intervention in Iraq at the end of the Gulf War to protect the Kurds in north Iraq, and the Shi'a Muslims in the south, against the regime of Saddam Hussein. This was approved without his consent, though in accepting the arrangements proposed, for instance, in a Memorandum of Understanding, that consent was later implied. On other occasions, such as that of the Security Council Resolution which first sanctioned UN involvement in Somalia, Resolution 733 adopted on 23 January 1992, action was in response to a request by Somalia, even though the government of that country was near expiry. In Resolution 794, which authorised the United States to dispatch 30,000 troops to 'establish a secure environment for Humanitarian Relief Operations in Somalia as soon as possible', approved unanimously on 3 December 1992, the explicit consent of the Somalia authorities was not mentioned, but by that time any pretence that such existed could be abandoned. In the major pronouncements of the United Nations (e.g. A/43/131 and A/46/182)[29] there was consistent reference to the primary responsibility of the target states for dealing with complex crises within their frontiers, although 46/182 implied some relaxation of this in its precise wording: it held that 'The sovereignty, territorial integrity and national unity of States must be fully respected in accordance with the Charter of the United Nations. In this context, humanitarian assistance should be provided with the consent of the affected country and in principle on the basis of an appeal by the affected country'. The use of the phrase 'in principle', and the normative 'should', implied that there could be occasions when government approval was not possible, but where intervention was nevertheless necessary.

The difficulty in sanctioning any relaxation in the principle of non-intervention should not, however, be underestimated. There could be occasions when states might be particularly fearful of intervention, for example if an army engaged in counter-insurrection activities was accused of gross violations of human rights. The government of India has been particularly concerned about any relaxation of the principle, and it is not difficult to think of reasons for this position: the Indian army is vulnerable to accusations of infringements of human rights in various parts of the country, such as Kashmir. Conversely newly independent states were likely to be suspicious of what might appear to be the granting of a licence to western developed states to intervene in their affairs: the unfortunate reference by British Foreign Secretary Douglas Hurd to the possible need for a new kind of imperialism, meaning the taking over of territories where orderly government had collapsed, by the United Nations — in a way reminiscent of the trusteeship system — could not have dampened such fears.[30]

One difficult case, therefore, was when there was clear evidence about the existence of a massive threat to human life and rights and a failure of the state concerned to permit intervention by organisations or other states to provide the help which it was unable to provide itself. The question was whether in these circumstances international society should accept the principle of non-consensual intervention. The point should be made that this is not quite the massive leap which it might appear to be at first sight. There are at least two international organisations, UNICEF and ICRC, which are not in their charters required to have the specific consent of a state before they might work within its frontiers. There may in some cases be acquiesence by default; if there is positive refusal then obviously the organisations cannot work in that state, but there are shades of non-refusal which are capable of being interpreted as implying consent.

Another difficult case is when the government in a particular territory has collapsed so that it is difficult to say that this still amounts to a state. There are two possible responses to this: one is to say that as there is no government, its consent is not required, and that therefore there is no barrier to intervention under international law. The Congo intervention is a version of this, except it operates in reverse; as the government had collapsed, after requesting UN assistance — thus legitimising its presence — there was no sovereign authority that was entitled to request the withdrawal of the United Nations force.

Another is a much more inflexible view, which is to say that as there is no authority to sanction intervention it cannot be permitted. Action cannot be undertaken until a new sovereign government has been created. Both of these positions have been taken in Somalia: the latter by UNDP when it argued that large sums of money in its control ($68 million) could not be used for relief purposes because they were intended for another purpose, namely development, in agreement with a sovereign government;[31] the former in Security Council Resolution 794 which sanctioned the dispatch of 30,000 US troops to Somalia territory without the consent of any Somali government, which did not exist, and against the wishes of the conflicting war lords.

Three modes of intervention

But it should be stressed that even the inflexible view — no intervention without consent — has softer variations which have emerged in recent years. The first of these has already been mentioned: UNICEF and ICRC do not require formal consent and may occasionally evade the strict principle, as in Cambodia in the late 1970s. But non-governmental organisations are also more flexible than most intergovernmental organisations in their attitude to the requirement of consent before intervention. The larger NGOs naturally always prefer to obtain such consent, and would find it difficult to establish a presence without it. But they are more likely to get that consent precisely because they are non-governmental, though there are some major exceptions to this, such as the profound suspicion of the Indian government about them, and the dislike of the Iraqis for some of them at the end of the Gulf War. But smaller organisations, or those with special interests and committed volunteers, may be less punctilious, and take greater risks in order to set up shop in defiance of governments' consent. In general NGOs are able to pursue more sophisticated strategies in order to establish a presence, for instance, in working through front or cover organisations. They are also much more adept at working across boundaries, either in the case of disputes within states, or across state borders. There are no known examples of intergovernmental organisations having done the latter.

A second approach was illustrated in the *corridors of tranquillity* in Sudan, when a very important diplomatic precedent was established, followed elsewhere in Africa, by the setting up of demilitarised zones. Armed conflict was excluded from them with the consent of the parties to the dispute, so that aid could be channelled through them to those needing assistance. This involved persuading the warring parties that their military presence in some areas was not essential to the pursuit of their cause, and also that the provision of humanitarian assistance would also not be prejudicial. The military were to be persuaded that ceding territory for a humanitarian cause was rational in terms of their own ambitions.[32] Although such zones of tranquillity are vulnerable — the warring parties may change their minds — the idea was a step towards the safe haven idea, but was not identical: the latter involved placing primary stress on the humanitarian principle, even if it compromised the strategic interests of a disputant, and was therefore a non-consensual intervention.

A third mode of intervention has been the use of arms to cut through the territories of the parties to a dispute, and to impose the humanitarian principle ahead of the strategic interests of the parties to the dispute. To assert a superordinate goal may also be seen as being consistent with the principle of neutrality in internal disputes, but it has an ambivalent relationship with sovereignty: on the one hand it implies impartiality in civil disputes, and a carelessness about their outcome; on the other it is in explicit contravention of the principle of the exclusive domestic jurisdiction of states.

One of the major innovations in humanitarian assistance in recent years, however, has been the use of military force, in Somalia, in Yugoslavia and Iraq, directly for humanitarian purposes. In Yugoslavia, for example, UNPROFOR 2 had the task under the terms of Security Council Resolution 770 of ensuring the delivery of humanitarian assistance; unlike UNPROFOR 1[33] it was not entrusted with a peacekeeping function.

In considering the arguments about the right to intervene which apply in the late twentieth century it is important to consider the sources of sovereignty. They rest upon the demonstration that a particular territory contains a people which wishes to organise itself in the form of a state, without excessive dissent, and under the control of a legitimately established government, set up according to procedures which are generally accepted among that group of people (see the arguments on this point advanced by Griffiths, Levine and Weller in their chapter in this book). In these circumstances the crucial step might be taken which establishes that territory as a constituent state member of international society, namely its *de jure* recognition by the other state members as a fellow state.

It is the conferring of recognition that essentially creates the barriers in the way of intervention, and it follows that those barriers against intervention might be altered, and weakened, by changing the process of recognition. This possibility becomes particularly important when there is some doubt about whether a government satisfies the conditions of recognition or not.

At the moment this is left to the separate states, acting on their own account, or as individual states in cooperation with other states, as was the case with the member states of the European Community when they recognised the states emerging from the collapse of Yugoslavia.[34] The recognition of these states was itself a fairly *ad hoc* business, driven by the interests of Germany, and imperfectly monitored by the Bartinder Commission set up under the authority of the Commission on Yugoslavia. The *ad hoc* character of the recognition of states, is matched by a corresponding *ad hoc*ery about their derecognition.

There seems to be considerable asymmetry between the formal if clumsy process of recognition, which has been considered in its implications over a long period of years, and the almost complete lack of any consideration of the process of derecognition except as a weapon in times of conflict in the hands of individual states, an act which is divorced from the justice of the target's claim to statehood. The point emerges from this that the lack of any general procedure for removing recognition is a difficulty in the way of intervention, as the states which separately continue to recognise a state are likely to argue that the sovereignty of that state cannot be compromised. Conversely any move towards asserting a right to intervene on humanitarian grounds would be facilitated by introducing procedures for recognising states through United Nations procedures. It becomes more important to make sure that states are well founded in the first place if there is to be an obligation to intervene. How can the process of recognition be left to individual states acting separately, and for reasons of their own, when failing states are to be put together again by the international community? It may be, however, that if collective recognition is impossible, a more activist intervention policy also has to be excluded.

Sovereignty and intervention

Several sets of circumstances involving recognition, sovereignty and intervention may now be extracted from the above.

First are the circumstances in which a state has collapsed, there is a general acceptance that its government has ceased to exist, and that intervention does not compromise sovereignty in the eyes of any other states. Arguably Somalia had reached this condition by late 1991.

Second is where some form of government exists, and there is a dispute about whether the state is still sovereign. In this case diplomacy will of necessity involve dispute about these questions and intervention may be delayed.

The third set of circumstances is where there is no dispute about the continuing sovereignty of the state, but where the question of non-consensual intervention arises because threats to life and rights are so gross as to sustain a general consensus amongst states in its favour.

Finally, there are cases where a state is accepted as remaining sovereign but where its government accepts its responsibility for humanitarian action and works in cooperation with the international agencies.

In this instance, in a strict sense, there is no intervention; paradoxically the Somalia case in its early stages was not one of humanitarian intervention, but rather of humanitarian assistance by international agencies and governments. Resolution 794 which sanctioned the American move into Somalia was also in a strict sense not intervention as by that stage the central government of Somalia had ceased to exist in the eyes of the majority of states, or at least in the eyes of the member states of the Security Council which approved the resolution unanimously.

The difficult cases, therefore, are those where there is a disagreement about sovereignty, or where a government flatly refuses intervention. In the first case the difficulty could be resolved by making the issue of recognition one of concern to the international community together, acting as an entity through the United Nations, thus removing the *ad hoc* character of both the recognition and the derecognition process. This would also be helpful in cases where an international organisation finds itself unable to provide forms of assistance because they follow from an agreement with a sovereign government which no longer exists. The capacity of the UN to confer and remove legitimacy needs to be exploited by matching it with formal mechanisms. In the case of the intervention in Somalia through the instrument of US forces it is arguable that such a sanction had been given. The African states had requested such intervention, and the others, including the permanent members of the Security Council, had accepted this advice.

The second difficult case would be helped by creating a procedure, such as that outlined in the evidence submitted by the Development Studies Association to the Foreign Affairs Select Committee of the House of Commons, which laid down the conditions under which there could be non-consensual intervention,[35] (i.e. without the consent of the target state; no intervention can be non-consensual in the sense that it does not reflect the consensus of the society of states!).

These conditions are as follows:

- that there should be clear evidence of a massive and immediate threat to human life and human rights;
- that the United Nations Security Council should agree that this is indeed the case, together with the approval of the General Assembly by a two-thirds majority;
- that the issues should be subject to the jurisdiction of the International Court of Justice, and that the terms of the intervention, including the conditions under which the mandate should be concluded, should be subject to its decision;
- and the mandate of the organisations responsible for the operation should be approved by the United Nations.

There is a further issue which is raised by these proposals. That is that the decisions of the Security Council are not subject to the jurisdiction of the Court: the latter cannot pass judgment on the legality or otherwise of the decisions of the former. This is different from the European Union, for instance, where the European Court of Justice can decide upon the legality of the actions of any of the other institutions. The question of whether this situation could be created for the United Nations institutions is one which needs serious consideration, as subjecting the Security Council to the Court is an essential safeguard if the doctrine of non-intervention is to be placed within a new set of principles. This arrangement would not be without precedent in relations between sovereign states as the practice in the European Union indicates.

The erosion of the strict interpretation of Article 2(7) of the UN Charter depends upon the creation of countervailing procedures in the global organisation. There can be no question of individual states, or particular groups of states, compromising the absolute prohibition on intervention. But the obvious danger also exists that even in cases of humanitarian assistance when a government has collapsed and lost recognition, or where it survives and cooperates fully with the international organisations as representatives of the international community, there are also dangers for sovereignty. Consideration of the changing circumstances in which intervention may be accepted cannot, however, be separated from two other issues: the issue of the process by which recognition is conferred, and the issue of the subjecting of the institutions of the United Nations to supervision by the International Court to measure their compliance with relevant international law.

There is the need to resist the ambitions of other states, such as neighbours, to use the occasion of the intervention to capture territory. There is also the problem that the sovereign government may seek to enlist the intervening agencies to promote a cause of its own within the state, for instance, to consolidate its hold over areas where there is a high level of dissent. These problems are considered in other sections of this chapter.

Operations: conducting a programme of humanitarian assistance

Economic and social concerns of the UN: the background

The problem of how best to coordinate the activities of the United Nations is one that has relevance to the activities of that organisation in general, but it has been discussed over a long period with regard to economic and social activities. Before turning to a specific discussion of the arrangements for humanitarian assistance, as they had emerged by the mid-1990s, it is desirable to look at the general character and problems of the UN's social and economic arrangements. It is necessary to begin from a view about what the United Nations system is in fact like. All too often proposals for reform start with principles, or a desirable state of affairs, rather than by addressing the present reality.

The underlying problems, which in the early 1990s afflicted the attempts to improve provision of humanitarian assistance, were that the system was stubbornly polycentric, and that it contained no organisation within it which could coordinate and manage its wide range of economic and social activities. The Specialised Agencies had constitutional independence from each other, and from the centre, and there was no central institution which had legal authority over them. This was how the system was designed, and the history of the system was not very encouraging for attempts to alter this. The polycentric character, and the resulting failures of management, meant that it was always easier to respond in an *ad hoc* fashion to new problems, rather than to adapt rationally within the system and to build according to the decisions of a coordinator and initiator upon existing arrangements.

In a polycentric system there are special problems in the way of internal adaptation in response to new problems: responses tend to be tentative and partially outside the system. The first reason for this is that by definition there is no central mechanism for deciding upon the nature of the response. Secondly the actors, in this case chiefly the Specialised Agencies, tend to see adaptation as requiring a reduction in their own areas of competence, or an unacceptable expansion of another's, or at best as a mutual limitation. This helps to explain the tendency of the Agencies' main coordinating mechanism, the Administrative Committee for Coordination (ACC), to send reports to the Economic and Social Council (ECOSOC) which conceal inter-Agency disagreements.[36] The members are as much involved in justifying positions adopted within each agency as in coordinating their activities in striving for a common purpose. Ameri concluded that 'towards the coordination of overall policy it cannot be claimed that the ACC has made more than a minor and intermittent contribution'.[37]

The general interest is to reject change, and to conceal the occasional pro-system response. At best, the least threatening actor may be allowed a minimum coordinating role. 'It is in most cases true that the UN Secretariat alone can carry the ball and make inter-agency cooperation meaningful.'[38] Any stronger response tends to be evaded and hence to be expressed outside the system.

A third reason for low intra-system adaptability is the lack of a single authoritative perspective on what is required, and the sheer volume of information and competing evaluations.[39] At meetings of the ACC, the Secretary-General has usually hesitated about taking a strong line. Hill commented that 'There exists no means of harmonising the thinking of executive heads and the senior staff of organs concerned with central policy issues, such as UNCTAD, UNIDO, UNDP, and directing it towards problems facing the international community and towards possible initiatives that the UN might usefully take'.[40] Research efforts in the various agencies have not been integrated. It is hardly surprising, then, that there is no authoritative viewpoint in the light of which changes can be introduced.

The Economic and Social Council was intended to manage the system, but has failed to live up to the expectations of the founders. In particular it failed, despite various institutional amendments, such as the setting up and subsequent reinforcement of its Committee on Programme and Coordination (CPC) in 1969, to coordinate the activities of the Specialised Agencies. This failure was seen by Gunnar Myrdal, as early as 1960, as 'almost scandalous in view of the declared purposes of the Charter'.[41] This judgement still seems to apply in the early 1990s, despite some marginal reforms, and is one measure of the difficulty of reforming the organisation. The main problems remain that it cannot direct the agencies or require that their operations be coordinated.

A further weakness in the mid 1990s is that the General Assembly lacks the authority to instruct the Agencies, though it can give them advice and address recommendations to them. It has tended not to consult the Agencies very closely when it has considered economic and social proposals — an omission which might be considered extraordinary — and it lacks the means of effectively monitoring the performance of the Agencies. For instance, it has no way of checking the relationship between the Agencies' budgets and their programmes; it has been said that the General Assembly checks budgets in a vacuum.[42] Its main watchdogs over the Agencies, the Advisory Committee on Administrative and Budgetary Questions (ACABQ) and the Joint Inspection Unit (JIU), though capable of providing good, hard-hitting reports, are essentially advisory.

Another route to effective management and policy coordination was sought when in Resolution 32/197 of 1977 it was recommended that a new Director-General for Development and International Economic Cooperation (DGDIEC) should be appointed within the Secretariat to ensure 'the coherence, coordination and efficient management of all activities in the economic and social fields financed by the regular budget or by extra budgetary resources'.[43] The post was established and was held most recently by Blanca: but it was largely unsuccessful with respect to its major goals. Blanca's office became largely ineffectual, and it was absorbed in the major reorganisation made by Secretary-General Boutros-Ghali in early 1991. The experience of the DGDIEC is relevant to the prospects of the Under-Secretary in charge of the most recent attempt to coordinate economic and social activity within the UN: the Department of Humanitarian Affairs (DHA) which was set up in 1992 to coordinate disaster assistance. This is discussed at length below.

Some characteristic deficiencies may be summarised. There has been, on the one hand, a tendency to *reiteration* which has taken two forms: first, a deliberate duplication of activities and institutions, and, second, a repetition of other activities and functions, which has been more the consequence of a carelessness or lack of conscious control in management. (The former is now referred to in the discussion which follows as *duplication,* and the latter as *fragmentation*). On the other hand, there has been a tendency towards the concentration of various functions in subsystems which has also taken two forms: the first has been a resistance to specialisation in functions, in other words a habit of performing tasks at the same time and place which are in important respects different and disconnected; and second is a tendency to resist the concentration in the system of key functions, so that there remain unresolved claims and counterclaims about where such functions should be performed. The former is called *aggregation* in what follows and the latter *reservation*.

Duplication is revealed, as was pointed out earlier, in the existence of a number of institutions within the system which claim to act as system managers and coordinators, sometimes in the central systems, sometimes in individual countries, or both. As has been already mentioned, ECOSOC should perform this role at the centre, according to the Charter. But the ACC also considered that it should manage and coordinate, and introduced in the 1970s new institutions to help with this, in particular the Consultative Committee on Substantive Questions (CCSQ). Bertrand commented upon 'the vagueness of the terms of reference; the similarity of jurisdiction between organs as important as the Economic and Social Council, UNCTAD, the Second and Third Committees of the General Assembly ... [which] have created in the United Nations system a state of confusion'.[44]

In relation to development issues the UNDP claims a central role.[45] At the country level, coordination takes place through the resident coordinators of UNDP, though for a while the World Bank attempted the same task through its Round Tables. Such unsatisfactory duplication and uncertainty about roles arose because of the habit of adding new institutions to existing arrangements, in order to solve a perceived problem rather than altering the arrangements.

The *reservation* of functions may be illustrated in a number of contexts. ACC's traditionally unhelpful approach towards strengthening central control has been reflected in its unenthusiastic attitude towards joint planning which 'should not be undertaken for its own sake'.[46] There are numerous reports of squabbling between the ACC and the CPC — reported as a 'sort of dialogue of the deaf'[47] — neither wishing to lose status to the other, and of rather low-key, half-hearted attempts to improve matters[48]. The Director-General for Development and International Economic Cooperation found it difficult to exercise his coordinating function with regard to the Agencies: indeed the latter in practice refused to recognise his authority. That he was not an elected officer, but was appointed by the Secretary-General, placed him below the Agency heads in the pecking-order.[49] This partly explained their refusal to accept the Director-General as chairman of the ACC in the absence of the Secretary-General himself, as had been envisaged. The ACC's welcome of the new arrangements of the DHA in 1993 remained lukewarm.

The duplication and reservation of roles is, of course, a reflection of the play of bureaucratic politics, but also of the failure of the member states to counter the anti-rationalisation tendencies which are inherent in bureaucracies. The governments have themselves been divided, so UNCTAD survived and competed with ECOSOC, the former favoured by the developing states and the latter by the developed. The interplay of bureaucratic politics and intergovernmental disagreement also explains the apparent increase in another form of duplication in the work of the institutions — the repetition of discussions about the same issues at various levels in the same institution and in different institutions. For instance, ECOSOC has too often gone over the ground already traversed in its own committees; and the General Assembly has repeated the debates already conducted in main committees. A US government official acidly complained: 'Should we accept the continuation and repetition of the experience of the last eight months, for example, during which the issues discussed at UNCTAD Six were reopened and repeated on at least three occasions?'[50] Such duplication arose because of the mistrust of governments of each other: rationalisation and specialisation increase the risk that a key function in the system can be 'captured' by a state or group of states of the wrong persuasion.

The *fragmentation* of the system was revealed in the tendency for available resources to be devoted to a wide range of small-scale, frequently unrelated projects, a habit which arises from the feeling that all the various demands, however small, from the various states, deserve some kind of response. Fragmentation has also been closely allied with what Bertrand describes as his 'fallacy number 2: that the development of the poorer zones in the world can be brought about by a sectoral and, therefore, non-integrated approach'.[51] 'The obligation to deal with all existing problems, in all fields, and in all sectors, because of the convergent pressure of the most diverse interests of all delegations, tends to a parcelling out, not to say fragmentation, of available resources between a very large number of small programmes and small projects endowed with extremely limited means'.[52] This multiplicity, together with the urge of most states to be involved and represented, also leads to what Bertrand described as an abysmally poor quality of staff.[53]

There has also been fragmentation in the financing of operational activities, both between institutions ('financing decisions are taken separately for each of the operational funds, UNDP, UNFPA, UNICEF, etc.') and between donors and beneficiaries ('no real dialogue between donor and beneficiary countries on the nature of the problems to which most attention should be paid'). 'It is not even certain that within each organisation there is agreement between headquarters and field personnel or between the various departments dealing with different but related problems'.[54]

Such a pattern of fragmentation is, of course, likely to be reflected and reinforced by the widely reported lack of coordination of the views of officers who come from the same country, but who are working in different institutional settings. On a number of issues the positions of governments are simply not thought through so that their various representatives adopt different and sometimes contradictory positions in the various institutions.

The United Nations social and economic system has also shown a tendency to treat together various activities which might be judged to deserve attention in different fora, the practice called here *aggregation*. The anonymous US official quoted earlier summed up this tendency rather well in a particular context.

> Rather than fulfilling specific niches in a well-defined system, subordinate bodies are attempting to assume the coloration and indeed the function of the whole system. This blurring of institutional lines has led to enormous duplication of effort and the consequent waste of human and natural resources, the spread of disagreement and confrontation to other forums and the injection of purely political and theoretical economic issues into previously practical discussions'.[55]

Such habits of aggregation also tend to undermine the practical working arrangements within institutions. But the main point is the tendency for particular institutions to broaden their mandates in a process which might be described as functional imperialism — a tendency also observable in NGOs.

The range of difficulties in the system are symptoms of the barriers in the way of change which are found in the interplay between bureaucratic politics and the interests of states. Any major restructuring of the system in the light of these difficulties has been strongly resisted by the officers, and the commentators who were close to them, who have developed a pride in their familiarity with the arcane complexity of the UN system and for whom any change has been seen as devaluing this asset. They have asserted the virtues of pluralism, whilst too many governments are too frequently indifferent and unknowing about what goes on.

These negative factors have been reinforced by fierce disagreements between governments on some matters, which have led to active opposition to change except on their own terms, and by hostility on the part of the majority of international officials to anything which might weaken their particular organisation or their role within it. Of course many of these problems were sharpened in the context of the Cold War, and by the pressures of a radicalised and relatively united Third World. This history of institutional development remains relevant to current problems.

Models of humanitarian assistance

It is in the context of this not very encouraging experience of attempts to coordinate the activities of the members of the UN system that the situation regarding humanitarian assistance has to be considered. This experience reveals some of the problems in the way of reform.

At another level, there are five specific difficulties which have been located by students of the system.[56] First is the problem that the mandates of the organisations are not clear: they overlap and duplicate each other, and leave gaps in competence, as with the issue of internal migrants, or recovery. Second, there are uncertainties in the minds of field officers about appropriate procedures and rules. An illustration of this problem, which deserves to be regarded as a classic of its kind, is the case of the Iraqi sugar allowances.[57] Third, there is not enough delegation of executive capacity to the field by the headquarters of international organisations, a failing that is sharply contrasted with the powers allotted to some of the new national rapid response emergency officers, such as with the US Disaster Assessment Relief Teams (DART) arrangement. Fourth, the lines of responsibility between the field and headquarters are not clear. And fifth, and in large part a function of the other factors, headquarters and field officers often have a quite different perception of the urgency of problems on the ground. These problems are considered further in the discussion which follows.

In the context of humanitarian assistance, discussion over the years focused upon the inadequacies of the UNDRO, which has been said to be too small, to be inadequate in various respects in its relations with the Agencies, and to be uncertain about its own mandate.[58] It has occasionally taken on an operational role itself, when that might have been better executed by other more experienced and specialised organisations: it sought such a role with regard to refugees in the Gulf War in competition with UNHCR, and its storage facilities in Italy duplicated the operation of UNICEF in Sweden.

More recently, in early 1992, the central system of the UN was altered by Secretary-General Boutros-Ghali in response to the recommendations of General Assembly Resolution 46/182 of December 1991. Attempts were also made by the Secretary-General to improve the functioning of the Agencies' own coordinating apparatus, the ACC. It looked as if there was some movement, however small, towards overcoming the problem of bureaucratic decentralisation, no doubt due to the emergence of great power consensus and the tightening of their control over budgetary procedures.[59] Later the Secretary-General proposed streamlining the representation of the United Nations system in member countries, by having single United Nations embassies rather than a multiplicity of missions from various member organisations. By the time of writing there had been no practical outcome of this proposal.

The primary effect of the changes on the humanitarian machinery was to bring UNDRO into the Secretariat, within a new Department of Humanitarian Affairs (DHA) under a 'high-level official' to be 'designated' by the Secretary-General to strengthen his 'critical leadership' role (A Res. 46/182, vi(a)). In consequence an Under-Secretary-General, Jan Eliasson, was appointed to head the new operation in the spring of 1992. This was his reward for having very skilfully piloted 46/182 through the Assembly: his early performance as head of DHA-UNDRO is evaluated below.

The purpose of the DHA-UNDRO was to 'combine the functions at present carried out in the coordination of United Nations response by representatives of the Secretary-General for major and complex emergencies, as well as by the United Nations Disaster Relief Coordinator' (A/46/182). The office was to prepare consolidated appeals for funds and provisions, 'be involved with the systematic pooling and analysis of early-warning information',and serve as a 'central focal point with the governments and intergovernmental and non-governmental organisations concerning United Nations emergency relief operations, and ... mobilise their emergency relief capacities, including through consultations in his capacity as Chairman of the Inter-Agency Standing Committee'. The new Department was also given a Central Emergency Revolving Fund (CERF) of $50 million to facilitate rapid and coordinated response. The Fund became operational on 22 May 1992 and by the end of May 1993 had disbursed $23 million. But there were several difficulties with the Fund. Funds could only be dispersed to UN operational organisations and agencies, and not to ICRC, NGOs and other intergovernmental organisations. Disbursements could only be made in the context of an existing or forthcoming consolidated appeal, and would have to be repaid; and the DHA could not itself use the money for taking early action before any agency had acted. The amount of money available to the new DHA was also very little compared with the resources needed to cope effectively with a complex emergency.

The prospects for DHA are considered at length below.[60] At this point, however, two broad approaches to managing the disaster relief process are sketched. On the one hand there is a strong, supranational, managerial approach, which seems to be excluded by the nature of the system as discussed above. On the other hand is a role which may be described as that of *facilitator*, when the coordinating mechanism assists other actors to harmonise their approaches and operations. As will become apparent, the latter image is closest to the optimum combination of what is desirable and what is possible, and much of the following argument reinforces this point.

Developing states are also likely to react against a supranational approach, seeing it as part of an attempt to dominate them by the developed states. This has been the experience with some of the attempts to approaches problems on the so-called New Agenda in this way: developing states reacted strongly against attempts to pin them down to a World Population Plan of Action, or to environmental programmes containing indicative targets.[61] A second problem is that a centrally managed system might not be effective in adjusting the effort to the precise contours of the specific crisis in a particular country. There is a case for encouraging a degree of *ad hoc*ery, so that a better fit between the problem and the efforts focused upon it emerges pragmatically.

In the history of the United Nations since the early 1980s, three broad systems of arrangements for dealing with humanitarian crises have emerged at the country or area level. In the first the operation is simply taken over by the UNDP Resident Coordinator, although, as is argued below, there are reasons for supposing that for complex or more serious humanitarian crises this is a less desirable arrangement. Around twenty countries could be identified in 1993 as 'failing' in the sense that they were at risk of collapsing as states: working through the established UNDP mechanism could make sense for the others. In the second system a lead entity from among the UN organisations takes responsibility for managing the coordination of the programme. Examples of this include UNICEF in Cambodia, and UNHCR in Yugoslavia, and in the Gulf after the war with Iraq.[62] This was the procedure recommended in General Assembly Resolution 36/225 of 17 December 1981. The way in which the lead organisation emerged was somewhat *ad hoc*. It might be the obvious choice, and accepted as such by the other Agencies, because of the nature of the problem. It might also be named as the lead organisation by the Secretary-General. Such a procedure is most likely to arise if the existing Resident Coordinator of UNDP has failed in some way, or has been withdrawn. It is possible that the various potential lead Agencies quarrel about their status. This seemed a danger in Angola in 1993.[63]

A third model is that of working under a designated officer, usually the Special Representative of the Secretary-General. In the past this has often worked through *ad hoc* mechanisms, which have emerged out of increasing concern about a crisis on the part of particular organisations or individuals, who have proposed setting up a specific coordinating structure. Thus, for example, James Grant of UNICEF and James Ingram of WFP took the initiative of proposing to the Secretary-General the establishment of a Special Office for Emergency Operations in Ethiopia in 1984.[64] The mechanism has then been created by recruiting staff from UN Agencies under the leadership of the Personal or Special Representative of the Secretary-General.

Another option has been to set up a permanent standing group for emergencies, on the model of the African Emergency Task Force (AETF), able to monitor problem areas and set up coordinating mechanisms as appropriate. It was made up of the representatives of the main agencies which had become involved in the area. The experience of AETF is thought to have been very favourable. 'It is the only UN machinery which, on a fully representative inter-agency basis, monitors potential emergency situations, periodically reviews data, meets at short notice to assess information leads from all sources and keeps the Secretary-General informed on significant developments'.[65] After the creation of the DHA the question arose of how far the country-level mechanism should be controlled by that body, and how far the chain of command should run through its structures and the Under-Secretary to the Secretary-General, with the latter's special appointment forming one of the links in that chain. By 1993 the strongest form of this arrangement appeared to be in Mozambique where agencies apart from UNHCR assigned officers to a coordinating committee with a single chain of command running from the Director, through the Special Representative and Under-Secretary-General Eliasson. In this case, also, the UNDP machinery was bypassed.

The two latter approaches appear to have a lot in common. Both systems reflect the imperative that the coordinating mechanism should be a *facilitating* framework rather than a directing one. This seems to indicate a need for devising better ways of communicating between organisations in a system which continues to be pluralistic, rather on the lines of the system of correspondents set up to link the foreign offices of the member states of the European Union in order to harmonise their foreign policies.

The functions of a facilitator may now be identified in outline as follows:-

1. to provide technical support, and information, to assist organisations to identify and harmonise their separate contributions to the relief effort. This and several other functions in this list includes servicing and monitoring the various relevant permanent and *ad hoc* committees of Agencies and other operational organisations.
2. to work up plans of action for countries indicating roles for organisations in areas and sectors, and to establish priorities.
3. to obtain information about the onset of a crisis, in cooperation with the machinery discussed above, and stimulate an initial response from the emergency relief fund.
4. to assist with the setting up of an *ad hoc* country framework under the authority of the Secretary-General, with the help of the UNDP country organisation, and any mechanism such as AETF.
5. to act as a reservoir of experience which can be accumulated and applied to other areas.
6. to ensure that effective communications are established between organisations, including those between NGOs and IGOs. (One step in this direction was the major effort made by Jan Eliasson to improve communications with the NGOs, and regular monthly meetings with them had begun to take place through officials in Geneva, and his own office in New York in 1993.)
7. to help with the process of generating financial and other resources for the provision of disaster relief.

Aspects of these problems are discussed in greater detail in the next sections.

The role of the DHA

COORDINATION: HEADQUARTERS AND COUNTRY

Here attention is focused on the coordination arrangements at headquarters level, centring around DHA and raising questions about its development. There are two major functions for DHA under this heading. First is the function of setting up and servicing the main committees, consultations and Task Forces in Geneva, where the various intergovernmental and non-governmental actors can be brought together; second is managing the process of producing consolidated appeals which is discussed below.

Chief amongst the headquarters committees is the Inter-Agency Standing Committee (IASC) in Geneva, set up on the recommendation of A46/182, which meets several times a year — six times by December 1993. It is intended to formulate priorities among the various tasks facing the international community in particular crisis situations, and in various parts of the world, and to integrate programmes and projects so that duplication is reduced to a minimum and each participant is encouraged to play to its strengths.

In early 1993 close observers argued that the meetings of the IASC needed to be more positive and focused: they had not moved beyond mere information exchange and lacked any capacity for rapid decision-making, particularly on the division of tasks between the members. And participants in the IASC Working Groups were frequently not senior enough to speak for their Agencies and take decisions.[66] Beneath the IASC Working Groups were Task Forces which had responsibilities in particular areas, such as the new states of Eastern Europe, and Iraq.

That on Iraq had met around 150 times by April 1993, and the evidence suggested that it had been successful. It had taken over from Sadrudin Aga Khan's Office of the Executive Delegate's emergency operation in Iraq with regard to protecting the Kurds, and acted under the terms of the Memorandum of Understanding, first negotiated by him with Iraq and thereafter renewed every six months. It could also rely on regular donations from member states, and from the income generated by an account (ESCROW) made up of the frozen overseas assets of Iraq.

With regard to the Iraqi working group the DHA had a stronger coordinating role than elsewhere. Ten staff were employed in Geneva, and a further thirty-three in Iraq and seven in Turkey. They had hands-on responsibilities, for instance in coordinating the flow of humanitarian assistance through convoys of trucks — about 6000 movements from Turkey into Iraq by April 1993. An unusual feature of the operation was the employment of UN guards in Iraq, recruited from the UN's own security staff.

But the case of Iraq was arguably a special one. In that context the group and the DHA had been empowered by the special circumstances at the end of the Gulf War and by the legacy of the arrangements set in place after the Iraqi surrender on the basis of Security Council Resolution 687. It may be misleading to draw too many conclusions from the relatively strong coordinating role of DHA in Kurdistan. It has also been accepted, though, that in the successor states of the Soviet Union there would have been much more confusion and greater shortage of resources without the DHA. It organised several airlifts of necessary materials to the area, though this function had been inherited from UNDRO. The general conclusions must be that, although coordination is a vitally important function, it cannot usually be about imposing a common framework of cooperation: as argued above, the Agencies and other organisations simply cannot be induced to accept this, and it may not be desirable anyway.

Each Agency has developed a strong sense of a proprietorial right to its exclusive mandate, and may be separately accountable for this to higher authorities. For instance, UNHCR Director Sadako Ogata is herself directly accountable to the Secretary-General and the General Assembly, according to the mandate of her organisation; and although this is also true of the head of DHA, there is naturally resistance in UNHCR to allowing the latter's responsibility to usurp that of the former. This point has also been made about relations between the World Food Programme and the DHA in Angola. In the latter case there was already an established line of authority as the WFP was accepted as always being the second in command to the UNDP coordinator in the field. The situation in Angola in mid-1993 had a potential for confusion as a lead agency had not emerged, and there were rival claims to this role from WFP and from DHA. The obvious solution was to place responsibility for overall coordination in the hands of a Special Representative of the Secretary-General.

Jan Eliasson, as the first head of DHA, seemed himself to be uncertain about how far the Department should develop its own strong coordinating, as opposed to facilitating, role: he strongly opposed the idea of a lead organisation, and it might be assumed that he challenged this orthodoxy because it pre-empted a stronger role for the DHA. In this position, however, he would inevitably attract the strongest opposition from the Agencies. The general point is that mandatory coordination is excluded by the separate mandates, and individual responsibilities of the Agencies: any attempt by the DHA to promote the principle that the channel of accountability should always pass through itself will be resisted.

The complaint has also been made in this context that too frequently the role of DHA is somewhat parasitical. Officers have been sent out from DHA who have become an extra drain on the Agencies already in the field, and their additional contribution to the coordination mechanisms already established there has been hard to detect. Clearly it is preferable for the work of DHA to be adequately funded, so that it is not seen as taking place on the backs of the operational organisations in the wrong sense.

PERSONNEL

For the DHA to be persuasive it is, of course, very important that it should be able to demonstrate that it has a level of expertise and understanding which is as good as and, if possible, better than that of the officers in the field — better in the sense that it combines an understanding of problems in the field with the capacity to formulate oversight positions. This requirement brings up a major problem in the arrangements of the DHA: in the eyes of too many officers with extensive field experience, the staff of DHA when it was set up contained too many of the old school of UN bureaucrats. They were career civil servants, whose experience hitherto had been largely at headquarters, and who had little or no understanding of the requirements of field operations.

It was said that staff seemed to have been dumped on the DHA as a consequence of the Secretary-General's efforts to shed officials from the central system in response to the injunction to make the organisation leaner but fitter. The working ethos for these staff had been defined during the Cold War period, and they were usually — and properly — concerned with development programmes that involved a leisurely six-year planning and implementation cycle. They were, however, also overly bureaucratic and used to a cautious evolution of plans in the Cold War context. There was now a visible clash between this traditional culture of diplomacy in the UN, and the new culture of relief provision, which required rapid response, impatience with routine, and imaginative innovation.

What should be done? More field people from NGOs and IGOs had to be brought into the DHA: DHA's coordination function was more likely to be accepted by the experienced NGO and IGO agencies if this were done. In 1993 there was some evidence of the beginnings of this, with SCF and UNICEF officers being placed on secondment with the DHA. This development is regarded as a major innovation, but the process needs to be taken much further.

There were complaints in Geneva about the siting of the DHA-UNDRO in both New York and Geneva, with the Geneva branch straining to take on a more modern set of clothes, and the New York side, being the political element, being much too prone to don the traditional pinstriped suit. The tension between the two, encountered in 1993 in discussions about bringing them together in one site, matched the struggle between the culture of diplomacy and the culture of relief. As is argued below, the DHA needed two major capacities, a functional one and a political one, the former being the resource, and the latter being the mechanism through which the resource was deployed. It may well be, there-fore, that the distinction between Geneva and New York reflected this dual need, as the New York side related DHA to the security and politi-cal mechanisms of the UN, whilst the Geneva office was closer to the operational Agencies. The identification of the complaint about staff with the New York–Geneva dichotomy may well reflect the lack of an appre-ciation of the role of the former by the latter. There was nevertheless a great need for more staff with field experience in both places, and there was a case for requiring that existing staff should spend time in the field.

Under-Secretary Jan Eliasson was credited with great skill as a diplo-mat, but he was not thought to have succeeded in generating a new dynamism in the DHA. Hence mistakes made before his appointment remained uncorrected: it was alleged that people who had been with-drawn earlier were returned without protest by him and stayed around too long; and, as already reported, there was a confusing multiplicity of offices and claims. It seems a little hard, however, to blame the Under-Secretary for failings which he inherited so early in his period of office (he was appointed only in April 1992). Obviously two qualities, that of mis-sionary activist and that of conciliator and pacifier, were needed, and per-haps these qualities are too much to expect in a single personality. Eliasson resigned 21 November 1993 (with effect from the end of January 1994).

There were problems which the head of the DHA needed, in summer 1993, to address. One was the understaffing of the parts of the DHA which had a particularly important role in coordination, those dealing with the IASU — the Inter-Agency Support Unit; and another was an uncertainty about the future role of the DHA: should it acquire a capac-ity for rapid response to emergencies in competition with the Agencies, such as UNHCR, which obviously had a long experience of such response? Eliasson and Ogata had not been on good terms. The right role for the DHA, it was pointed out by Agency officers, was to send in fol-low-up teams to monitor cooperation between the Agencies immediately after the initial response.

To quibble about the timing of such interventions in this way may appear at first sight to be over-fussy, but it involved fundamental ques-tions regarding the role of the DHA and the Agencies. The DHA was treading on the toes of the operational actors, and claiming a role for which the latter thought it was not equipped. They feared that Eliasson wanted a more activist supra-organisational role for the DHA, rather than a facilitating one, and this led to unnecessary hostility towards the organ-isation from the Agencies. Indeed the history of the UN, particularly as regards the experience of the Director-General for Development and International Economic Cooperation, suggested that any claims to a more activist managerial role were likely to be fiercely resisted.

THE DHA AND CONSOLIDATED APPEALS

The second DHA function as facilitator is managing the process of producing consolidated appeals. The DHA had succeeded early in its existence in putting together a number of impressive appeals. A series of country-specific appeals produced as part of the Special Emergency Programme for the Horn of Africa (SEPHA) in early 1993 were illustrative of this. Another was the special appeals for the Iraq programme, which had attracted up to 95 per cent of the funding sought: $700 million had been raised, including $40 million from the ESCROW account holding the frozen overseas assets of Iraq.

But there were a number of problems. First the usual success level was below that for Iraq, frequently not going up to 60 per cent of the sum requested. Between January and the end of May 1993, $4 billion had been called for, but only 25 per cent of that had been made available.[67] The point was made that in addition to well-prepared appeals, the DHA needed a more aggressive approach to donors, and this led back to the problem of leadership and staffing. There was also a great danger if there were too many appeals: in April 1993 it was reported that there had been twenty consolidated appeals in the last few months, and the cost of getting one such appeal going could be as high as $70,000. Of course flexibility and updating had to be built into the process but too many consolidated appeals could be as confusing for donors as none at all.

Second was the danger that the consolidation of appeals would detract from the separate efforts of the participating actors to attract their own funds. Separate efforts in fact continued in a number of different ways, such as UNICEF's use of its own very effective fund-raising machinery. In 1992 this generated $240 million from the private sector. There were also major appeals by UNHCR both for emergencies and for regular programmes. It was important that the consolidated approach should not lead to an overall reduction in giving. It was also essential that the donors should keep the standing funding arrangements for regular programmes in place. There was some concern that this principle of additionality was not always upheld.

Third was the problem that there were too many discontinuities between field inputs into the appeal process and those from headquarters. One illustration was where funding was attracted on the basis of a particular field input, but was then redirected as the result of headquarters' decisions without reference back to the donors. The converse of this was when donors earmarked contributions specifically for particular countries, projects or agencies, thus building inflexibility into the funding process. The general problem here was that of reconciling the need for flexibility with the need to construct consolidated appeals on the basis of calculations about specific needs, and the appeal for money and resources on that basis.

The non-governmental organisations had a major complaint in this context. Their achievements were used in calculating the needs base in the construction of the consolidated appeals, but they were not in their view fully involved in the assessment and planning process, and they received too small a share of the proceeds. These went mostly to the intergovernmental agencies and might or might not then be transferred on to the NGOs. (The US experience was somewhat different from this: see below.) Some NGOs felt that this aspect of the appeals was unfair. They also pointed to the 1993 Strategic Plan in Somalia which included an assessment of achievements, including those of NGOs, which had not been financed out of the earlier appeal. They also complained about these problems with particular reference to the 100-day programme, which it was claimed had started out as a plan of action initiated by the leading NGOs, but which had been highjacked by UNICEF, under whose auspices it eventually appeared, and turned into a mere shopping list.

Fourth was the risk that such appeals, in focusing on emergencies, would divert excessive amounts of money from longer-term development and humanitarian needs. UNICEF pointed out that, in 1992, 50,000 children died in the area of so-called 'loud' crises such as Somalia and ex-Yugoslavia, whereas 13 million children died because of more mundane causes such as measles, diarrhoea, and dysentery every year.[68] Too little attention was also given to the problems of reconstruction after a crisis, and indeed there was no single agency which had a mandate for reconstruction.

This is not to say that Consolidated Appeals were not necessary, but rather to point out that there were problems which could arise in their construction. Country-level arrangements for gathering relevant information needed to be adequate, and this involved establishing good relations with all those organisations, including NGOs, which were present, working through the resident coordinator, establishing priorities with regard to funding and ensuring that the appeal represented a programme that was integrated.

Indeed appeals could not be effectively consolidated in the absence of effective coordination between all the agencies and organisations involved, both in the UN system and the NGOs. It was necessary to have an institution like the DHA to perform the interrelated roles of information-gathering and establishing priorities, which were fundamental to the success of the relief process. By the spring of 1993 there had clearly been much progress, but the dangers discussed here remained and further improvements were obviously necessary.

DHA AND COOPERATION BETWEEN NGOs AND THE UN SYSTEM

With regard to cooperation between the NGOs and the IGOs there appeared to be some progress in the early 1990s, but perhaps not as much as the NGOs would have liked. Certainly the point was accepted that the

NGOs played a vital role in dealing with crises, and they had greatly increased in size. The media publicity given to the crisis in Ethiopia in the mid-1980s greatly boosted the popularity of the NGOs and significantly enhanced their capacity to attract funding. The claim was also made that in Somalia it was demonstrated for the first time that in some circumstances the NGOs could do work which the UN system could not do. Despite some fears that too many inexperienced young people had been sent into the field (CRS had this view in early 1993), and too many NGOs were still 'here today, gone tomorrow',the larger NGOs displayed in Somalia an appropriate professionalism which the Agencies lacked.

In addition there was evidence that the NGOs had adapted to the greater pressure on them resulting from the increasing number of complex emergencies. For instance, Catholic Relief Service set up a Disaster Response Committee in 1987 which was based at CRS headquarters in Baltimore, USA. Oxfam also established a separate Emergencies Unit.[69] SCF (UK) was unique among the large NGOs in not putting in place emergency-specific arrangements on the grounds that they would lead to active searching for work, rather than providing for a considered and measured response as necessary. It was felt that establishing a special unit would promote bureaucratic politics within the organisation: the organisation as a whole was required to be involved in responding effectively to emergencies.

A positive view of the general role of the DHA with regard to the NGOs was that it could help promote transparency ('there are no secrets')[70] by explaining each to the other, and could create the bureaucratic and political space in which they could operate. In Iraq a weekly newsletter had been set up through the DHA, and there were regular routine meetings between DHA and NGO officials. The DHA could also help to establish the credentials of NGOs with host governments — for instance, protect them against accusations that they were merely spies from the West. This was not to say, however, that there was no further room for improvement in relations between the main intergovernmental agencies and DHA and the NGOs. The problems of their participation in the consolidated appeal process have been discussed above, and there was some evidence of a certain gap between the principles enunciated above and the practice.

For instance, a number of NGOs, amongst which SCF (UK) was most vociferous, concluded that DHA still had not fully understood the importance of the role of NGOs when it accepted the condition on which the Iraqis had insisted, in the Memorandum of Understanding negotiated at the end of 1992, that all NGOs in cooperation with the UN Agencies would have to sign an agreement with the central Iraqi authorities. This condition was accepted by DHA, and put NGOs in a difficult position as it seemed to compromise their political neutrality and their absolute commitment to the provision of humanitarian relief based on need. Under the agreement organisations would have to lodge with the Iraqis details of personnel and operations. Oxfam and CARE had previously accepted conditionality imposed by host governments, and they did so on this occasion. Other NGOs, including SCF (UK), declined. The result of this was somewhat confusing: it appeared that as a result they could not enlist the support of UN Agencies in Iraq, for instance with regard to logistical support, but that they could remain present.

The DHA improved the consultation procedures between NGOs and IGOS in the sense that the leading NGOs were brought into discussions with the Inter-Agency Standing Committee, set up by the DHA as the main overall meeting point of the Agencies, and were represented there through federations of national NGOs in Geneva, when they existed, such as the Federation of Red Cross and Red Crescent Societies. But other relevant organisations were invited to attend on an *ad hoc* basis; the relationship between them and the IASC was rather a 'grace and favour' one. The NGOs were also involved in the subcommittees of the IASC, which were the committees concerned with the various specific country problems, Iraq, Eastern Europe, and Somalia. More of these were being created.

One problem with the method of organisation in the early 1990s may be noted. The federations were inevitably rather weak organisations, being concerned primarily with facilitating links between the national organisations, defining their common interests, guarding their interests, including the protection of logos and titles, promoting research and occasionally prompting and assisting action by constituent members. The problem was that there were inherent difficulties in trying to coordinate the coordinators: how far could they commit, and lead, and be sure of reflecting what their members actually wanted and were prepared to do? The main actors were the national ones.

The impression gained by this writer in Geneva in early 1993 was, however, that there was a slow process of strengthening the leagues or federations. It was also indicated that the DHA would prefer to consult through federations or umbrella organisations, and that it often found the enormous number of claimants for attention hard to handle. The American NGO umbrella, INTERACTION, was the primary consultative partner in New York, and played a part in involving particular NGOs on particular issues. In Europe, in the absence of an overarching framework, the choice was between the stronger national NGOs or the federations. The Federation of Red Cross and Red Crescent Societies was seeking a more active role for itself, and in 1990 commissioned a study to find ways of achieving this.[71] The International Save the Children Alliance (ISCA) was contemplating moving to a system for raising its own money: in 1993, 85 per cent of its funds came from the four largest national member organisations. The ISCA was also the agency through which the members dealt with the EU in Brussels, and as the EU was an important donor this was likely further to enhance the Alliance's role. It was for the moment, however, often necessary to have both the main national actors as well as the federations involved in the meetings of the more active coordination committees.

The point emerged that one of the difficulties experienced by UN Agencies in dealing with NGOs was finding the right NGO partners: should they be the Federations or individual national organisations, and if the latter, how many and which? As the main NGOs were actively involved in building up further national organisations in other countries, this seemed to be a problem that could get worse. In the early 1990s there were only half a dozen or so major relief NGOs, but these were themselves all nationally based, and the rules of the game which they had constructed could encourage greater competition between them and new national members in the future: with the waxing and waning of the fortunes of particular national members, there could be no guarantee of avoiding serious rivalries. The structure of the NGO universe also allowed the governmental agencies with which they dealt to play off one against the other: the present writer found some evidence in UNICEF, and in the DHA, of a certain hostility to SCF (UK), and a partiality for other national children's NGOs. These points favoured the strengthening of the Federations, to simplify the NGO universe and make it more intelligible to outsiders, but also to avoid future counter-productive rivalries, with fewer opportunities for others to exert differential leverage.

In their structures NGOs are themselves paradoxical organisations: they tend to challenge the orthodoxies of sovereignty, but in some ways are a reflection and promoter of it. Although all the evidence suggested that they found ways of working together rather quickly in crisis situations, there was always the danger of conflicts over mandates. One of the striking features of the leading NGOs was that although each had a core activity there had been a tendency to move out from this towards a more general responsibility, thus increasing the risk of treading on each other's toes. The case for the NGOs themselves seeking to find more formal ways of coordinating their activities and defining their mandates was reinforced by this tendency. As they got larger and richer compared with the Agencies, the risk increased of simply duplicating at the non-governmental level the problems of the latter. In some ways it could be worse as the larger NGOs had such clear national roots.

The trend towards the strengthening of the umbrella organisations was relevant here. As has been mentioned, the Save the Children Fund Alliance was weak in 1993, but it was at least on the cards that it could become more powerful, and there was some interest in increasing its budget to a third of the funds of the national members. This position was particularly supported by the US partner, though it was pointed out that they got more of their money from the US government than Save the Children in Britain. The latter got a third of its funding from the government, but the former two-thirds. The elevation of the SCF to Category One status in the ECOSOC in April 1993 if anything encouraged this development, as, although the organisation could now submit evidence without its having been requested, and could now speak at meetings, it had to do this through the Alliance. Other organisations such as CARE had not got this far, but the question of the future strengthening of CARE International was clearly on the agenda. The model for the NGOs seemed to be the Federation of Red Cross and Red Crescent Societies, which had a more dynamic initiating and managing function, and some modest operational capacity of its own. NGOs are themselves in a phase of structural evolution, and they could in the medium term emerge as more clearly transnational. One advantage of this would be that it could simplify relations between the UN system and the major NGOs.

On the NGO side there were in 1993 a number of coordinating bodies. The oldest was the International Council of Voluntary Agencies, established in the inter-war period. More recently, in 1973, a committee emerged which was specifically concerned with emergencies. This was the Steering Committee for Humanitarian Response, which by 1993 was made up of seven of the leading NGOs — Caritas Internationalis, Catholic Relief Services, International Federation of Red Cross and Red Crescent Societies, International Save the Children Alliance, Lutheran World Federation, Oxfam and World Council of Churches. (Save the Children Alliance was the most recent new member, having joined in 1992.) There are some conspicuous absentees, such as CARE International. The Steering Committee meets with the representatives of the UN Agencies every third Thursday. It was described as being mainly concerned with advocacy: promoting agreed causes and positions to governments and agencies. It maintains links with the Humanitarian Liaison Working Group of Ambassadors of the Missions of the OECD states in Geneva, which was concerned with more political questions.

The individual operational agencies for their part also sought to improve their contacts with the NGOs in the 1980s and early 1990s, so that routine NGO contacts could be rapidly augmented to deal with emergencies. The 1993 UNICEF Report (E/ICEF/1993/11), though lacking in detail, did lay great stress on the importance of such contacts in dealing with disasters, a feature of their attitudes which the main NGOs said was rather recent. There are three general meetings a year with the umbrella groups and *ad hoc* meetings with national groups. But the specific mechanisms for such contacts are underdeveloped, consisting as they do of two somewhat overworked junior officials. They were finding it difficult to cope with the additional burdens of liaison resulting from the increasing number of emergencies. In New York, UNICEF links with NGOs had been improved because of a personal initiative by a senior official.

The best equipped for dealing with the NGOs in 1993 was UNHCR, which had an office staffed with six full-time officials for that purpose. Under Mrs Ogata's predecessors, cooperation had not been as close, and in the first phase of humanitarian intervention after the end of the Gulf War was reported as having been poor.[72] The World Bank also had an NGO coordination officer and there was a welcome trend of seconding NGO staff for short periods to the Agencies.

There were, therefore, two forms of IGO-NGO contact, one tending to be through both groups collectively, and the other tending to be between individual leading NGOs and individual leading agencies. This is not to deny the existence of a third set of channels: that between individuals on both sides on an informal basis. Very often the point was made that a great deal depended on the people involved and their individual qualities and inclinations. The NGO complaint was too often, to put it politely, that the IGOs were staffed with career officials who disliked having their routines disturbed, and who were out of touch with the realities of field operations. The best thing that could be done, they said, was to change the IGO staff, to have a seconding of staff from one to the other, and especially to have a large contingent of NGO people in DHA-UNDRO. For their part the IGOs often complained that the NGO personnel, though energetic, lacked experience and the ability to sustain responsible action in the long term. Too often they were 'here today, gone tomorrow', leaving the UN system to carry the can.

THE US EXPERIENCE: A MODEL FOR DHA?

There are two big differences between the European and the US way of managing relations between government and the NGOs for the provision of disaster assistance.[73] First the US organisations obtain a large proportion of their income for this purpose from the Office of Foreign Disaster Assistance (OFDA) located within the United States Agency for International Development (USAID) in the Department of State: the Administration is the major funder of US NGO activities. The primary condition of fund allocation was that it should be focused upon humanitarian concerns, but there is also a clear preference for dealing with US-based NGOs; others do, however, receive funding if they are on the spot and can do the job. ICRC and WFP are favoured partners, but in 1991–2 a number of non-US NGOs, such as SCF (UK), received substantial support. Second, the overall structure of the US NGOs' system is much more tightly organised than that in Europe. The larger part of them are linked within a single umbrella agency called INTERACTION, but, within that institution, some thirty-odd NGOs are members of the *Disaster Response Committee*, chaired in 1993 by the representative of the Save the Children Fund (USA). This committee may also be regarded as evidence of the adjustment of the NGO system to disaster relief, since it was established in 1989. The chairman of INTERACTION is a member of the board of UNICEF.

The question obviously arises as to how far the US groups are agents of US Administration policy: the answer appears on the whole to be in the negative. Most US disaster aid, outside food relief, has gone to the NGOs. It has been allocated on the basis of the NGOs' proposals for dealing with problems in their area of specialisation, after close consultation about the best way to deal with the crisis. The OFDA does not give detailed instructions as to the spending of the money — it does not 'micromanage' — though money is designated for particular projects and countries, and a funding report is expected at the end of the financial year. Political reasons for the non-fulfilment of a contract are noted. NGOs, such as CRS, have no sense that the Administration has been dictating the terms of the contracts.[74] The doubt remains in the mind of this writer, however, as to how far US NGOs can continue to rely on funding if they propose working in states of which the Administration disapproves, such as Cuba.

Nevertheless the US model has a number of useful lessons for the DHA. Indeed one argument is that the process of strengthening the DHA should involve emulation at the multinational level of the arrangements already working in the United States. As the United States does not seem prepared to scale down its bilateral arrangements, it looks as if a stronger DHA would be the multilateral equivalent of OFDA for the other developed countries. One lesson is that a fast response is more likely in the bilateral arrangement because a USAID representative is usually present in the countries likely to need disaster assistance, and his advice, and perhaps that of the US Ambassador, is likely to be believed and acted upon by the US agencies.

After the fall of Siad Barre in January 1992, and the withdrawal of US Embassy and USAID staff because of security risks, US reinvolvement was rapid. By 21 February an AID/OFDA relief coordinator, Jan Westcott, had been based in Nairobi to coordinate US assistance through ICRC, UN Agencies and the NGOs. Later, in 1992, Jan Westcott worked with an EC representative in Somalia. Meetings between OFDA officials and NGO representatives in Washington were speedily triggered by consultations with INTERACTION. The consequent convening of the latter's thirty-member Disaster Response Committee with OFDA officials could lead to the rapid agreement of a plan of action and its implementation. There is clearly a strong potential for rapid response and considerable financial muscle to back this up in the US system.

Rapid response is greatly helped by a unique feature of the US system which DHA would do well to emulate.[75] These are the DARTs (Disaster Assessment Relief Teams), which are constructed very rapidly from amongst the OFDA's own staff and/or qualified outsiders and sent to a crisis country for rapid assessment of needs. Such teams were sent to Nairobi and Mombasa on 21 August 1992; the US air force began airlifting support into Mombasa for distribution to Somali refugees on 22 August, and into Somalia on 27 August 1992; and later a DART team went into Mogadishu. Members of the US team were transferred to UNOSOM 1 in December 1992, as the latter was set up and began work.[76] The DART teams rapidly got to grips with the Somalia problem, even though they did this initially from neighbouring countries when security problems discouraged direct involvement. The application of resources was combined with flexibility, early warning and flow of information, and a high degree of technical competence.

THINKING ABOUT DHA

At the time of writing in early 1993 there was much debate about the kind of role which should be given to the DHA. A spectrum of roles was conceivable, ranging from a basic bureaucratic service role at one end to a managerial role at the other. Between these two poles were a facilitating role, concerned with the provision of key resources, such as information, and funding appeals, and communication between organisations, and the active construction of country-specific disaster plans; and, nearer management, an active coordination role, seeking to direct participating organisations within defined slots in the overall plan, and acting as a link in a chain of command going up to the Secretary-General.

The strongest option appears to be for the DHA to take on facilitating functions, dealing with issues like information gathering, analysis and dissemination, and the delineation of responsibilities for organisations, but under the authority of an official appointed as the permanent representative of the Secretary-General.[77] Increasingly the habit of the system appears to be for the Secretary-General to appoint Special Representatives to countries where more pressing emergencies have arisen: on 18 May 1993 two further Special Representatives were appointed — for the Sudan and Zaïre. As in Somalia the Secretary-General's appointee has overall responsibility for overseeing the three primary aspects of the operations in complex crises: the humanitarian aspect, the security/military aspects, and the political aspects. Under the Special Representative the normal procedure is for the appointment of a trinity of Humanitarian, Security and Political Coordinators. The problem is to decide when a complex crisis has arisen, and when this particular response is appropriate: this could be a primary task of the DHA. A major development in thinking about the system, however, is the conclusion that the 'Leading Agency' concept should now be abandoned. UNHCR, and others, might not like this, but this is thought to be the way of the future.

The best approach appears to be for decisions to be made in advance of a crisis on the basis of UNDP-generated data. The DHA should ensure that the data are comprehensive and reliable. It would then have responsibility for alerting the UN, especially the Secretary-General, if circumstances tip over towards disaster. UNDP Resident Coordinators would be in charge of dealing with immediate efforts to avert the disaster. DHA strength should be at the country level where staff should be put to collect and analyse information, not in Geneva or New York. In this model the DHA would be expected to invest a great deal in the planning function: preparedness would be its goal. In countries tending towards failure, the DHA would be expected to have plans for sector and area management, with plans for slotting in the various Agencies in the light of their strengths. There should, however, be no direction about this: it would depend upon consultation and consensus among the operational organisations, be they IGOs or NGOs. The suggestion has also been made that, as with peacekeeping forces, resources and personnel should be stocked in advance. The Under-Secretary should have a 'little black book' of individuals who would be prepared to play a role in the management of the assistance process, and who would be a part of the country-level management committee. Such individuals might come from outside the system altogether, but more usually they would be selected from organisations according to the primary dimensions of the specific crisis. The whole point would be to facilitate rapid response, and to establish a facilitating process.

What emerges from this discussion is a proposal for two loops of function and authority with regard to each emergency, one concerned with information-gathering, analysis and funding, which could use existing development machinery within countries, in addition to the DHA-UNDRO arrangement; and another to do with response and operations, which would bring a new coordinating mechanism into each crisis, though doing this rapidly through the Secretary-General, and where necessary after Security Council approval.

The failure hitherto to develop the kind of facilitating arrangements inherent in this 'two-loop' approach has meant that the UN system has again begun to respond in characteristic fashion — on the lines discussed earlier with regard to the general economic and social area. It is a response which involves what was described in terms of 'duplication' and 'fragmentation'.

In the early 1990s various national and regional organisations began to move into the area of responsibility of the established Agencies. For instance, the ODA in Britain acquired an operational capability in mid-1991 which it incorporated into a Disaster Relief Initiative; 165 personnel, recruited on a short-term basis, were sent to the Kurdish area of Iraq, and a part of Turkey that had been affected by earthquake.[78] Similarly the European Community set up its own relief organisation in early 1993 under the title of the European Community Humanitarian Office (ECHO).[79] Other states, especially in Scandinavia, were developing such capacity.

There are two difficulties that arise from these new arrangements. One is that it is unclear as to how far they will take resources from the efforts made through international organisations. NGOs are especially concerned that the EC's increasing operational role may threaten their traditional function as a conduit for EC relief assistance. Despite protestations to the contrary in 1993 it seemed unlikely that there would not be some diversion, if only because contributions to the international effort would not increase as they might otherwise have done. The other difficulty is that in responding to an apparent failure of the international system in this way the problem is made worse rather than better. Difficulties of coordination and management are compounded rather than simplified.

A general dilemma affecting improvements in humanitarian arrangements appears at this point. As has been shown, better management has to be based on improved coordination in a pluralistic system, rather than on the introduction of supranational management principles. But states have a natural inclination to do things for themselves. Even the Nordic states allocate only around 40 per cent of their relief budget to the multinational system, the rest being allocated on a country to country basis. This seems the most attractive procedure from the point of view of the donor state, and it accords with the principles of the international system when the receiving state has kept its integrity and capacity. This is where the dilemma emerges: the donor states adopt a kind of two-tier view of international society. Some states are seen as having failed catastrophically, and are therefore considered to be suitable cases for treatment by the international welfare system, whilst others, having retained integrity and capacity, are able to opt out of that system and, as it were, 'go private': they arrange things bilaterally.

The problem, therefore, is that there will be a continuing tendency of fragmentation in the system for humanitarian assistance until all states, donors and recipients, accept that they share equally a general interest in improving international arrangements; bilateral arrangements inevitably reflect the lack of credibility of that principle and get in the way of its being more widely supported.

A new structure for international humanitarian assistance: looking backwards and looking forwards

What should be stressed in the agenda for reform of the structure of the humanitarian assistance machinery? The following proposals may be extracted from the above arguments.

1. *There should be two loops of functions with regard to crises, a reporting and disaster mitigation loop, and a crisis management and operational loop.*
2. *The resident country development machinery should be entrusted with*

the collection of information with reference to development and crisis indicators. These should be forwarded to the DHA-UNDRO, which should be present in the country if the indicators are negative. Agencies should provide information through the country machinery.

3. *The permanent inter-agency group, the Inter-Agency Standing Committee (IASC), in Geneva with a branch in New York, should be developed as the central executive agency of the system, and its membership should also include the lead NGOs. It should have global responsibilities for receiving and forwarding information on development and possible disasters, and produce coordinated recommendations. It should learn from the experience of OFDA-INTERACTION meetings in the US system: it should meet at the highest level and should seek to allocate roles not just for the Agencies but also for the NGOs represented through the Disaster Relief Committee in Geneva. It should be equipped to meet at very short notice in the event of a crisis, with powers to draw on the DHA's revolving fund.*

4a. *If a country moved from mitigation to crisis the DHA-UNDRO should immediately inform the Secretary-General who would immediately appoint a special country representative, or ensure that a lead organisation was in place to set up and lead the country coordinating mechanism. This would bring together the Agencies and NGOs in the country, collect and collate appropriate information, and recommend action.*

4b. *Efforts should be made to improve the staffing and procedures of DHA-UNDRO and of a Standing Inter-Agency Group for Emergencies (IAGE) in the light, and on the lines, of the above arguments.*

Apart from the quality of staff, those dealing with the DHA from the outside have had difficulty with understanding the logic of its internal structure, and so they have problems in deciding on the appropriate section or subdepartment with which to deal. But the logic of the DHA's organisation is linked with the logic of the IASC's internal organisation. At the moment the latter does not have any dedicated staffing of its own.

At this point a comparison might usefully be made with the Council of Ministers of the European Community, which does have such a permanent staff. Moreover the comparison also suggests the desirability of developing much closer direct links between the participating organisations, as the states in the EC have developed close links between themselves through such devices as the system of European Correspondents. At the moment the organisations do not have such offices, or any technical machinery, telex systems, or dedicated phone connections, which would facilitate such links. This lack is itself a striking failing and is a measure of the weakness of the coordination machinery. Once such devices were in place, and a staff specific to the IASC had been created, a matching staff could be set up in

DHA. In that way the logic of the internal structure of the latter would become more readily accessible to outsiders.

5. *Much of what has been said about the problems of coordinating the activities of the Agencies applies equally to the NGOs. They tend to talk too little to each other and their transnational liaison mechanisms are too weak, both between national representatives of particular NGOs through their federal institutions, and between the NGOs in general. The Disaster Relief Committee should be beefed up.*

There is a danger, as the NGOs become more powerful, of simply recreating at a higher level all the problems of the Agencies. Indeed the further risk for the NGOs is that their national structures will dominate as they get stronger and richer, thus in some ways reinforcing the problems of sovereignty.

6. *There can be no single model for coordinating the disaster operations within countries, though there is a strong argument in support of always appointing and giving a key role to a Special Representative of the Secretary-General. Much depends on the gravity and nature of the crisis, whether or not a government still exists, and whether there is a need for active security support. The precise form of the country machinery should be determined by IASC on the basis of a DHA-UNDRO report and recommendation.*
7. *The country mechanism should act with IASC to produce consolidated fund appeals. The country mechanism would also generate and transfer information concerning performance. Probably the appeal after consolidation should be addressed to the main donors by IASC, which would be seen as representing the active assistance system.*

Reconstruction and humanitarian assistance

In this discussion of the experience of humanitarian assistance one theme has as yet been addressed only obliquely. This concerns the guidelines which should be followed to facilitate withdrawal from crisis situations. Clearly questions about rehabilitation and recovery should form a part of thinking during involvement in, and the conduct of, such operations. The NGOs and IGOs and governments involved should be putting three questions simultaneously: how to get in, how to be effective, and how to get out.

The reader will not be surprised to discover that this is a fairly brief section, in view of the slight experience of international organisations in successfully concluding a programme of humanitarian intervention. The best that can be done is to state the various issues that arise in this situation and which need to be noted during the conduct and establishment of such operations.

The withdrawal phase can be broken down into at least three subphases. The first is the direct provision of relief to the human suffering and repair of the damage caused by the disaster. Second is the process of rehabilitation, the reinstatement of the integrity of individuals and their relationships, so that a potential for self-reliance is generated. Third is the process of reconstruction, during which economic, social, administrative and governmental arrangements are built up and made effective: the civil structure of the state is regenerated.

One of the parts of this spectrum which has received relatively little attention is that concerned with rehabilitation and reconstruction. It should be focused at three levels, and at each of them there has been some evidence of new concern. At the local level it is necessary to work with and to enhance the capacity of existing local authority structures. It is also necessary to work with existing economic structures, for example to provide food for work except in the worst of situations. Local merchants need to be enlisted in support of distribution programmes by allowing them to purchase food and sell it in the markets. Ingenuity has to be used in finding ways to provide currency for such purchases which does not appear simply to be given. CRS reported its experience with regard to moving from food aid to food self-sufficiency. This problem has indeed been much discussed in its technical aspects. But it is evident that the need for the effective micro-management of the process is still understressed. Too often this delicate evolution depends on the relatively uncoordinated interaction of a large number of groups, ranging from NGOs like CARE, Oxfam and SCF, to UNICEF, WFP and FAO. There is need for sensitive micro-management, and hence issue-specific coordinating mechanisms at the local level, which despite the good intentions of individual organisations are not always available.

This suggests a need for links between the organisations dealing with the disaster, but also links between them and the development agencies, as well as the closer involvement of the Bretton Woods organisations, in order to promote rehabilitation and development out of disaster relief.

Second, there is need to deal with the country level. There was evidence in Somalia in the summer of 1993 of the beginnings of a major effort to regenerate the country's governmental and administrative structures. The DHA had embarked upon a major programme involving the setting up of regional administrations, and in 1993 was looking to recruit up to 1000 advisers to man these operations. The intention was not to subdivide the country, but to shape local government in consultation with established local clan authorities. Similarly an attempt was being made to link the relatively stable, and semi-detached, northern part of Somalia now called Somaliland, with this process — not to force unity, but to generate reconciliation. The CRS was, unlike ICRC, very proactive in this — anxious to bring about reconciliation between conflicting groups wherever possible.

Third, there is a need to do something at the international level. There is some evidence of greater concern on the part of the leading states with this process. The US Congress, for instance, allocated money specifically to reconstruction, as opposed to development or relief, for the first time in autumn 1992. One hundred million dollars were allocated for Relief, Rehabilitation *and Reconstruction* in the Sub-Saharan region. Fifteen million dollars were allocated for reconstruction through OFDA in three countries — Angola, Mozambique and Ethiopia — though, because of the Somalia crisis, in the event only the money for Mozambique was allocated. There was also a more widespread realisation among the leading developed countries that the relief of debt repayment obligations was a necessary part of the reconstruction process.

In sum:

Wherever possible, food aid should not be allowed to interfere with the process of growing local produce. In other words there should be help with seeds and the survival of livestock whenever this is feasible as an alternative to food aid.

There should be serious study of the process of reconstruction after an emergency. The United Nations system and indeed the NGOs have not yet acquired special expertise in this area. Emergency provision should not be at the expense of longer-term relief and development operations. It is dangerous if 'hot' crises attract such a level of funding that more routine programmes suffer. The UNICEF evidence is striking in this context: 50,000 children died in 1992 in hot crises, but 13 million died because of ailments like diarrhoea and dysentery in longer term 'cold' crises.

In promoting recovery and reconstruction more effort needs to be given to support for internal migrants; no organisation had a mandate to deal with this problem in 1993, though UNDP and UNHCR had both acted in this context. One aspect of the problem is that the provision of assistance should not lead to large movements of population. The setting up of the special feeding centres by Oxfam and other agencies in the Ethiopian crisis in the mid-1980s was generally regarded as a mistake, as bringing together large numbers of people increased the prevalence of diseases and led to many more deaths.

The UN should build on local authority structures and set up an apparatus for the recovery of the state. This involves a role in conferring legitimacy to a new regime, and in helping it with the training and supply of administrators. To say this implies a position which would have been regarded as being 'politically incorrect' just a few years ago. It implies a frontal challenge to the terms of the General Assembly Resolution of December 1960 under which claims for independence by colonies were to be allowed unconditionally, i.e. they were not to be dependent on meeting any kind of educational, social or economic standards. The result of this policy, which was first resisted by the countries of the developed world, and then welcomed as a way of abandoning their responsibilities, led to the setting up of a number of utterly incompetent and sometimes corrupt regimes which completely failed to provide for the welfare of their citizens.

In reconstructing states which have experienced major humanitarian crises, and the collapse of administrative and political structures, the United Nations could take on a kind of modified trusteeship role. It could help create well-founded states. It could also issue certificates of legitimacy to new regimes, which is in fact what it aimed to do when it helped set up and supervise elections in Namibia, Cambodia and Angola, and acted to ensure proper respect for human rights in El Salvador.

It should not be forgotten, though, that General Assembly Resolution 46/182 required that humanitarian assistance should be provided 'in principle on the basis of an appeal by the affected country' and that 'the affected state has the primary role in the initiation, organisation, coordination and implementation of humanitarian assistance within its territory'. Wherever possible, therefore, the structures of the recipient states should, according to the resolution, be fully involved with the operation, and help to formulate their own demands of the international community. There are cases where this principle does not seem to have been followed. For instance, the Kenyan authorities felt that their own Drought Recovery Programme (DRP) had been dealt with in a fairly cavalier way in the SEPHA consolidated appeal in 1992. The Kenyans had drawn up an appeal in close consultation with the agencies involved, so that when the programme was launched in October 1992 they were confident that it had the full backing of the UN. But subsequently 'they felt uncertain about how far funds contributed to SEPHA would be used for the DRP' — to use the tactful words of a report written by an official. In this instance the principle of working through national structures and helping with their operations did not seem to have been respected.

A great difficulty for the humanitarian assistance process is encountered at this point. In general it is, of course, necessary to work with and to sustain national authorities. The traditional view of sovereignty would lead to a relative indifference to the character of a regime except *in extremis*. But how is the decision to be made that a government has become excessively abhorrent, so that to work with it in some areas of humanitarian assistance is to defend the indefensible? And at what point, and how, is the judgement to be made that the failure of the government has been so catastrophic that some kind of rebuilding from a lower level of organisation in the state is necessary? Working with acceptable regimes on what appears to be a manageable crisis can be through the UNDP system and in particular the Resident Coordinator; but if there is a collapse of such a magnitude as to constitute a complex emergency, and if the government is discredited, then a different mechanism is indicated, brought afresh into the country on the pattern already discussed. The worse the crisis, and the greater the scale of necessary humanitarian assistance, the more important it is to make a judgement about a regime's acceptability.

This reveals an irony in the position of the United Nations with regard to sovereignty and Article 2(7) of the UN Charter. A more flexible view of sovereignty is sought in order to facilitate more effective humanitarian assistance. At first sight, as the Secretary-General admitted (BBC Radio 4 programme, *The Thin Blue Line,* Sunday, 25 April 1993), this might appear to be a licence for the richer states to act as a world policeman and to trample on the interests of the weaker and less developed states. But the purpose of UN activities at the end of the day is to make states stronger not weaker: to make the world safe for sovereignty. It is recognised that the Geneva Conventions, and international law regarding human rights, rest on the sovereignty of states. It is the states that sanction them and which are required to uphold them. States that are properly constituted, in respecting human rights, and in promoting human welfare effectively, are more likely to be the strong and stable pillars of such a system.

Notes

1   I am grateful for the help provided for this study by a large number of officials in Geneva, New York and Washington, in intergovernmental and non-governmental international organisations, and in offices of national representatives. Although they prefer to remain anonymous, I acknowledge with thanks that without them what follows could not have been written.

2   See Paul Taylor, *International Organisation in the Modern World*, London, Pinter (1993), 159–78. For a good discussion of the role and problems of the Specialised Agencies see Douglas Williams, *The Specialised Agencies and the United Nations: The System in Crisis*, London, Hurst (1987).

3   For an excellent account of the main problems and issues see Randolph C. Kent, *The Anatomy of Disaster Relief: The International Network in Action*, London, Pinter (1987). For a critical account of the aid process see B. E. Harrell-Bond, *Imposing Aid: Emergency Assistance to Refugees*, Oxford, Oxford University Press (1986).

4   On the emergence and role of non-governmental organisations see Peter Willetts (ed.), *Pressure Groups in the Global System*, London, Pinter (1982); there is an extensive literature on the issue of sovereignty and intervention in states: see Michael Waltzer, *Just and Unjust Wars*, London, Allen Lane (1977); and John Vincent, *Nonintervention and International Order*, Princeton, Princeton University Press (1974). For recent discussions of the issue see *International Affairs*, **69**, 4 (Autumn, 1993). See also Gene Lyons and Michael Mastanduno (eds.), *Beyond Westphalia? National Sovereignty and International Intervention*, Berkeley, University of California Press (1993).

5   The classic text on peacekeeping is Alan James, *Peacekeeping in International Politics*, London, Macmillan in association with the International Institute for Strategic Studies (1990).

6   See Kent, op.cit. (note 3). An indication of the wide range of problems resulting from man-made crises is contained in the International Federation of Red Cross and Red Crescent Societies, *Operations Report 1991/92*, and in the Committee of the Red Cross, ICRC 1992 *Review of Operations*, Donor Report, Geneva, April 1993.

7   Complex emergencies included Afghanistan, Angola, Azerbaijan, Cambodia, Iraq, Liberia, Mozambique, Somalia, Sudan and former Yugoslavia. See United Nations, Economic and Social Council, *E/ICEF/1993/11* (Report from United Nations Children's Fund, Executive Board).

8   See Krister Eduards, Gunnar Rosen and Robert Rossborough, 'Responding to emergencies: the role of the UN in emergencies and ad hoc operations', in Nordic UN Project, *The United Nations: Issues and*

Options, Stockholm, Nordic UN Project (1991), 81. In 1989 the cost of support for each of 600,000 displaced persons had been $375. But 'the total foreign development assistance to the Sudan during the 80s averaged $30–40 per person per year'.

9 For a graphic account of this dilemma see E/ICEF/1993/11, op.cit., (note 7) at paras 5–8.

10 Reported to the writer by a UNICEF official, March 1993.

11 See Kent, op.cit. (note 3).

12 For a discussion of these issues, and the nature of 'entitlements', a concept which he elaborated, see Amartya Sen in Jean Drèze and Amartya Sen (eds.), *The Political Economy of Hunger, Vol 1: Entitlement and Well-being,* Oxford, Clarendon Press (1990).

13 This seems to be the recommendation of the General Assembly in United Nations, General Assembly, *A/Res/46/182,* 14 April 1992, at para. 19.

14 Ibid., para. 19.

15 See written evidence from Angela Penrose and Andrew Timpson of Save the Children Fund (UK) to House of Commons Foreign Affairs Select Committee, November 1992.

16 This point is made very forcibly by the British Ambassador to the United Nations, Sir David Hannay, in his evidence to the House of Commons Foreign Affairs Select Committee. See House of Commons, Foreign Affairs Committee, *The Expanding Role of the United Nations and its Implications for UK Policy,* Minutes of Evidence, Tuesday 27 October 1992, 11.

17 See *International Herald Tribune,* 4 August, 1992.

18 By an official interviewed in New York, September 1992.

19 See Penrose and Timpson, op.cit. (note 15).

20 United Nations, General Assembly, A/Res/43/131, 20 March 1989, Preliminary Statements, 2.

21 See Maggie Black, *A Cause for Our Times: Oxfam, the First 50 Years,* Oxford, Oxford University Press (1992), esp. 219–21.

22 Hedley Bull, 'Introduction', in Hedley Bull (ed.), *Intervention in World Politics,* Oxford, Clarendon Press, (1984), 4.

23 The United States accepted the principle of non-intervention at the seventh International Conference of American States in 1933.

24 See Leslie Bethell, *The Abolition of the Brazilian Slave Trade: Britain, Brazil and the Slave Trade Question, 1807–1869,* Cambridge, Cambridge University Press (1970).

25 Inis L. Claude Jr., *National Minorities: An International Problem,* Cambridge, MA, Harvard University Press (1955).

26 Ibid., 30.

27 See contributions from Yufan Liang and Wang Baoliu in the proceedings of the Conference, *The New World Order and the Role of the*

United Nations, forthcoming.

28 In his *Report* on the work of the United Nations of 6 September 1991, Perez de Cuellar, then UN Secretary-General, reflected this view when he wrote: 'It is now increasingly felt that the principle of non-interference with the essential domestic jurisdiction of States cannot be regarded as a protective barrier behind which human rights could be massively or systematically violated with impunity.' General Assembly, *A/46/1,* 6 September 1991, 10.

29 United Nations, General Assembly, A/Res/46/182, 14 April 1992, approved at the 78th Plenary Session, 19 December 1991.

30 See comments on this question by two British ex-ambassadors to the United Nations, Sir John Thomson and Sir Crispin Tickell, in their oral evidence to the House of Commons Foreign Affairs Select Committee, in Foreign Affairs Committee, *The Expanding Role of the United Nations and its Implications for UK Policy: Minutes of Evidence,* London, HMSO, 17 February 1993, 175–6 and *passim.*

31 *Observer,* 6 September 1992, 2.

32 See Overseas Development Institute, *Briefing Paper: Recent Changes in the International Relief System,* January 1993.

33 See Paul Taylor and Spiros Econimedes, *Relations between Global and Regional Organisations in the Maintenance of International Peace and Security: The UN and the EC in the Case of Yugoslavia,* forthcoming.

34 See, for example, James Gow, *Yugoslav Endgames: Civil Strife and Inter-State Conflict,* London Defence Studies No.5, London, Brassey's for the Centre for Defence Studies (June 1991) and John Zametica, *The Yugoslav Conflict,* Adelphi Paper 270, London, Brassey's for the IISS (May 1992).

35 Issued as Development Studies Association, *The United Nations Humanitarian Response,* November 1992, 13–24.

36 Houshang Ameri, *Politics and Process in the Specialised Agencies of the United Nations,* Aldershot, Gower (1982), 92.

37 Ibid., 93.

38 Ibid., 96.

39 See, for example, *Reporting to the Economic and Social Council,* prepared by Maurice Bertrand, Joint Inspection Unit, JIU/REP/84/7, Geneva, 1984, para. 5, 2, and *passim.*

40 Martin Hill, *The United Nations System: Coordinating its Economic and Social Work,* Cambridge, Cambridge University Press (1978), 95.

41 Quoted in John P. Renninger, *ECOSOC: Options for Reform,* UNITAR, New York, 1981, 5.

42 Hill, op.cit. (note 40), 44.

43 General Assembly, A32/197, 127, para. 64.

44 Ibid., 7, para. 20.

45 *Operational Activities for Development of the United Nations System,*

A/38/258, 3 June 1983, 9, para. 9(a).

46 *Restructuring of the Economic and Social Sector of the United Nations,* A/37/439, 6, para. 16.

47 Bertrand, op.cit. (note 39), 16, para. 35.

48 See A/37/439, op.cit., 4, para. 10.

49 Interview with UN official, April 1985.

50 From an anonymous internal US administrative document headed *North/South Dialogue and UNCTAD,* dated 16 February 1984, Section 11, 2.

51 Bertrand, op.cit. (note 39), 45–46, para. 138.

52 Ibid., p.29, para.63.

53 Ibid., 12, para. 38.

54 Ibid., 19, para. 42.

55 Ibid., 2.

56 See Larry Minear *et al., United Nations Coordination of the International Humanitarian Response to the Gulf Crisis, 1990–92,* Occasional Paper Number 13, Thomas J. Watson Jr., Institute for International Studies, Brown University, Providence (1992).

57 Ibid., 8–9. This hilarious episode started with a request for an increase of 15 grams of sugar a day per person for a group of refugees in the desert in view of the bitter cold. The request was sent to UNDRO in Geneva, which referred it to WFP in Rome, which referred it to UNHCR in Geneva — which then rejected it!

58 See Eduards, Rosen and Rossborough, op.cit. (note 8), esp. 89–90.

59 See Administrative Committee on Coordination, *Future ACC/1993/14,* 23 April 1993, being a *Summary of Conclusions of the ACC Meeting, First Regular Session of 1993,* at Rome, 19-20 April 1993. 'ACC expressed appreciation for the Secretary-General's decision to establish the Department of Humanitarian Affairs and the appointment of Under-Secretary-General Eliasson to strengthen inter-agency coordination', but: 'ACC members noted the assurance that DHA's role was not to assume operational responsibilities but to ensure effective coordination and better utilisation of the distinctive capacities and expertise of the organisations and agencies of the UN system' (para. 15). A wary welcome indeed!

60 Most of the material on DHA-UNDRO results from extensive interviews with officials in Geneva in April 1993 and in New York in May 1993.

61 This point comes out very clearly in Paul Taylor, 'Working for global population control', in Paul Taylor, *International Organisation in the Modern World: The Regional and the Global Process,* London, Pinter (1993), 181–204.

62 See Minear *et al.,* op.cit. (note 56). See also Paul Taylor and A.J.R.Groom, *The United Nations and the Gulf War,* Discussion Paper

No.38, Royal Institute of International Affairs, February 1992.

63 Interview with officials in Geneva, April 1993.

64 *Nordic Project,* op.cit. (note 8) 90–91.

65 Ibid., 91.

66 Views of officials in Geneva, April 1993.

67 From the Secretary-General's *Report* to the High Level Coordination Segment of the Economic and Social Council, 31 May 1993, 28.

68 United Nations, Economic and Social Council, *UNICEF Emergency Operations, E/ICEF/1993/11,* 24 February 1993, paras. 5 and 6.

69 For an excellent account of these adaptations see Robert Dodd, 'The marketing of mercy: A review of the emergency response capability of the League of Red Cross and Red Crescent Societies, and of other agencies', prepared for LRCRCS, May 1991, unpublished.

70 An official's view in DHA Geneva, April 1993.

71 This was the report by Dodd, op.cit. (note 69).

72 See Minear, *et al,* op.cit. (note 56), pp.32–3.

73 Most of the evidence for this section was the product of interviews with officials in CARE, Catholic Relief Services, INTERACTION, and OFDA in New York, Baltimore and Washington, DC in May 1993.

74 According to CRS officials interviewed in May 1993.

75 In his *Report to the High Level Coordination Segment of the Economic and Social Council* of 31 May 1993, the Secretary-General reported that DHA was establishing a UN Disaster Assessment and Coordination Standby Team (UNDAS) which could be dispatched immediately to the disaster site. This looked like the DART arrangement.

76 For an account of the steps in US involvement in Somalia see Office of US Foreign Disaster Assistance (OFDA), *Situation Report No.20,* 30 March 1993.

77 See the Report of the Secretary-General to the Economic and Social Council, High-level Coordination Segment, *Coordination of Humanitarian Assistance: Emergency Relief and the Continuum to Rehabilitation and Development,* 31 May 1993. The Secretary-General pointed out (p.4) that working under his authority was the best way of bringing the strengths of the organisation to bear simultaneously on humanitarian, political and security issues. He concluded: 'recent experiences have demonstrated the need for the appointment of Special Representative of the Secretary-General *(sic)* to oversee the entirety of the UN operations' (p.13).

78 See Overseas Development Institute, *Briefing Paper,* ODI, Regents College, London, January 1993.

79 See Colin Scott, *Mapping European Community Development Policy,* Save the Children Fund, Overseas Department Working Paper No. 4, London, January 1993.

4

Evacuation, intervention and retaliation: United Nations humanitarian operations in Somalia, 1991–1993

Hugo Slim and Emma Visman

Virtue itself turns vice being misapplied.
Shakespeare, *Romeo and Juliet*

This chapter examines Save the Children's experience of the UN's emergency humanitarian assistance to Somalia from 1991 to 1993, and identifies key issues of humanitarian policy emerging from the Somalia emergency. As one of the few INGOs which continued to work in Somalia throughout the period, Save the Children's experience gave it a special position from which to observe and comment on the international community's humanitarian response. The chapter draws on SCF's criticisms of the operation through the press and written statements as events unfolded, and on more considered comment produced retrospectively and privately in SCF reports.

Introduction

The Somalia emergency has been seen by many as an opportunity to experiment in the new interventionist options available to the international community since the end of the Cold War (Drysdale, 1994, 1–2 and De Waal, 1994). For the policy-makers of the UN and its more powerful member states Somalia has become a laboratory for the new world order and for attempts to invent new models of conflict resolution, peace enforcement, humanitarian assistance and peacebuilding. In the process, a number of important issues of humanitarian policy and practice have come to a head before and after military intervention. Many of these issues remain a feature of the international community's wider response to similar complex emergencies, and the failure to resolve them continues to compromise the UN's humanitarian operations worldwide.

In the case of Somalia, it seems possible that if initial UN humanitarian policy and practice had been better informed and its mandate been more flexible, the military intervention of December 1992 might not have been made to appear so necessary or inevitable. Once military intervention had taken place, the progress of events shows that military-led humanitarian intervention in Somalia did not lead to a rapid and durable solution to the crisis. The short but tragic history of the Somali emergency shows that in complex emergencies interventions of this kind by the international community can complicate matters still further. The priority for the international community should be to ensure that the mandates and capacity of *routine* UN humanitarian operations are sufficiently flexible and well resourced that large-scale military intervention and dramatic rescue-style operations do not become the norm.

Four phases

In what follows, the events of the three-year period are divided into four distinct phases. The first phase covers the year 1991 which has been dubbed by SCF's Africa Director 'the UN's year of missed opportunities' (Bowden, 1992). In phase two, the period from January to December 1992, UN ceasefire negotiations dominated proceedings and displaced concerted humanitarian action. Phase three saw the first phase of UN military intervention by UNITAF from December 1992 to May 1993. Subsequently, in phase four, when the handover to UNOSOM II took place, there was a brief 'honeymoon period' and then an escalation of conflict following the killings of twenty-five UN Pakistani troops on 5 June 1993 and the impact of subsequent UN military operations on humanitarian aid.

It is necessary, however, to provide some background to the crisis in order to understand the origins of the political vacuum, and the civil war which has undermined Somali government; and also to examine the way in which the Somalia emergency has been presented in the West — a factor which played no small part in determining the actions of the international community.

Political background

Farer has observed that after its independence in 1960, 'the Somali government was initially a mere political superstructure resting on the tectonic plates of the main organising units of Somali society, the clans' (Farer, 1993, 4). A system of client and patron built upon traditional clan relationships, successful government depended on a delicate balancing act.

When Siad Barre, the head of the army, came to power in a *coup* in 1969, the principle of Somali politics remained the same but gradually lost its balance. Barre continued to increase the huge military arsenal which had brought him to power, first under Soviet patronage and then, after the Soviet Union's famous superpower switch to support Ethiopia in 1977–8, with American backing. Under his regime, Somalia became one of the five main recipients of US aid in Africa, its strategic importance valued highly by successive American governments.

After Somalia's defeat in the war against Ethiopia, Barre's increasingly ruthless and authoritarian regime became ever more reliant on a narrow and exclusive clan base and the years that followed saw a 'reign of terror' (Samatar, 1991, 18–20). In the name of modernism and Somali nationalism, his regime purged political, religious and clan-based opposition. An increasing tide of opposition organised by different clan leaders swelled up and eventually swept him from power in January 1991. Barre's departure, however, left a vacuum at the centre of Somali politics which the southern warlords have since been trying to fill, while the north broke away claiming independence as the Republic of Somaliland in May 1991. The vacuum in the south was exacerbated by the socio-economic legacy of the Barre years and by the widespread destruction of the war to remove him. In early 1991 there was a total lack of political parties, trade unions and other national or regional civic organisations, all of which had been suppressed under the Barre regime. On an economic level, the commercial system was one of corruption and patronage, and during Barre's fall the banking system had been destroyed, resulting in the cessation of much of the once substantial remittances from abroad. The war against Barre in early 1991 also resulted in the massive destruction of infrastructure and the disruption and collapse of local food markets. From 1991 to 1993, civil war continued between the main warlords and their respective clan and subclan supporters in an attempt to fill the gap left by Barre and to attain national supremacy, or to secure regional fiefdoms.

A question of image

During the three years from 1991 to 1993, the Somali emergency was characterised in two different ways by the western media and politicians. In the initial period, the Somali emergency was represented as a 'basket case' (the term 'basket case' was first used by Henry Kissinger to describe Bangladesh in the early 1970s). In the second period it became something of a crusade. Both images were misrepresentations. More akin to caricature, they were simplistic and detrimental to a more informed understanding of the crisis. Nevertheless, as political and media images they were both extremely influential.

Throughout the first two years of the Somalia crisis, Somali society was portrayed to the world by the majority of western media and politicians alike as an extremely complex web of internecine intrigue, defying logic and essentially incomprehensible to the outsider. The word 'anarchy' was most commonly used to describe political, social and economic conditions in the country. The overwhelming tendency was to condemn Somalia to that select group of 'basket case' nations whose problems seem to lie far beyond the pale of assistance and solution, and in the face of which the international community can only wring its hands. This kind of fatalism is convenient for international political expediency. It allows western politicians to shake their heads in pity while keeping a 'tragic' and perhaps 'intractable' humanitarian crisis firmly at the bottom of the foreign policy priority list Unfortunately, such caricature is also an essential part of the way in which much of the western media present 'Third World' crises until such time as a disaster is ripe for more sensationalist coverage (Benthall, 1993). For a significant period, therefore, a coincidence of interest existed between the media and the western political establishment which kept the spotlight off Somalia. The picture of a dangerous, dark and hopeless case dominated by civil war was the predominant image surrounding Somalia throughout 1991 and early 1992.

Events began to turn as famine became more obvious in the second quarter of 1992. The appearance of starving women and children replaced the pictures of wicked gunmen and allowed for more conventional and sympathetic disaster images. The vocal interventions of the new UN Secretary-General Boutros Boutros-Ghali around this time also made for a significant shift. From Bosnia, he observed how the enormous tragedy in Somalia was being eclipsed by the overwhelming international attention being paid to the 'rich man's war' in former Yugoslavia. The media and the international community began to reframe the crisis in Somalia in terms more accessible to western public opinion.

This change in image marked the second development in the West's portrayal of the Somalia emergency. If the first image had been one of a hopeless 'basket case', then the second was characterised by the more familiar image of a crusade with good guys, bad guys and innocent women and children. This new image dominated the Somalia emergency from late 1992 to the end of 1993, albeit becoming gradually more tarnished over time. It helped to make the case for military intervention and for the UN military operations which followed in June 1993. As Tom Farer (the former legal consultant to the United Nations Operation in Somalia) has pointed out, this portrayal of events reached its most extreme form in the demonisation of General Aideed (militarily the most powerful of the rival Somali warlords) in the second half of 1993 (Farer, 1993). As events unfolded, it will be seen how these different representations of the Somali crisis justified and underpinned action taken by the international community.

The year of missed opportunities: January – December 1991

After fierce fighting Siad Barre was eventually overthrown and defeated in January 1991, and on 29 January the United Somali Congress (USC) declared itself as an interim government under the presidency of Ali Mahdi Mohammed. UN staff in Somalia had been evacuated during the fighting and were still based in Nairobi, on the grounds that insecurity did not allow for UN operations. On 4 February SCF began a relief programme in Mogadishu with material support from UNICEF and by 15 February had set up five emergency feeding centres in the city.[1] By this time there was still no evidence of any return of UN staff to Mogadishu and no plans developed for UN involvement. On 18 February SCF issued the first of many press releases which called for UN involvement during 1991. This was followed up on 22 February by a letter to the *Independent* newspaper calling for the UN to re-establish operations in Somalia as a matter of urgency. The press release stated that 're-establishing a UN presence is a vital step in ensuring that communities have a chance to rebuild normal life … a large scale relief operation under UN auspices is urgently needed to avert the threat of an open famine which faces the city [Mogadishu]' (Save the Children, 1991).

Throughout February and March, SCF staff in Somalia noted that several national and regional structures remained intact and that ministries were still functioning to some degree in the face of sporadic violence. They believed that 'opportunities for re-engagement [with these structures] still exist' and that international aid could be channelled through them in an effort to rebuild the economy, health and education services. In March the UN sent a reconnaissance team to Mogadishu but still no UN return was planned. In April and May, the UNDP Resident Representative for Somalia made two one-day visits to Mogadishu but did not meet with NGOs working in the city and beyond. Similarly in May, the WHO representative visited Mogadishu for a mere two hours. Meanwhile, malnutrition levels worsened and in April and May SCF increased the number of its feeding centres to twelve. But still there was no UN presence and no obvious plan. Finally, in August — some seven months after the first calls for its reinvolvement — the UN returned to Somalia and posted UNICEF and WFP staff to Mogadishu on fortnightly rotations from Nairobi. However, fierce fighting between Aideed and Ali Mahdi in September caused the UN to evacuate again, this time until December. SCF also evacuated some of its staff in August but for seven days only, and in September it expanded its emergency feeding programme still further to sixteen centres in an attempt to meet increasing food needs.

The last quarter of 1991 saw an increase in fighting matched by a serious shortage of food stocks in Mogadishu. The 7000 metric tonnes of food which arrived in Mogadishu in September were blockaded in the port. In

November SCF noted 'evidence of great social distress with a resultant increase in looting and outbreaks of fighting'. SCF staff in Somalia also noted that this period 'signified the end of nascent structures, and Mogadishu became factionalised on a clan basis'. The opportunities identified in February to re-engage with the vestiges of Somali services and infrastructure had passed. In November the United States joined the calls for the UN to return to Somalia. Andrew Natsios, head of the Office of Foreign Disaster Assistance (OFDA), and the US congressional hearings on Somalia (at which SCF representatives repeated their fears of an 'open famine') both called for the UN to return. On 24 December, UNICEF staff returned to Mogadishu, but did not communicate with NGOs there for ten days. But in many ways it was now too late. In early 1992 SCF's Director for Africa, Mark Bowden, lamented the absence of UN efforts in Somalia and criticised the 'unwillingness of the international community to engage in a systematic manner to try and restore government and to try and create [service provision] structures. That is the opportunity which has been missed' (Bowden, 1992).

By the end of 1991, SCF was particularly disturbed by the attitude of the international community and the UN to the new self-proclaimed Republic of Somaliland. Unable to recognise Somaliland without international consensus on the issue, the UN was in a difficult diplomatic bind. UN agencies on the ground, however, made matters worse by not appreciating the potential of the north's administrative organisations, many of which were still intact. The UN appeared reluctant to work with these organisations and to support Somaliland's leaders and its governing structures. Politically bound to a single policy for 'greater Somalia', UN agencies were constrained from pursuing a twin-track humanitarian approach which might have allowed them to respond separately to the existing but under-resourced regional structures in the north. In a press release in January 1992, SCF observed that 'the reluctance of the international community to work with local structures [in Somaliland] is counter-productive and a major obstacle to recovery. Whatever the political outcome, Somaliland needs local authorities which can provide services to children and communities' (Save the Children, 1992a). In SCF's view, the refusal of the UN to engage with local health, educational, and law and order services in Somaliland put a major brake on rehabilitation and reconstruction in there throughout the period 1991–3 (Gilkes, 1993). With security and political stability so much better in Somaliland than in the south, this was especially frustrating and an even greater opportunity was wasted.

Ceasefires, airlifts and plans: January – December 1992

The second major phase of the Somali emergency can be seen to have lasted from January to December 1992. It was initially dominated by intense UN political activity under the auspices of Under-Secretary-General James Jonah, who set out to negotiate a cease-fire in Mogadishu between the two main warlords, Generals Aideed and Ali Mahdi. Jonah's first mission began on 16 January, during which he made clear that the provision of UN humanitarian aid would be conditional on a cease-fire.

While the UN continued to suspend humanitarian assistance pending a cease-fire, SCF went on distributing food and began to develop a mother and child health programme (MCH) in Mogadishu. ICRC also began to move food into Merca during January. As NGOs continued to expand their work, SCF found the UN's lack of response and the conditions laid down for its involvement hard to understand. An SCF press release on 27 January described the UN as 'disastrously ill-prepared' and expressed its 'dismay at the continuing failure of the UN agencies to adopt appropriate measures to aid both [Somali] territories' (Save the Children, 1992a).

On 2 February, still with no cease-fire, the UN nominated Bassiouni as its representative to Somalia and later that month UNICEF began to plan a feeding and health programme. Fighting continued and a total of 7000 metric tonnes of wheat flour and dried skimmed milk was looted during February. In March Jonah achieved a cease-fire in Mogadishu and in April (four months after the first cease-fire negotiations began) UNICEF became operational with a feeding programme and the distribution of tents. In March SCF had carried out an assessment of conditions in Belet Weyne and expanded its feeding and MCH operations into the area in May.

On 24 April, UN Security Council Resolution 751 established a United Nations Operation in Somalia (UNOSOM). It appointed Ambassador Sahnoun as the Secretary-General's Special Representative (SGSR) in Somalia and ordered the deployment of a UN security force to observe the cease-fire along the 'green line' between Mogadishu north and south. Sahnoun arrived in Mogadishu on 4 May and began to coordinate the UN agencies and to establish excellent contacts with a broad range of Somali factions and communities. The first 2000 metric tonnes of UN food aid since the cease-fire arrived, and Sahnoun drew up a relief plan for Somalia which divided the country (including the north west) into four distinct zones for the distribution of food aid. Finally, in May and June with the cease-fire holding in the main, UN operations seemed set to increase.

Between 10 and 12 August a UN inter-agency mission, including James Grant (Director of UNICEF) and Jan Eliasson (Under-Secretary-General for Humanitarian Affairs and head of the UN's new Department of Humanitarian Affairs) also visited Somalia 'to determine ways to accelerate the relief effort' (United Nations, 1992a). Towards the end of August the UN Security Council approved Sahnoun's relief plan, and accepted the logistical support of the US air force to airlift food into the four zones from neighbouring Kenya. The airlift got under way on 28 August and continued to move food into Somalia for the next six months up to 28 February 1993. Following the inter-agency mission, and with the assistance of NGOs operational in Somalia, the UN worked throughout September on the preparation of a '100 Day Action Programme for Somalia'. The paper was finally presented to donors in Geneva on 12–13 October. However, in November (almost two years after the beginning of the Somali emergency) NGOs were still undertaking 80–90 per cent of all relief and rehabilitation work in the country (Save the Children, 1992b).

Progress on the deployment of UN observers, however, was beset by 'tortuous negotiations' with Aideed and Mahdi (Drysdale, 1994, 39–53). In July, Sahnoun eventually obtained their agreement for the team of fifty UN observers to monitor the Mogadishu cease-fire. On 12 August, Sahnoun and the various Somali factions agreed to the deployment of 500 Pakistani soldiers as UN 'security personnel' responsible for escorting humanitarian supplies at the port and airport in Mogadishu but no further. The Pakistani Battalion (PakBat) began to arrive in August, and in strength on 14 September.

UN failure to respond

UN performance in Somalia during 1991 and 1992 raises several important issues: its lack of response to early warning; its severe problems in engaging with Somali society and the vestiges of state structures; its extreme reluctance to operate in conditions of insecurity; the tendency of UN political negotiations to stall UN humanitarian assistance initiatives; and its obvious lack of sufficient social and political analysis.

In a written submission requested by the British Parliament in November 1992, SCF observed that 'although it must be acknowledged that there are increasing demands being made on the UN, the lack of urgency in responding to the Somalia situation is difficult to understand in view of warnings from other agencies and the UN's own early warning systems' (Save the Children, 1992b). As has been seen, throughout 1991, NGOs like SCF, ICRC and MSF were restarting and expanding their programmes in Somalia and alerting the international community to initial opportunities and subsequent deteriorating conditions in the country.

Loud messages for assistance were also being sent within the UN system, most notably through UNICEF and through two UN Security Council Resolutions put forward by Cape Verde, in January and July 1992. The January resolution requested 'the Secretary-General immediately to undertake the necessary actions to increase humanitarian assistance of the United Nations and its specialised agencies to the affected population in all parts of Somalia, in liaison with the other international humanitarian organisations and to this end appoint a coordinator to oversee the effective delivery of this assistance'.

Despite all these warnings, however, the UN humanitarian response throughout 1991 and the early part of 1992 remained one of extreme hesitation, inactivity and withdrawal. Subsequently, in October 1992, Ambassador Sahnoun, who had been very effective in his role as Special Representative of the Secretary-General, was forced to resign when he was thought to have become over-critical of the UN's inadequate response. The UN's failure to get involved in humanitarian assistance not only meant that no major attempt was made to meet Somali needs during 1991 and early 1992, but also that the UN and its logo were discredited in Somali eyes by the time the UN did become very deeply involved in 1993.

It is apparent from the above analysis that the UN's main operational dilemmas in Somalia centred on questions of partnership and insecurity. What was the appropriate institution or structure for the UN to work with in Somalia in the absence of a strong and recognised central government? What level of risk to its staff and supplies could the UN accept if it resumed operations in Somalia?

In search of legitimate partners

The UN's failure to engage with nascent government structures and non-governmental organisations in Somalia during this period reflected a problem of mandate. As an organisation of states, the UN is mandated to relate to state authorities and respect national sovereignty. This essentially state-centric mandate also dictates the operations of the UN's Specialised Agencies. Political uncertainty over the international legitimacy of the initial USC government in the south and the self-proclaimed Republic of Somaliland in the north west meant that UN agencies were unsure about whom they could work with and relate to in Somalia. While there were many calls for UN involvement by NGOs and Somalis, the UN could find no internationally recognised party offering it official cooperation. Instead UN representatives were caught between the competing claims of the two main rival Somali factions.

In this dilemma over governmental legitimacy, UN officials experienced an extreme crisis of protocol, and one that was at first to paralyse and then limit their operational options. In both Somalia and Somaliland it meant that UN agencies were forced to bypass vestigial or nascent government structures and prioritise international NGO partners. With an apparent lack of long-term partners the UN also confined its humanitarian assistance to relief interventions rather than longer-term rehabilitation or development aid, as would have been more appropriate during 1991.

Is it safe?

Even more pressing to UN officials on a daily basis than the question of government legitimacy and partnership was the question of security. Persistent insecurity was more routinely given as the reason behind the continued UN evacuation to Nairobi in 1991 and early 1992. The UN's security guidelines in Somalia seem to have been excessively restrictive and consistently prevented UN operations from getting under way. The situation for all humanitarian organisations was indeed extremely dangerous. The Somali Red Cross, the ICRC, UNICEF and other NGOs all had Somali and international staff who were killed and injured. However, most NGOs took the view that humanitarian operations were still possible and could be negotiated and managed on the ground. Most NGOs developed security strategies and guidelines which facilitated their work. Generally, these involved the use of armed guards and intensive information-gathering. The UN made little attempt to develop and experiment with similar strategies. Instead, evacuation seemed to be their only protection strategy. The fact that the period of UN evacuation was so long compared with other agencies suggests that UN security guidelines need to be modified to allow for more flexibility in acute emergencies. Of all the UN agencies, only UNICEF consistently showed a commitment to being more flexible over security issues and sought a middle way between guaranteed safety and outright evacuation. Its secondment of staff to SCF was one example of this and an imaginative attempt to circumvent the extremes of UN security policy.

UN political initiatives take precedence

Another feature of the UN's response in Somalia during early 1992 was the priority given to its political peacemaking efforts, at the expense of humanitarian operations. Cease-fire initiatives dominated UN efforts during the first half of 1992, and UN humanitarian assistance was made conditional on a peaceful resolution to the battle for Mogadishu. The fact that UN humanitarian assistance was subordinate to UN peacemaking negotiations rather than run in parallel meant still further delay in the mobilisation of UN humanitarian operations.

The UN Secretary-General's *Agenda For Peace* (Boutros Boutros-Ghali, 1992) makes it clear that political and humanitarian action must be linked, but in Somalia the linkage was simply one of conditionality. There was no attempt to develop and articulate a more sophisticated overall UN strategy which combined political and humanitarian initiatives. It could be argued that the war in Somalia did require a tough conditional linkage to be made between the two. Such a view, however, simplifies the Somali situation. It fails to distinguish between the need to broker the political goals of the Somali warlords on the one hand, and the need to cater to the wider humanitarian needs of the Somali people and the reconstruction of Somali society on the other. As SCF observed in January 1993, the lack of an integrated political and humanitarian strategy 'meant that no strategic decisions concerning a relief effort could be made ... Somalia presented problems that required a combined approach and creative thinking' (Penrose and Timpson, 1993).

Ill-informed and ill-prepared

For the great part of 1991 and the early part of 1992, the UN had no consistent presence in Somalia. Instead it was monitoring the situation from Nairobi and by occasional flying visits. Throughout this period events in Somalia were moving fast and the situation was extremely complex. Two things were needed to survive and succeed as a humanitarian agency in Somalia at the time: good information and good contacts. The UN had neither. This meant that UN agencies were in no position to gauge the current situation and make effective judgements on how and when to resume operations. It also meant that when they did resume operations they were a long way behind in their local knowledge — the new kid on the block, lacking the hard-earned wisdom and credibility of the street.

The UN's lack of information and contacts meant that its analytical capacity in Somalia was extremely weak when it attempted to renew activities in 1992. This seriously compromised its ability to plan appropriate humanitarian assistance programmes. While NGOs were undertaking detailed surveys, accumulating important local knowledge and learning from experience during 1991, the UN was isolated and uninformed. The two UN Action Plans, which SCF described as 'little more than lists of projects with price tags' (Save the Children, 1992b, 8), gave little evidence of how the UN intended to implement these plans and served mainly to show how totally under-resourced UN agencies currently were. Any UN humanitarian operations would have to start from scratch and would take several months to mobilise effectively.

Military intervention and UNITAF: 3 December 1992 – April 1993

The third phase of the Somali emergency was signalled by UN Security Council Resolution 794 on 3 December 1992. The Security Council accepted an offer of US forces and acted under Chapter VII of the UN Charter to authorise the Secretary-General and cooperating member states to 'use all necessary means to establish as soon as possible a secure environment for humanitarian relief operations in Somalia' (United Nations, 1992b). The US-led 'Operation Restore Hope' was launched immediately and expectations among Somalis and in the international community were generally high. On 9 December the first US marines came ashore in Mogadishu, their timing coinciding with prime-time TV in the United States and their landing taking place under the arc-lights of the international TV media. The first French forces also arrived on 9 December and the combined UN force implementing Operation Restore Hope became the United Nations Task Force (UNITAF).

During December 1992 and January 1993 UNITAF forces fanned out beyond Mogadishu but their deployment, which was concentrated on major cities, relief centres and road routes, was largely confined to the south. UNITAF control omitted regions north of the line beyond Mogadishu, Jalalaqsi and Belet Weyne, and also steered clear of the Kenyan border area. Deployment of UNITAF forces beyond Mogadishu was slower than expected by Somalis and international NGOs as transport and communications support took time to establish. UNITAF forces were deployed to Baidoa (16 December), Kismayo (20 December), Bardhere (23 December), Hoddur (25 December), Jalalaqsi (27 December), Belet Weyne (28 December), and Merka (31 December). On 31 December US President Bush visited US forces in Somalia. From January to April, individual UN member states' military contingents began to take responsibility for general security and relief protection in particular zones. The Australians took over in Baidoa, the Canadians in Belet Weyne, the Belgians in Kismayo, the Botswanans in Bardhere, and the Pakistanis in Mogadishu and Merka. Later the Italians and Nigerians also took up positions in Mogadishu, and Germany provided logistical support forces to UNITAF. During this time UNITAF forces reached a total of 38,300 troops, but were only ever effectively in control of 40 per cent of the country (Visman, 1993, 21–2).

Disarmament

One major problem during UNITAF's initial deployment lay in the extent to which its mandate related to disarmament. In the first few days of UNITAF operations there was uncertainty about whether or not UNITAF forces should disarm Somalis as part of their role to ensure a 'secure environment'. It was decided that they should, but this met opposition from international NGOs which had been employing armed guards to protect their convoys and compounds, and would still need to do so in areas beyond and between UNITAF control. Exemptions were agreed on but over the next few months a series of colour-coded weapon permit systems made gun control extremely complicated for NGOs, as systems and regulations frequently changed and armed guards hired by NGOs repeatedly had their weapons confiscated, slowing down relief operations.

Improvements?

The period from December 1992 to April 1993 was characterised by a general improvement in nutritional status and overall security in Somalia. An SCF report noted that 'UNITAF forces did enable the major food deliverers to provide a much improved service'. In particular, UNITAF's effectiveness in securing the main ports and airports, and providing convoy security to regional centres, was considerable. UNITAF's provision of safe storage for the cash supplies of international NGOs was also an important contribution in the wake of recent lootings (Visman, 1993, 34–6). While conflict decreased around aid convoys, however, violence began to flare up in areas beyond UNITAF control throughout January, February and March. During this period targets changed and attacks were no longer focused on food convoys, but aimed at higher-value items like vehicles and cash. UNICEF, ICRC and MSF Holland premises were all attacked and robbed in early 1993, and the number of expatriate relief worker deaths in January and February 1993 was more than those in the whole of 1992. These attacks were often linked to personnel and employment disputes within aid agencies, and to an increasing Somali resentment of UNITAF operations (Visman, 1993, 24 and 35).

The UNITAF force was initially welcomed with some enthusiasm by many Somalis. This was due in part to the fact that it was perceived as a US and not a UN force. But both the purpose and the conduct of the UNITAF operation raise serious policy questions about the justification, practicalities and advantages of military humanitarian intervention.

Mixed motives and bad timing

The timing and motives behind the UNITAF operation are open to a variety of interpretations. De Waal has shown how the US aid agencies led by CARE and INTERACTION, together with the US media, mobilised US public opinion on intervention in Somalia during the last days of the Bush presidency (De Waal, 1994). He suggests that the mobilisation of public opinion coincided with the desire of certain policy-makers in the UN and the international community to engage in military-led humanitarian intervention as a possible precedent for similar complex emergencies. To many of them, Somalia seemed 'do-able'. It can also be argued that US intervention in Somalia was a political opportunity for President Bush to go out on a high, and perhaps to leave his successor a difficult and diverting foreign policy legacy.

The main humanitarian arguments given for intervention were continued starvation and the high levels of looting of relief supplies. Some press stories quoted pilferage rates of up to 80 per cent. A similar figure of 'between 70-80 per cent' of food losses was officially reported to a UN Security Council meeting on 25 November 1992 by the UN Special Envoy in Somalia. However, these extreme estimates of levels of looting and of the severity of the famine at this stage were challenged by other agencies. It was argued that protection and extortion rackets did account for regular losses but not as high as 80 per cent, and not much greater in fact than in comparable African food emergencies (African Rights, 1993, 2–4). Most agencies were suffering significantly lower losses and were witnessing an upturn in nutritional status as the famine passed its peak towards the end of 1992 (De Waal, 1994). A strong view exists among some agencies, therefore, that the humanitarian reasons for intervention were exaggerated, and that although UNITAF improved the passage of relief supplies, they did so only after the worst had already passed. A 1993 ICRC bulletin is a good example of this view:

> Following the arrival of UNITAF in December 1992 the security situation for moving food supplies within Somalia improved, which in turn helped accelerate an already visible general improvement in the nutritional status of the most vulnerable groups of the population. (ICRC, 1993)

Like several other NGOs in 1993, ICRC felt that UNITAF had caught an already changing tide in famine conditions, rather than having been responsible for turning that tide. As an exercise in famine prevention, therefore, UNITAF was definitely late. As an attempt to ameliorate existing famine conditions it was largely late as well.

This dissonance between humanitarian timing and political timing raises important questions about the policy-making behind the Somalia operation and the success of any future military-led interventions. If improved timing is considered to be one of the main advantages of a rapid military-led humanitarian intervention, then this advantage was not borne out in the Somalia operation. International humanitarian operations are consistently late, and in this respect the UNITAF intervention was no exception. The evidence suggests that like other international humanitarian operations, military-led humanitarian interventions will also be determined largely by public opinion and political will rather than humanitarian timing and acuteness of need. There is no evidence from the Somalia experience to suggest that in military-led intervention the international community has found a new and more timely way of responding to humanitarian emergencies. On the contrary, while military intervention may offer a new approach with certain advantages for providing a 'secure environment', its timing is still dependent on the same old process of political arbitrage which determines and selects the international priority given to particular emergencies at particular times irrespective of actual need. So long as this system of international humanitarian decision-making continues to prevail, most emergencies are likely to receive a late response. No matter how fast and effective military intervention can be, it will never be fast enough if it is already too late when it sets off.

UNOSOM II and the operation against Aideed: April 1993 – December 1993

On 26 March the UN Security Council passed Resolution 814 which authorised a new UN force of 28,000 troops to take over from UNITAF. This new operation took the name of previous UN operations in Somalia and became UNOSOM II under a new SGSR, the US Admiral Jonathan Howe, with Lieutenant-General Bir of Turkey in command of UNOSOM forces. UNOSOM II assumed control from UNITAF on 4 May 1993 with an initial six-month commitment until 31 October and a budget of US $437,022,000 (United Nations, 1993a). But with a smaller force — which by 28 May had still only reached 19,134 troops — UNOSOM II was given an expanded and more complex task (Visman, 1993, 40). Resolution 794 had committed UNITAF to establishing 'a secure environment for humanitarian relief operations'. Under Resolution 814, UNOSOM II was intended to 'assume responsibility for the consolidation, expansion and maintenance of a secure environment *throughout Somalia*'; emphasis added (United Nations, 1993b, para. 14). The resolution also included a policing or peace enforcement role, insisting that 'all Somali parties ... desist from all breaches of international humanitarian law and reaffirming that those responsible for such acts be held individually accountable' (United Nations 1993b, para. 13). In this mandate lay the seeds of a more complex and potentially confrontational task.

Throughout May, resentment at the continuing lack of Somali involvement in UNOSOM's policy-and decision-making continued to grow. Anti-UN demonstrations increased and UNOSOM II was also militarily tested almost immediately when 100 armed SPM-Jess supporters entered Kismayo on 7 May and engaged UNOSOM Belgian troops and the forces of Jess's rival General Morgan. Some sixty Somalis were estimated to have been killed and a further 100 injured in the battle. On 17 May, Admiral Howe made clear UNOSOM's position on such attacks in accordance with its mandate in Resolution 814: 'UNOSOM II will not be content with simply repelling such attacks on the people of Somalia or on UNOSOM forces ... we will pursue and bring to justice not only those who violate the ceasefire, but also those who order them to do so' (UNOSOM, 1993).

Also during May, UNOSOM II set about developing the organisational structure with which to carry out the various aspects of its mandate. Seven main departments reported to the SGSR: force command (known as 'UNOSOM Military'); political affairs ('UNOSOM Political'); humanitarian relief and rehabilitation ('UNOSOM Humanitarian'); a justice section coordinating civil police offices; UN agencies; administration and logistics; and public affairs. In the middle of May, UNOSOM Humanitarian produced a Mission Statement which identified five priority areas: continuing emergency relief operations; resettlement of the displaced; resuscitation of commerce and trade; reinvigoration of the productive sector; and rejuvenation of social services (cited in Visman, 1993, 42). UNOSOM Humanitarian asked the World Bank to take the lead in developing a medium-term economic plan with UNDP, but the relatively low level of pledges after consultations at a donor meeting in Paris in May meant that UNOSOM Humanitarian remained in perpetual financial crisis for the rest of 1993. On 21 July Jan Eliasson, the UN's Under-Secretary-General for Humanitarian Affairs noted that 'only US$1 was being spent on humanitarian assistance for every $US10 spent on the military peace-enforcement operation and that the US$166 million requested by the UN for humanitarian operations in Somalia remains underfunded' (cited in Bradbury, 1993).

5 June

The events of 5 June marked a major turning point in the Somali emergency. Twenty-three UNOSOM II troops from the Pakistani Battalion (PakBat) were ambushed and killed in Mogadishu and a further nine were taken hostage while inspecting premises of USC/SNA Aideed weapon cantonment sites.[2] On 6 June the Security Council made a swift response to the killings in Resolution 837, which called for investigation into those responsible. In the next few days UNOSOM recommended the 'relocation' of all non-essential expatriate humanitarian staff to Nairobi in anticipation of large-scale retaliatory action by UNOSOM Military and the likelihood of heavy collateral damage. Any humanitarian personnel remaining in Mogadishu were 'centralised' in particular locations. The evacuations took place and most international NGOs temporarily moved to Nairobi where they issued a joint statement warning against the long-term implications of UNOSOM military retaliation. All NGOs agreed that such action was misguided.

SCF's main concerns at this time were twofold: first that an escalation of the conflict would make continuing humanitarian relief and reconstruction work impossible; second, that by entering the conflict in this way the UN would become like one of Somalia's factions and lose its neutrality and credibility. In a statement on 8 June, SCF declared:

There has been a call for rapid military reprisals from the UN Security Council. To do this would be to entirely misjudge the current situation in Mogadishu and the mood of ordinary Somalis. This would lead to a rapid escalation of violence. There must be further opportunity for the intensification of diplomatic, political and peaceful initiatives. Open and honest dialogue would reassure Somalis that the UN intention is to work for a permanent solution. (Save the Children, 1993)

Two days later on 10 June in an open letter to the British Foreign Secretary, Douglas Hurd, published in the *Independent* newspaper, SCF's Director-General, Nicholas Hinton, urged that:

military action will have a destructive effect on the perceived neutrality of the UN [and] is likely to polarise further the current situation in which the UN is increasingly seen as an occupying force rather than a guarantor of the security and future well-being of ordinary Somalis ... The myriad of longterm problems of Somalia require exhaustive diplomacy, an understanding of the Somali context and above all a willingness to work alongside Somalis.

Hinton continued that any military response threatened 'to destroy the neutrality of international humanitarian assistance' at a time 'when with the Somali people, SCF and others are making substantial progress in the long haul to put basic services and infrastructure back together again' (Hinton, 1993).

UNOSOM's military response began in the early hours of 12 June with heavy bombardment of 'key' USC-Aideed premises. For the next five months there was a series of attacks or engagements between UN forces and Somali factions, most notably those of General Aideed whose arrest and detention were made a priority by Admiral Howe. In effect, the UN found itself fighting a counter-insurgency war in Somalia, killing and injuring hundreds of Somalis and losing UN troops from its multinational force. On 30 August UNDP and NGO (Oxfam and AICF) premises suffered collateral damage from UNOSOM forces. One of the worst incidents occurred on 3 October when US UNOSOM forces injured an estimated 700 Somalis during a 'sweep' in Bakara market. On 8 October the US government authorised deployment of a further 5000 US troops under direct US command.

Humanitarian repercussions

Throughout this five-month period UNOSOM military operations did, as expected, have a significant impact on humanitarian programmes. Although most military activity was confined to the Mogadishu area, its impact affected relief and development operations in the rest of the country in a number of ways during the second half of 1993. First, as Mogadishu was a 'logistical hub' for many humanitarian operations, the disruption there presented major difficulties to NGOs attempting to service or initiate programmes outside the capital. Secondly, as increasing numbers of UNOSOM troops and resources were required for military operations in Mogadishu, fewer were available for normal convoy duties in the central regions or in the Kenya border area. Thirdly, humanitarian assistance programmes within Mogadishu itself were severely affected by the UN military retaliations. CARE's large-scale food distribution programme in Mogadishu was suspended for several weeks in June and faced constant disruption throughout July and August. Fourthly, the intense media focus on the fighting in Mogadishu acted as a deterrent to donor involvement and dissuaded them from funding longer-term rehabilitation programmes, so stalling Somalia's reconstruction process once again. Finally, in their determination to show a return to 'normalcy', UNOSOM senior staff were particularly keen that NGOs should step up visible and high-profile activities like food distribution, over and above less telegenic rehabilitation and development activities which they were now trying to prioritise. This concern continued to skew the humanitarian agenda away from long-term priorities.

UNOSOM II's interventionist style

UNOSOM II's operations raise serious issues about the style and extent of military humanitarian interventions. Security Council Resolution 814 gave UNSOM II a complicated and far-reaching mandate which enabled UNOSOM to enforce peace and assist in the rebuilding of a democratic state. UNOSOM's commanders and the UN Secretariat chose to make this role as explicit as possible. Instead of creating a secure environment within which the various Somali factions could come to terms and rebuild a national government, UNOSOM took the lead role in actively reconstituting a Somali body politic via a system of regional and district councils and by entering into military conflict with the most powerful faction.

Neutral force or UN faction?

Farer has identified this extremely activist interpretation of Resolution 814 as the main reason that the UN and various parts of Somali society ended up on an inevitable collision course. He argues that by giving the UN operation 'the central role in guiding the evolution of Somali politics', the UN leadership

> chose to make [UNSOM II] the mentor and disciplinarian, the main creative force. They chose an active tutelary role, one in which they would

hand out black and white hats respectively to favoured and disfavoured Somali politicians. Thus they made the UN a player rather than an honest broker in the country's unruly political life, and set the stage for confrontation (Farer, 1993, 11).

There is little doubt that UNOSOM II's extremely interventionist style gave rise to a strong feeling of exclusion amongst many Somalis who felt uninvolved in the rebuilding of their country. In policy terms, the experience of this approach proves that strong and unilateral UN political and military action is no substitute for the more intricate process of mediation. A UN presence which had set out to facilitate peacemaking amongst Somalis rather than enforce peace might have avoided the fierce confrontations of 1993 and their bitter legacy for UN–Somali relations.

Overriding the humanitarian agenda once again

If the bloody confrontations between the UN and Somalis during 1993 signalled a failure of UN political strategy, they also led once again to a derailment of humanitarian assistance strategies. The events of the latter part of 1993 proved for the third year in succession that the UN found it difficult to maintain a combined political and humanitarian strategy in Somalia. From 5 June onwards political and military strategies took precedence over humanitarian assistance programmes. It seemed to many NGOs that the latter were put to one side while UN military objectives were pursued, and UNOSOM II found no way to develop UN and NGO humanitarian assistance as a vital part of peacebuilding after the events of 5 June. Instead the partnership between UNOSOM political and military departments and UNOSOM Humanitarian became increasingly uneasy. Their lack of common purpose and cooperation came to a head in August 1993 when UNOSOM Humanitarian finally moved out of UNOSOM II headquarters in an effort physically to distance itself and disassociate its operations from UNOSOM II's political and military activities.

Lessons learned

UNOSOM Humanitarian's office move is powerfully symbolic of the difficulties UN humanitarian assistance programmes have in living alongside UN political and military operations. The need for a combined approach between the three UN roles in complex emergencies is one important lesson from Somalia. Another lies in the fact that military humanitarian interventions can no longer be assumed to be a panacea for humanitarian emergencies grounded in disputed sovereignty, warring factions and government breakdown. Because political timing rather than humanitarian timing still looks set to dictate such interventions, it also seems likely that military humanitarian interventions will frequently be late. In addition, the Somalia experience shows that the mandates of such interventions need careful consideration. Military intervention and peace enforcement are no substitute for political negotiation actively combined with timely and well planned humanitarian assistance. As UNOSOM II's activities have shown, a UN mandate which takes too active and authoritarian a role in reconstructing the body politic can disempower and frustrate the society in question, and exacerbate conflict.

These arguments were recognised by a commission of enquiry established by the Security Council in November 1993. According to a report in *The Times* (London, 31 March 1994), the three-man commission included the chief justice of Zambia, and two generals with experience of peacekeeping operations, from Ghana and Finland. In their report, which UN officials had attempted to keep confidential, the commissioners were strongly critical of UNOSOM II for exceeding its mandate by trying to impose a political settlement by force, and they argued that 'In peacekeeping ... enforcement action should be regarded as the last resort, after all peaceful means have been exhausted'. They added that 'There was no one to teach the basics of peacekeeping to UNOSOM HQ and contingents'; and concluded that the UN should abandon policies of 'peace enforcement'.

It is most important, however, that the lessons from the early part of the Somali crisis should not be eclipsed by studies of the more dramatic military interventions of 1992–3. The greatest lessons of all must emerge from the period of UN inactivity during 1991–2, an inactivity which can be said to have bordered on negligence. At a time when international NGOs and various Somali organisations were appealing for help and expanding their humanitarian assistance programmes, UN agencies were confined to Nairobi. The main questions to arise from the Somali emergency, and the ones which need to have the loudest echo around the headquarters and meeting rooms of UN policy-makers are, therefore: where were the UN agencies in 1991 and 1992 and why could they not find ways to engage effectively in a crisis of such magnitude? It is these questions which now need to exercise the policy-makers of the UN agencies and the member states who support them so as to ensure that the UN is never so absent again.

Notes

1 These details of dates and descriptions, and those that follow, are taken from SCF's 'Chronology of Events in Somalia', Annex 1 of its *Case Study on Somalia*, prepared by Angela Penrose and Andrew Timpson and presented to the Development Studies Association's Seminar on 'The United Nations and Humanitarian Assistance', Oxford, January 1993.

2 Cantonments are areas designed as storage sites for weapons. The idea was that factions would store all their heavy weapons in such sites, securing hardware that could be useful for a future Somali army, until such time as the establishment of an effective government could take place.

Bibliography

African Rights (1993), *Somalia Operation Restore Hope: A Preliminary Assessment,* London, African Rights.

Benthall, J. (1993), *Disasters, Relief and the Media,* London, I.B. Tauris (Chapter 5 includes detailed discussion of the media's predominant narrative format of disaster relief).

Boutros-Ghali, Boutros (1992), *An Agenda For Peace,* New York, United Nations.

Bowden, Mark (1992), '1991: the year of missed opportunities', *Report on a Meeting on Conflict and International Relief in Contemporary African Famines,* Save the Children and the London School of Hygiene and Tropical Medicine, March 1992.

Bradbury, Mark (1993), Summary of consultations with UK-based agencies on peacemaking in Somalia, Oxfam UK/Somalia, July 1993.

De Waal, A. (1994), 'Dangerous precedents: Somalia 1991-1993', in J. MacRae, and A. Zwy, (eds.), *War and Hunger: International Humanitarian Policy in Complex Emergencies,* London, Zed Books.

Drysdale, J. (1994), *Whatever Happened to Somalia? A Tale of Tragic Blunders,* London, Haan.

Farer, Tom (1993), 'United States Military Participation in United Nations Operations in Somalia: Roots of the Conflict with General Mohamed Farah Aideed and a Basis for Accommodation and Renewed Progress', Submission to the Committee on Armed Services of the House of Representatives, 14 October 1993.

Gilkes, P. (1993), *Two Wasted Years: The Republic of Somaliland 1991–1993,* Save the Children, London.

Hinton, N. (1993), Open letter to Douglas Hurd, British Foreign Secretary, *Independent,* 10 June 1993.

ICRC (1993), *Information Factsheet,* International Committee of the Red Cross, Geneva, September 1993.

Penrose, A. and Timpson, A. (1993), '*A Case Study on Somalia*', Save the Children presentation to the DSA Seminar on 'The United Nations and Humanitarian Assistance', Oxford, January 1993.

Samatar, S. (1991), *Somalia: A Nation in Turmoil,* London: Minority Rights Group.

Save the Children (1991), press release, London, dated 18 February 1991.

Save the Children (1992a), press release, London, dated 27 January 1992.

Save the Children (1992b), Submission by Save the Children to the House of Commons Foreign Affairs Select Committee, London, November 1992.

Save the Children (1993), press release, London, dated 8 June 1993.

United Nations (1992a), Introduction 100 Day Action Programme for Somalia, 6 October 1992.

United Nations (1992b), UN Security Council Resolution 794, 3 December 1992, para. 10.

United Nations (1993a), Security Council 3188th Meeting Summary, 26 March 1993, cited in E. Visman, 'Military humanitarian intervention in Somalia', Save the Children, London, December 1993, 38.

United Nations (1993b), UN Security Council Resolution 814, 26 March 1993.

UNOSOM (1993), Weekly Report on Regional Activities, 17 May 1993, cited in E. Visman, 'Military Humanitarian Intervention in Somalia', Save the Children, London, December 1993, 39.

Visman, E. (1993), 'Military Humanitarian Intervention in Somalia', Save the Children, London, December 1993.

5

Short-term interventions and long-term problems: the case of the Kurds in Iraq

David Keen

Introduction

This chapter looks at some of the medium- and longer-term problems that can arise in the wake of an essentially short-term humanitarian intervention.[1] It takes the establishment of a 'safe haven' in northern Iraq as a case-study and assesses the efficacy of attempts to protect and assist the Iraqi Kurds[2] in the wake of this intervention. The chapter examines some of the special problems that can arise when refugees are encouraged (and perhaps pressured) to return to countries where the existing government remains hostile to them. It looks at the effect of continued Iraqi government hostility on the welfare and safety of the Iraqi Kurds. And it suggests that international responses in the wake of the safe haven have tended artificially to separate the problems of providing aid and providing protection, without taking adequate account of the connections between these tasks.

The creation of the safe haven in northern Iraq was a bold and in many ways unprecedented challenge to national sovereignty. It was hailed as breaking new ground in humanitarian assistance. However, with the international spotlight shifting elsewhere, inadequate attention has been paid to *sustaining* protection and assistance for those in need. This issue is particularly important in the case of Iraqi Kurdistan, where returning refugees were given assurances of safety and where people remain vulnerable to an openly hostile government in Baghdad.

The position of the Iraqi Kurds has often been portrayed rather simplistically. An emphasis on relatively recent military events has tended to dominate public conceptions of the problem: the 'safe haven' is often seen simply as a military solution to a refugee problem arising from a sudden outbreak of violence against the Kurds on the part of Saddam Hussein's forces in 1991.

What is typically missing from this kind of account is any recognition of the important historical and economic dimensions of the Iraqi Kurdish problem. This shortcoming appears to have encouraged an inappropriate pattern of international protection and assistance in the wake of the Kurdish repatriation. Critically, Baghdad's strategy against the Kurds, notably since the mid-1970s, has been based not so much on random cruelty but on a long-term and in some sense rational strategy aimed at controlling the Kurds politically by undermining their economy. This has embraced the destruction of much of Kurdish agriculture and, since October 1991, a tight economic blockade on northern Iraq. Because the pattern of international aid since 1991 has tended to perpetuate the severe economic weakness in Iraqi Kurdistan created by the Baghdad government, the international community risks assisting Saddam Hussein in his strategy against the Iraqi Kurds.

Although the United Nations (and conventional wisdom in international aid policy) has urged that aid efforts should move away from a focus on emergency relief towards promoting self-sufficiency, it is precisely this self-sufficiency (at least in a collective sense) which a loose but powerful coalition of international interests seems anxious to avoid. Many Kurdish officials and ordinary people have expressed the view that there may be an international 'conspiracy' to keep Iraqi Kurdistan weak. The pattern of aid to the Iraqi Kurds since the safe haven was established (and in particular the serious neglect of economic rehabilitation) makes this view difficult to contradict.

Meanwhile, if the international community has to a large extent turned its back on the Iraqi Kurds, the recent neglect of the plight of the Turkish Kurds has been even more marked. Although the Kurds in Turkey are not the focus of this article, it should not be forgotten that the suffering of the Iraqi Kurds is part of a much wider Kurdish problem. Significantly, it appears to be deference to Turkey — whose pursuit of European Union membership should provide the opportunity for substantial leverage — which lies at the heart of many of the weaknesses in aid to Iraqi Kurds as well as underpinning international neglect of the Turkish Kurds.

A question of responsibility

If the international community has a humanitarian responsibility to the Iraqi Kurds, it also has responsibilities arising from a variety of historical contributions to the current problems faced by the Iraqi Kurds.

When modern-day Iraqi Kurdistan was incorporated into the new state of Iraq after the First World War, Kurdish nationalist aspirations — having been encouraged by the 1920 Treaty of Sèvres (signed by the allied powers and the government in Constantinople) — were largely abandoned. Bringing the Iraqi Kurds within the new British mandate of Iraq offered to bolster British access to oil that was abundant in Kurdish parts of Iraq, whilst at the same time appeasing Turkish fears of a Kurdish state. Kurdish dissent was violently suppressed, and when the British surrendered their mandate over Iraq in 1930, the British failed to ensure any written guarantees protecting Kurdish autonomy.

Kurdish nationalism was again encouraged by the West in the early 1970s when the United States, apparently reacting to Iraq's oil nationalisation programme and seeking to bolster its ally the Shah of Iran, supported Kurdish resistance against Baghdad, only to abandon the Kurds in 1975 when the Shah resolved his border dispute with Iraq. The Kurds were to pay a heavy price for this resistance in the form of widespread government retaliation and destruction of agriculture, with the first major wave of repression coming in 1974–5.

In the 1980s, with western governments increasingly emphasising the threat from Iran, the Iraqi government was given important assistance in building up its military strength — strength that was to be turned not only against Kuwait but also against the Kurds.

A range of evidence — including first-hand accounts from Iraqi Kurds[3] — suggests a powerful western responsibility for the Kurdish uprising in 1991. This uprising was precipitated by the war over Kuwait (which weakened Saddam Hussein's repressive machinery and increased prices), by UN sanctions against Iraq (which further boosted prices) and by western encouragement (for example, on the Voice of America radio station). When the uprising led to brutal retaliation by Saddam Hussein, western governments stood by.

Once the Iraqi Kurds fled to Iran and to the Turko-Iraqi border, the international community failed to ensure adequate protection and relief. In choosing to return to the interior of Iraq, the Iraqi Kurds were influenced by the inadequacy of relief and protection on the Turkey-Iraq border and in Iran, by the prospect of forcible ejection from the border areas by Turkey, by a vigorous allied military campaign to persuade them to return, and by guarantees of their safety made by the allies.[4]

All this imposes a clear obligation to ensure that Iraq is indeed safe for the Kurds. Within northern Iraq, the UN encouraged resettlement in areas that the government of Iraq (GOI) still considered to be 'forbidden' areas (largely because of its continuing attempts to isolate Kurdish resistance). These included, notably, the areas along the Turkish and Iranian borders. The heightened danger for those who have returned to these areas further underlines the responsibility to provide continued protection.

At the time of the safe-haven operation, western governments stressed that the Kurds would be able to return to their home areas, that allied protection would remain resolute, and that a continuing strong humanitarian effort would be a vital element in securing continued protection for the Kurds.

Despite humanitarian and historical responsibilities, and despite commitments made by western governments, protection and assistance have both been inadequate, as the following two sections make clear.

Inadequate protection

A major component in the increasing vulnerability of the Kurds has been the rebuilding of the Iraqi military. Compared with reports at various points in 1992 and 1993 of some 100,000 Iraqi government troops in position near the Kurdish-controlled zone, Kurdish forces numbered perhaps 30,000. By mid-1993, Iraq had rebuilt an estimated 80 per cent of its military manufacturing capacity.[5] In this, it will have been assisted by machine tools that were purchased from Matrix Churchill among others. No one seriously doubts the ability of Iraqi government forces to overpower Kurdish resistance in the absence of international protection.

The GOI's continuing aggressive intent towards the Kurds is most obviously manifest in the positioning of large numbers of Iraqi troops along the 'front-line' which separates Kurdish-controlled from GOI-controlled areas. Saddam Hussein has repeatedly flouted UN Security Council resolutions — by inhibiting weapons destruction and by engaging in renewed internal repression. Apart from blockading the north and sponsoring terrorism there, internal repression has taken the form of direct attacks on Kurdish and Shi'a populations. Some 300,000 Kurds were forced to flee their homes in or near government-held areas between October 1991 and January 1992 amid continued government shelling and Kurdish/GOI skirmishes. Torture has continued in Kirkuk.[6] Aid staff reported in December 1993 that the movement of families from the GOI-controlled Iraq was continuing, with Kurds being periodically forced out of Kirkuk and Mosul by the Baghdad government. Meanwhile, Saddam Hussein has branded the new Kurdish administration illegal and its ministers bandits. He has said foreigners want to turn the Kurdish area into 'a termite that will devour the whole of Iraq'.[7]

While it is true that the Kurds have been better protected than the Shi'ite Muslims (not least because GOI ground troops have not been able to move around the area of northern Iraq that is under the administrative control of the Kurds), protection for the Kurds remains fragile, and it has been significantly eroded over time. The fact that this has happened in stages has tended to mute public protest at any given moment. Four key flaws in international protection for the Kurds can be discerned.

First, the international community failed in 1991 to create conditions for a political settlement within Iraq that could provide genuine safeguards against renewed repression for those who were moved back into the interior of a hostile state. Western ground troops were pulled out of Iraq (and then out of south-east Turkey) before the Kurds had been able to use the presence of these forces to negotiate a favourable political settlement. This was despite a clear promise from the British government that western forces would not be pulled out before negotiations between the Kurds and the GOI came to an end. Kurdish intellectuals' suggestions that a domestic political settlement be backed by international guarantees were not taken up.

A second flaw in the system of protection has been the limited usefulness of the UN guards. The UN guards in northern Iraq were originally billed as a force that would protect returning Kurds, and indeed they were used to persuade Kurds to come down from the mountains bordering Turkey. However, the UN Guards Contingent in Iraq (UNGCI) has gone so far as to state clearly that it has no brief for protecting the Kurds. The UN guards in northern Iraq bear no resemblance to the kind of 'UN line' set up in Cyprus — a model favoured by some allied officers involved in setting up the safe haven.

The numbers of UN guards were never likely to be an adequate substitute for the more than 20,000 allied troops in Iraq: a figure of 'up to 500' was agreed. The number of UN guards deployed in Iraqi Kurdistan (and indeed in Iraq more generally) has often been far below the figure of 500. At one low point, in October 1992, there were only thirty UN guards in northern Iraq.

It is not clear that the UN guards possess the *means* to offer any real protection (other than their mere existence) to anybody. The fact that UN guards have been unable to protect themselves against terrorist attacks calls into question their ability to protect anyone else. The presence of UN guards in Kalar and Kifri (near to the 'front line' with GOI forces) did not prevent Iraqi forces from shelling these towns in late 1991; in fact, the lightly armed guards fled the area once the shelling began. UN guards (like personnel of the UN High Commission for Refugees [UNHCR]) have not been admitted to certain strategic areas such as Kirkuk, where — as noted -reports of GOI abuses have been persistent. If the guards were offering serious protection to the Kurds, this is where their presence would be most needed.

UN guards have provided only intermittent protection to relief convoys, although this is potentially their most useful function. While the United Nations undertook that the UN guards would protect non-governmental organisations (NGOs) linked with the UN humanitarian programme, this commitment has not been fulfilled. The inability of the UN guards to provide the protection claimed (and the need for greater international involvement in protecting aid workers and aid operations) has been highlighted by a number of terrorist attacks directed at aid agencies. Baghdad is known to have sponsored attacks on aid agencies, and in early 1993 one aid worker summarised some of the dangers agencies have faced:

Typical attacks include bombs placed on or under agency vehicles, grenades thrown into areas in which staff are congregated, rockets fired at agency buildings, agency vehicles being shot at with automatic weapons as they drive along the road and other such threats.

The third main weakness in the current system of protection centres on the inadequacy of current monitoring of human rights among the Iraqi Kurds. Before UNHCR phased out its operations in Iraqi Kurdistan in April 1992, the organisation (which had a specific brief for protecting the Kurds) was repeatedly refused permission by the GOI to set up an office in Kirkuk. UNHCR withdrew at a point when Kurds still faced profound insecurity. UNICEF — which took over as the main UN agency in the north — has no protection brief.

Western government officers at the Military Coordination Centre (MCC) in Zakho near the Turkish border have a responsibility for monitoring abuses against the Kurds. But they report that while they are able to drive around the western governorate of Dahuk, they are unable to proceed much beyond this. This leaves Kurds in Sulaimaniya and Erbil governorates inadequately covered, not to mention the Kurds in the GOI-controlled area of Kirkuk. MCC officials express the hope that other abuses will be 'covered' by UNICEF, the UN guards and NGOs. But the UN has been largely inactive in publicising abuses; indeed, its public statements (in relation to proposed aid operations) have often suggested that the GOI wishes to cooperate in aiding the Kurds. The UN guards — billed by the UN as the 'moral witnesses' of the international community and 'the eyes and ears of the United Nations'[8] — are not trained to monitor abuses. To a considerable extent, the monitoring of abuses in northern Iraq has depended on *ad hoc* reports from NGOs, whose continued presence is uncertain and who have varying degrees of dependence on the cooperation of the UN and Baghdad.

The fourth and most important weakness in the current system of protection is the fact that existing systems of military cover for the Iraqi Kurds provide only a precarious and ambiguous protection.

The number of ground forces positioned in Iraq or nearby to protect the Kurds has been scaled down from more than 20,000 during the creation of the safe haven to virtually zero.[9] In June 1991, European and US officials talked of positioning a 5000-strong force in Turkey to protect the Kurds once allied forces had withdrawn from Iraq. The figure was later reduced to 2500-3000. In September 1991, ground troops were withdrawn from Turkey altogether.

Strictly, allied prohibition of Iraqi ground troops applies only to the rather limited 'security zone' centred on Dahuk governorate in the north west of Iraqi Kurdistan. There have been many serious attacks carried out by the GOI against Kurds outside this zone in Erbil and Sulaimaniya governorates.

Five problems with the 'Operation Provide Comfort' (OPC) air protection based in south-east Turkey should be noted.

First, air cover may be an ineffective way of monitoring or correcting human rights abuses (including outright attack) on the ground. Hoshyar Zebari, a Kurdish spokesman, has noted: 'If Saddam is determined to send his troops in, it will be really very difficult for the allies to stop him just from the air. That is the nightmare that hangs over us.'[10] Saddam Hussein will be aware of the West's reluctance to commit ground troops to Iraq once more. This point has been emphasised by the continuing abuses of the Shi'ite Muslims despite the imposition of a 'no-fly zone' below the 32nd parallel.

Second, the geographical coverage of OPC patrols is limited. Whilst a no-fly zone prohibiting Iraqi aircraft has been imposed north of the 36th parallel latitude line (a zone patrolled by allied planes), large parts of Kurdish-controlled Iraq (including the city of Sulaimaniya) lie below the 36th parallel, and so are not covered by allied patrols. Substantial numbers of Kurds living outside Kurdish-controlled areas (for example, in the vicinity of Kirkuk) are also not covered by this 'no-fly zone'.

Third, allied willingness to use planes to respond to repression even above the 36th parallel is open to question. For one thing, it is likely to be limited by the need for Turkish consent for specific military actions under OPC. In January 1993, Turkey made it clear that OPC planes should strike only in self-defence.

Fourth, the OPC agreement has to be renewed by the Turkish government every six months, and the agreement is unpopular in Turkey. This creates a strong feeling of insecurity among the Kurds. It also provides encouragement to Saddam Hussein to maintain his pressure against the Kurdish-held areas and wait for the (eventual) withdrawal of allied protective cover.

A fifth weakness in the OPC air cover is that it does not protect the Iraqi Kurds from military incursions *by Turkey,* such as that initiated in October 1992 with a view to 'flushing out' PKK (Kurdish Workers' Party) guerrillas (Turkish Kurds) from their bases inside Iraqi Kurdistan. These attacks led to deaths and injuries among Iraqi Kurds.

Inadequate assistance

In addition to the flaws in the system of protection for the Iraqi Kurds, international aid directed at the Kurds has also been seriously inadequate. This has been particularly damaging in the context of a double economic blockade on Iraqi Kurdistan arising from UN sanctions and a tightening GOI embargo.

UN sanctions have prohibited exports as well as the import of goods

that are needed for rehabilitation. The sanctions have also boosted con-
sumer prices by causing a sharp devaluation of the dinar, the Iraqi currency.

The GOI blockade was imposed on the Kurdish-controlled zone following the withdrawal of GOI forces from towns and lowland areas of the
three northern governorates in late October 1991. This blockade — a clear
breach of UN Security Council Resolution 688 forbidding repression of the
Kurds and other Iraqis — has affected trade, government services, flows of
government rations, and payment of government salaries and welfare benefits. Its effects have been particularly severe because of the Kurds' previous heavy economic dependence on Baghdad and GOI-subsidised food.
This economic dependence in turn reflected Baghdad's twin policies of
destroying Kurdish productive activities (especially agriculture) and at the
same time providing significant state patronage and subsidies.

Among the government services that have been gravely disrupted in the
GOI blockade are veterinary services, agricultural inputs, education,
health, and water and sanitation. NGO staff report an increasing shortage
of drugs, especially for chronic conditions. There have been outbreaks of a
variety of preventable childhood diseases.

In the course of 1992, the GOI tightened its blockade, and supple-
mented it with a tightening *military* encirclement by reinforcing GOI
troops on the 'front line' with the Kurdish-controlled zone. A partial loos-
ening of the blockade from August 1993 has seen small amounts of fuel oil
moving from GOI-controlled Iraq to the north, where it is sold at a large
profit.

Outside the Kurdish-controlled zone, government rations have provided
considerable protection against inflation. Yet even the full Iraqi ration provides slightly less than half the energy intake of an average person prior to
the Gulf crisis. Assessing the period April–December 1993, the UN estimates that between only 7 and 10 per cent of GOI-subsidised food has
been reaching the Kurdish-controlled area.[11]

Under the influence of GOI and UN blockades, price rises in Kurdish-
controlled areas have been very steep. They have far outstripped moderate
rises in wages. Wheat prices rose by a factor of 405 between November
1990 and November 1993.[12] People's ability to buy fuel and food has been
severely eroded. Rural and (in particular) industrial production has also
been hampered by shortages of inputs.

Most observers agree that the main aim of the GOI blockade is to
weaken the Kurds as a prelude to the re-establishment — whether through
negotiation or through crude military force — of GOI control over the
northern parts of Iraq.

A further blow to the Kurdish economy came at the beginning of May
1993, when the Baghdad regime withdrew the 25 Iraqi dinar note from cir-
culation, wiping out an estimated US$ 20 million of Kurdish savings.[13]

Many Iraqi Kurds had been paid in these notes for crops that were sold in desperation to traders supplying the market in GOI-controlled Iraq.

Stymied by a stagnant economy and by a variety of trade restrictions, the new Kurdish administration has often been able to pay only token salaries. Even these salaries — which represent by far the greatest drain on the resources of the Kurdish administration — are now threatened by the administration's shortage of revenue. This revenue has been hit by the restrictions on the Turkish trade in particular.

A continuing drift of people to Turkey and Iran has been reported, apparently linked to economic hardship, and much of this hardship remains unrelieved by international aid.

The task of rebuilding the Kurdish economy has been largely neglected. The much promised shift from relief to rehabilitation has repeatedly proven elusive. Iraqi Kurds and international NGOs expected the United Nations Development Programme (UNDP) and the Food and Agriculture Organisation (FAO) to develop substantial programmes in agriculture and rural rehabilitation, and a joint undertaking to support agricultural rehabilitation was made by the UN and the GOI in November 1991. However, UNDP has so far had no involvement in the north, and the World Health Organisation and FAO have had very little. The potential for self-sufficiency in Iraqi Kurdistan's fertile lands remains unfulfilled, whilst the inability of the Kurdish administration to match GOI trader prices has encouraged the previously noted 'leakage' of Kurdish grain to the south. The exploitation of significant oil reserves within the Kurdish-controlled area, meanwhile, has been impeded by UN sanctions and international inaction.

While exploitation of Kurdish oil reserves might in theory be encouraged by UN Security Council Resolutions 706 and 712 (which require Iraq to sell oil to pay for humanitarian supplies), in practice these resolutions have tended to encourage underfunding of international assistance, with donors sometimes arguing that aid programmes should be funded by sales of Iraqi oil.

A key result of the international neglect of development and rehabilitation is that the Iraqi Kurds remain dependent on expensive (and generally belated) relief operations. The emergency shelter programme of the winter of 1991–2 was succeeded by an emergency food and fuel distribution in the winter of 1992–3 and by continued relief distributions in 1993.

The lack of developmental assistance has impeded a return by the Iraqi Kurds to the villages from which they were forcibly displaced (notably in 1987–8, but also in 1991 and in some cases in 1974–5). Many farmers have been unable to farm their lands because of poverty, mines, and lack of infrastructure. While most farmers *have* been able to farm (at least on a temporary basis), a great many still live in economically depressed 'collective towns', unable to return permanently to their villages. The collective towns were originally created by the GOI, which used forced urbanisation to increase its surveillance and control of potentially rebellious Kurds.

The lack of encouragement of productive activities like agriculture and industry has encouraged many Kurds to resort to activities likely to *detract* from production in the long term. Favoured economic strategies have included selling capital assets, smuggling and plundering the environment. A climate conducive to investment in farming and livestock has not been created. Meanwhile, the deteriorating physical infrastructure (including water and sanitation) has had a detrimental impact on health.

Even the international assistance that *has* been attempted has often fallen victim — and has been allowed to fall victim — to GOI obstruction and severe delays. The UN's continuing deference to the priorities of the GOI has been a particular obstacle to effective, independent aid operations that emphasise rehabilitation rather than relief.

The GOI has stated that it welcomes humanitarian aid and 'undertakes to support and co-operate in those endeavours'. In practice, the GOI has used many means to obstruct aid operations, as well as levying what is effectively a severe tax on international aid by insisting that international funding be exchanged at the official rate.

Diplomatic obstruction by the GOI included the GOI's refusal — between 30 June and 22 October 1992 — to sign a new 'Memorandum of Understanding' giving government sanction to UN operations (and to NGOs operating under the UN umbrella). This helped bring UN operations to a virtual standstill. Pressures on the GOI to make an agreement — including the threat of an independent aid operation with or without Baghdad's consent — did not become strong until October 1992.

Terrorist attacks directed against NGOs and the UN have helped deter NGOs from setting up or expanding their programmes. Repeated attacks on UN relief convoys that passed through GOI-controlled areas caused significant delays in the delivery of essential emergency relief in the winter of 1992–3. The UN had not secured GOI agreement that these convoys be accompanied by UN guards, and did not do so until six weeks after the first attack.

Other GOI tactics for obstructing aid have included harassment of UN guards and drivers, and blocking of visas and travel permits. GOI obstruction was assisted by the premature departure of UNHCR — before its protection mandate had been properly fulfilled — and the assumption of many of UNHCR's roles by UNICEF, which has tended to seek Baghdad's approval for its operations. The GOI obstructed UN vaccination drugs for the north in 1993.

In a number of other ways, the UN has designed aid operations on the basis of assumptions that seem to reflect administrative convenience (and deference to Baghdad) rather than an objective assessment of needs and how they can best be met.

In the UN's plan to meet the emergency needs of the Kurds for the 1992–3 winter, the UN based its appeals for assistance on the assumption that the GOI would provide substantial rations to Kurdish-controlled areas. This assumption turned out to be erroneous. Further, the UN assumed that 'targeting' assistance to a relatively small number in Iraqi Kurdistan would be possible, and acceptable to the Kurdish authorities — without properly considering how this targeting would be achieved in practice. Despite recognising the needs of 2.25 million people, the UN's emergency Winter Plan for 1992–3 proffered food and fuel for only 750,000. There was little indication of how this figure had been arrived at, of who the intended beneficiaries were, or of how they would be targeted. In the event, the UN came under political pressure to increase the number receiving relief and to take into account political pressures rather than simply need. A small amount of relief was spread very thinly.

In a context where funds for contingency stocks are scarce, the UN based provisions for a renewed mass displacement on the assumption that most of the Iraqi Kurds will head for Iran and Turkey and will not have to be provided for. This ignores the powerful political obstacles to emigration that were evident in 1991. The danger of renewed mass flight is an acute one, particularly now that so many Iraqi Kurds are openly associated with a dissident regime.

Significantly, the UN has tended to play down problems with its own operations. The UN has sometimes reported on its own operations in a way that conceals the shortcomings of the assistance. For example, the deadlines by which it was deemed essential that winter supplies reached the north in 1992–3 were repeatedly revised by the UN as agreement on the operation was stymied in Baghdad. In this way, humanitarian needs were brought into line with the inadequacies of the existing response. Despite severe delays in fuel deliveries from Turkey, the UN declared in March 1993 that it would meet its end-March 1993 'deadline' for delivery of supplies. It did not mention that the original deadline had been mid-October 1992.

In the period April–December 1993, the UN distributed food to what it called a 'monthly average of 300,000 beneficiaries'. This group was described as a 'reduced target group', some 40 per cent of the 750,000 the UN had previously planned to target. (Even this 750,000 'target group' was smaller than the figure originally planned: the envisaged total number of beneficiaries for Iraq as a whole had been reduced from over 2 million to 1.3 million due to what the UN acknowledged to be a lack of resources.)[14] Significantly, even the figure of 300,000 did not represent a single, particularly needy group who were targeted in distributions, for the World Food Programme actually made distributions to a new group of beneficiaries every few months. This practice of rotating the distributions proved more politically acceptable to the Kurdish authorities than targeting the poorest, but the UN failed to make clear that targeting was being severely watered down. Indeed, its use of the phrases 'target group' and 'monthly average of 300,000' tended actively to disguise the lack of effective targeting.

While support for the Kurdish enclave was relatively strong through the second half of 1991 and up until April 1992, shortcomings in international assistance became more marked thereafter. In 1993, there were major delays in the release of donor funding for rehabilitation work. NGO workers report that it was not until July 1993 that programme funding started to come through, meaning NGOs were hard pressed to implement programmes before the winter set in. Compared with an estimated need for US$467 million in the year from April 1993, less than 43 per cent of this had been pledged and/or made available by 10 December 1993.[15]

One aid worker reports: 'Much of what was provided arrived so late in the year that some government authorities openly speculated that there was a political conspiracy to minimise its impact.' The shortage of aid resources also appears to have encouraged government resentment of funds going to local and international NGOs.

Despite the fact that the main emergency attracting international attention occurred in 1991, the emphasis in international aid programmes has continued to be on relief work. According to a UN report on aid operations in the last nine months of 1993: 'There is a broad consensus amongst the UN agencies and NGOs in Iraq to the effect that the Programme has already entered a rehabilitation phase.' However, the report adds, somewhat contradictorily, 'If security (UN Guards Contingent in Iraq) costs are added, the expenditures incurred or committed during the last nine months included 60% for relief.'[16]

Patterns of UN assistance have continued to be strongly influenced by GOI obstruction, which particularly inhibits anything resembling promotion of 'self-sufficiency'. In addition, the UN's need to use official Iraqi exchange rates when spending money inside Iraq has tended to encourage expenditures made outside Iraq, which in turn has encouraged spending on relief supplies. A shortage of UN staff in Iraq has also discouraged spending on rehabilitation work within the country. Meanwhile, the potential for involvement of development banks (whether Kurdish or international) has been neglected.

Noting the weaknesses in rehabilitation efforts in particular, many among the Iraqi Kurds and in the aid world suspect that western governments are responding to Turkish fears that a self-sufficient and politically autonomous Kurdish enclave in Iraq will serve to encourage Kurdish nationalism in Turkey. Certainly, repressing Kurdish separatism within Turkey has become a pressing priority for the Turkish government. British sensitivity to Turkish concerns about a possible 'Kurdish National Home' is evident in British government papers as far back as 1925. This sensitivity lay at the root of a shift in British policy through the 1920s, with the British government turning away from a League of Nations stipulation (made at the time of the incorporation of Kurdish areas into the British mandate of Iraq after the First World War) that steps should be taken to bolster Kurdish autonomy within Iraq.[17]

Connections between protection and assistance

The connections between the twin tasks of protecting and assisting the Kurds have often gone unnoticed. However, many Kurdish officials and international aid staff stress that there can be no lasting protection without adequate assistance, and there can be no adequate assistance and development without proper protection.

Improved support for rehabilitation in Iraqi Kurdistan, and for the new Kurdish administration, appears to be essential if even the minimum promises made by the UN and Western governments — of security, 'autonomy', and a 'safe-haven' — are to be met. Without these forms of support, the Kurds face prolonged economic deprivation and their new, democratic administration faces bankruptcy. Without proper international aid, a major danger is that the Iraqi Kurds will be forced, eventually, to make a political settlement with Baghdad from a position of weakness. This would make it very difficult to carve out safeguards against future abuses.

The GOI has a long-standing strategy of controlling the Kurds politically by undermining their economy, while at the same time holding out the prospect of state patronage for those who cooperate. The massive destruction of agriculture in the GOI's *Anfal*[18] campaign in 1987–8 was part of this strategy, as is the GOI's economic blockade on the north and the GOI's obstruction of international aid. Correspondingly, the Kurds' ability to retain some degree of autonomy from Baghdad — and some degree of protection from Saddam's genocidal policies — depends on international support for the economy which the GOI has been trying to undermine.

While most Kurds remain resolutely opposed to Saddam Hussein, Baghdad has long exploited divisions *among* the Kurds, and certain Kurdish tribal leaders have retained long-standing ties with Baghdad that have in the past brought them significant economic benefits and a degree of immunity from violence. Many actively participated in the repression of fellow Kurds. In the absence of a healthy economy and a strong administration, the GOI will be in a good position to promote, and profit from, these divisions. Other divisions that stand to deepen with worsening deprivation are those between rival Kurdish parties, between the central administration and tribal leaders, between residents and the displaced and even between officials and non-officials. In view of the danger of divisions and in view of a frequent (and understandable) reluctance on the part of Iraqi

Kurds to acknowledge such divisions, it may be worth devoting the rest of this section to a discussion of some of the potential fissures in Iraqi Kurdistan.

With much of the real power in Iraqi Kurdistan continuing to lie with the parties (and outside the parliament), deepening conflict between the parties poses real dangers. Rivalries, which have a long history, have sometimes even recently spilled over into violence. For example, 1993 saw fighting between members of the Iraqi Communist Party and members of the Patriotic Union of Kurdistan (PUK) in Dokan, Sulaimaniya governorate.

Evidence is emerging of growing economic disparities within Iraqi Kurdistan, and an increase in political tension that appears to mirror this increasing inequality. In addition to rapid inflation and the fact that large numbers of Iraqi Kurds remain unable to return to the villages and farmlands from which they were forcibly displaced by the Baghdad government, the level of unemployment is very high in Iraqi Kurdistan.

Returning to home villages has been inhibited not only by continuing insecurity but also by poverty and in some cases by the vested interests of Kurdish élites reluctant to relinquish land to which they gained access during the *Anfal*. In this context of growing inequalities, the profitability of many commercial enterprises and the relatively high (though still inadequate) salaries within the administration can be a cause of resentment. The Kurdish administration receives very little direct funding from the international community (and considerably less than Kurdish and international NGOs). As noted, the administration's chronic lack of resources means it has little left to spend on services after paying the salaries of officials. Some Kurdish critics have suggested that the Kurdish army (relatively well paid) could be usefully employed in work that will help displaced people return to their home areas and rehabilitate industry.

An additional source of tension is the fact that high prices in Iraqi Kurdistan have offered significant benefits for a relatively small group of traders, particularly those with good connections in Iran, Turkey and Baghdad-controlled Iraq. Also significant have been profits from property abandoned by Ba'athist officials after the uprising, with some of the *jash*[19] who cooperated with Baghdad benefiting in this way.

Some Iraqi Kurds have voiced resentment at what they see as the division of government jobs by the two main political parties, the PUK and Kurdistan Democratic Party (KDP). The presence of some former *jash* within the ranks of the main parties has been particularly galling for them. The widespread export of capital goods (like factory machines and machine tools) from Iraqi Kurdistan has also attracted criticism. State assets such as police cars have often been sold off for private profit. While the Kurdish administration has important achievements to its credit (for example, the unification of the party armies, or *peshmergas,* into a single Kurdish military force), its reputation can be gravely damaged by what

Duffield (in the context of his work on Sudan) has called the 'use of public office to further private gain'.[20]

With competition in petty trading and labouring increasingly intense, international aid staff report that the position of the displaced has been deteriorating.[21] However, the poorest groups within Iraqi Kurdistan have found little favour with the administration. Attempts by international organisations to target these groups have met with resistance from the Kurdish administration, with local officials often not regarding the displaced as part of their political constituency. Those displaced into urban areas, often working as petty traders, have been seen in some quarters as creating an 'undesirable atmosphere' and as contributing to rising prices. They have sometimes been subject to harassment by military forces and allegedly to attempts at involuntary relocation.[22] One Kurdish journal based in London reports official harassment of the increasingly popular Kurdistan Unemployed Union (KUU). The KUU demanded an investigation after the killing of leading member Nazer Omar in August 1993. KUU officials said they were exercising some self-restraint in their protests partly because of fears that Saddam Hussein would take advantage of open divisions.

Economic hardship has also contributed to insecurity and internal divisions by making impoverished Kurds more vulnerable to the temptation to take money from Baghdad in return for participation in terrorist activities.

Whilst the links between hardship and insecurity would seem to suggest that the international community should step up its assistance to the Iraqi Kurds, insecurity is sometimes cited as a reason why this assistance may need to be limited. Thus, in a recent assessment of assistance during the period April – December 1993, the UN noted:

> The security situation in the three northern governorates has been tense throughout the reporting period, and still remains so: violent armed clashes between different political parties took place in the last week of December 1993. It must be stressed that northern Iraq is a high risk area. Therefore, the implementation of the UN Humanitarian Programme in general, and rehabilitation projects in particular, depends, to a great extent, on the security situation in the area.[23]

At the same time, Western aid officials (for example, at the US Office of Foreign Disaster Assistance, State Department) have sometimes suggested that 'corruption' within the Kurdish administration (which, in so far as it exists, is in large part the *result* of inadequate international assistance) is a *justification* for low levels of assistance. In these various ways, the inadequacies of international assistance help to generate their own justification: the consequence becomes the excuse.

Promoting security to stimulate economic revival

Providing proper protection is essential if conditions are to be created for development and rehabilitation. As Simon Mollison, former SCF Field Director in northern Iraq emphasises, a degree of security is essential if people are to return to their villages and invest time and money in infrastructure and productive activities. A lack of security encourages economic activities — like sale of capital assets, smuggling and plundering the environment — which diminish production in the long term. NGOs and UN agencies also need a degree of security if they are to be encouraged to invest resources in Kurdish development.

The continued severe needs among many groups in Iraqi Kurdistan reflect the international community's partial failure to follow through on promises that the Kurds would be able to return to their home areas. Among the Kurds who have been unable to return home are many from the Kirkuk area and from near the 'front line' between Kurdish and GOI forces. Many were displaced from near the 'front line' *after* the suppression of the 1991 uprising. Large numbers of Kurds remain internally displaced and living in inadequate accommodation like dilapidated public buildings.

It is not just the threat from Baghdad which inhibits productive activity. Bombing and shelling from Iran has displaced thousands of villagers in eastern border areas. Turkish attacks have also inhibited farming.

Conclusion

This chapter has pointed to a pressing need for improvements in military protection for the Iraqi Kurds, for better monitoring of human rights, and for an upgrading of the UN's role in protecting the Iraqi Kurds. It has also suggested a pressing need to step up levels of international support for the fragile Kurdish economy and administration. This means substantially increasing development/rehabilitation programmes in the north and removing international sanctions from the Kurdish-controlled areas. These measures would go a long way towards countering the Baghdad government's long-standing attempts to control the Kurds by undermining their economy. They would support Kurdish efforts to provide themselves with a degree of political security.

Proper support for rehabilitation and for the administration also offers the only realistic way to prevent repeated and costly emergency operations.

Whereas agencies like UNDP, FAO and WHO have been used to working through national governments, the UN needs to find ways of working directly with the Kurdish administration.

UN sanctions are deepening the suffering of a people whose access to necessities has already been severely hit by the GOI's blockade. They are also inhibiting the rehabilitation of Iraqi Kurdistan and thereby helping to undermine the security they are intended to bolster. A particularly glaring paradox is the Iraqi Kurds' dependence on fuel from outside the region and the abundance of oil lying unexploited within the Kurdish-controlled area.

A more general movement towards democracy in Iraq might also be encouraged by offering wavering groups inside Iraq the clear prospect of a removal of sanctions and a reduction in war reparations for any democratic government.

As the international response to the plight of the Iraqi Kurds has evolved, it has seemed increasingly evident that the strong international response in 1991 sprang from exceptional circumstances, in particular from the visibility of the Iraqi Kurds (on television), the strong hostility towards Saddam Hussein in the wake of the war over Kuwait, and the perceived need to save Turkey from a sustained influx of Kurds from Iraq. These exceptional circumstances have all lapsed to some extent, and regional anxieties in relation to Kurdish self-sufficiency have come more to the fore. Countries like Turkey, Iran and Saudi Arabia are anxious that the Kurds should not become too strong, fearing the effect of a break-up of Iraq on their own minority populations. Turkey and Iran have periodically closed their borders with Iraqi Kurdistan, constraining its rehabilitation. For their part, western donors seem reluctant to provide the kind of economic support that would underpin the new political freedoms in Iraqi Kurdistan. Some US reservations about supporting the Kurds' experiment in democracy are conveyed in a 27 January 1994 statement by Ronald Neumann, Director of the Office of Northern Gulf Affairs, US Department of State. Neumann stressed that the US government had 'devised a humanitarian policy for the north which exists within, and is entirely consonant with, our overall Iraq policy of maintaining the territorial integrity of the state and seeking stable conditions in the region'. He went on to note the importance of 'coordination with local authorities on issues such as security while steadily avoiding any suggestion that we would support any territorial division'.[24]

The tasks of meeting humanitarian needs and protecting human rights have often taken the form of providing emergency supplies and wielding a military stick. Indeed, attention to the continuing repression of the Kurds may be taken in some quarters as justification for military action against Iraq. However, the recent emphasis on punishing 'bad government' in Iraq through military action is inadequate and often counter-productive: it allows Saddam Hussein to portray himself — to a domestic and international Arab audience — as standing up to 'western imperialism'.[25] An alternative, and more productive, approach would be based on rewarding 'good government', and in particular the experiment in democracy which the Kurds began with elections in May 1992 and which risks a slow death from economic deprivation unless there is a substantial increase in international support.[26] This means providing aid of a kind that helps people to carve out economic and political security for themselves, rather than simply feeding people in high-profile relief operations. Rewarding good government offers the prospect of a *lasting* solution to humanitarian problems, instead of an international system that lurches from one expensive emergency intervention to another.

Notes

1 This chapter draws on a detailed report by the author, commissioned by Save the Children Fund. Called 'The Kurds in Iraq: How Safe is Their Haven Now?', the report was based on a field trip to Iraq in October 1992 and on a range of documents and interviews dealing with the efficacy of international assistance. I am indebted to many people, but especially to the local staff of Save the Children Fund for their kindness and knowledge and to Simon Mollison and Joan Anderson for their encouragement and intellectual input. Although the original report was broadly endorsed by Save the Children Fund, the views expressed here should not be taken as the official view of Save the Children Fund.

2 Although (for simplicity's sake) this chapter speaks of the Iraqi Kurds, there are important non-Kurdish groups in northern Iraq, for example the Assyrians and the Turkomen.

3 Some of these are quoted in Keen (1993), 4–6.

4 A fuller account is given in Keen (1993), 4–12.

5 *Financial Times,* 13 July 1993.

6 Keen (1993), 27–8.

7 *New York Times,* 12 March 1992.

8 Keen (1993), 18–19.

9 That is, the handful of officers in Zakho.

10 *Independent,* 1 July 1993.

11 UN Inter-Agency Humanitarian Programme in Iraq (1994), 4.

12 Ibid., 4

13 *Hawkar* (newsletter of Hawkarani Kurdistan), July/August 1993.

14 UN Inter-Agency Humanitarian Programme in Iraq (1994), 4–5.

15 Ibid., 1.

16 Ibid., 3.

17 Keen (1993), 2.

18 The word means, literally, plunder from the infidel. Taken from the Koran, the word was applied to attacks and looting directed at the (mostly Muslim) Kurds.

19 This is a derisory term, with the literal meaning of 'baby donkeys'.

20 Duffield (1990), 21.

21 Mollison (1993).

22 *Hawkar* (newsletter of Hawkarani Kurdistan), July/August 1993.

23 UN Inter-Agency Humanitarian Programme in Iraq (1994), 3.

24 Quoted in *Middle East Economic Survey,* 7 February 1994.

25 Members of the Iraqi opposition have long argued that military intervention from outside might tend to strengthen Saddam Hussein, unless coordinated with an internal uprising.

26 A similar case can be made for supporting the administration in Somaliland, where there is still some prospect of avoiding the kind of expensive (and heavy-handed) emergency interventions seen in much of Somalia.

Bibliography

Duffield, M. (1990), 'Sudan at the crossroads: from emergency preparedness to social security', Institute of Development Studies paper, DP275, May 1990.

Keen, D. P. (1993), *The Kurds in Iraq: How Safe is their Haven Now?* London, Save the Children Fund.

Mollison, S. (1993), 'SCF (UK) Field Director's Annual Report, Northern Iraq, January–December 1993'.

UN Inter-Agency Humanitarian Programme in Iraq (1994), 'Progress Report on the Implementation of the 1993/1994 Cooperation Programme during the period 1 April 1993–31 December 1993' (draft), Office of the UN Coordinator in Iraq.

Index